A History of Public Broadcasting

Chapters 1-8

Tribal Memories

By John Witherspoon and Roselle Kovitz

Condensed by J.J. Yore and Richard Barbieri
from *A Tribal Memory of Public Broadcasting*

Chapters 9-11

Mission v. Market

By Robert K. Avery and Alan G. Stavitsky

Edited and designed, with captions by Steve Behrens

Current
The Public Telecommunications Newspaper
Washington, D.C.

For information, contact:
  Current Newspaper
  1612 K St., N.W., Suite 704
  Washington, D.C. 20006
  Phone: (202) 463-7055, ext. 37
  Fax: (202) 463-7056
  E-mail: current@ix.netcom.com

Printed in the United States of America

ISBN 0-9677463-0-2

Acknowledgments

Thanks are due to many individuals who helped us collect information and photos for this volume, particularly Tom Connors and Karen King of the National Public Broadcasting Archives; Lori Kaplan and Jackie Nixon of NPR Research; and John Fuller of PBS Research. Also: stations KERA, KUHT, WETA, WGBH, WILL, WNET, WOI, Columbia University, the Iowa State University Library, the Vermont Historical Society, Morton Silverstein, and Nancy Neubauer of APTS.

Cover photos

Clockwise from top left: filming *The U.S. Mexican-War, 1846-1848,* by George Stone for KERA; Anna Deavere Smith in *American Playhouse*'s "Fires in the Mirror," by Adger Cowans; Jeff Folmsbee shooting for WNET's *City Arts* series, by Joe Sinnott; Juanita Buschkoetter in David Sutherland's *Frontline*/ITVS series *The Farmer's Wife,* by John Schaefer; 1930s radio engineer W.E. Phillips of WILL, University of Illinois; NPR's *All Things Considered* co-host Robert Siegel.

Contents

Tribal Memories
By John Witherspoon and Roselle Kovitz

Mission v. Market
By Robert K. Avery and Alan G. Stavitsky

This book began as a selective historical study by John P. Witherspoon and Roselle Kovitz. Witherspoon, a former Corporation for Public Broadcasting official during the corporation's early years, was professor and director of the Center for Communications at San Diego State University. Kovitz was a graduate student who worked with Witherspoon, and who has until recently served as a regional director of the Public Television Outreach Alliance.

CPB commissioned the original study in 1985 with the intent of generating a document that could serve as a prologue to the corporation's strategic planning for the entire public telecommunication field. As such, the history focused on important system-wide issues and provided the reader with a general orientation as to how public broadcasting evolved over time and came to be structured, governed and financed the way it did. That study, released in 1986, was entitled *A Tribal Memory of Public Broadcasting: Missions, Mandates, Assumptions, Structure.*

The importance of this story to both those working inside the system and those outside who labored on the system's behalf prompted the CPB to seek the study's widest possible distribution. Toward that end, J.J. Yore and Richard Barbieri of *Current* newspaper edited the original manuscript for publication in *Current* as a series of historical essays. They subsequently revised and augmented these essays for publication in book form in 1987, as *The History of Public Broadcasting.*

The present book contains the original eight chapters by Witherspoon and Kovitz, and our three new chapters that bring the story of public broadcasting up to date. In addition, *Current* editor Steve Behrens has contributed photographs, illustrations and captions throughout this expanded edition to enhance and enrich the narrative. This edition also contains an expanded timeline, a selected bibliography, and references to original texts of documents on a new Public Broadcasting PolicyBase web site created by *Current* and the National Public Broadcasting Archives to assist readers' continued exploration of the subject.

As noted in Chapter 9, many social, economic and technological changes during the decade of the 1980s had a direct impact on the evolution of public broadcasting in the United States. These same trends, as well as changes in the terrain of mass communication research during that time, influenced the attention given to public broadcasting by academics. The death of the National Association of Educational Broadcasters in 1981 was most certainly a contributing factor as it eliminated the only national forum where there was intellectual cross-fertilization between public broadcasters and academics, as well as the principal publication outlet for that thought, *Public Telecommunications Review.* Then, two seemingly unrelated events took place that helped reposition public broadcasting as a research priority.

First, the translation of communication theorist Jurgen Habermas' seminal work, *The Structural Transformation of the Public Sphere*, into English in 1989 provided a theoretical framework that illuminated the importance of public broadcasting in our highly mediated social environment. Habermas' account of the "public sphere" as a normative ideal for democracy struck a responsive chord with a new generation of critical mass communication scholars who found the commercial broadcasting system generated by American corporate liberalism to be woefully lacking. Second, the attempted "zeroing-out" of all federal funding for public broadcasting by Newt Gingrich and his colleagues awakened public attention to the importance of taxpayer support for an alternative broadcasting system. With the sudden jeopardy and the grassroots response, the topic of system survival moved into the mainstream of public discourse.

Unlike several of the recent books that responded to this publication opportunity, *A History of Public Broadcasting*, does not contribute to the fatalistic rhetoric that forecasts the demise of the U.S. system. Since its beginnings in the 1920s, the system has survived an abundance of doomsayers. And that it *has* survived and continues to evolve to address current conditions of the marketplace is the best evidence for its long-term good health. We intend for this revised edition to provide the reader with an orientation to what has transpired to date, and also afford a glimpse as to how the system is preparing to meet the challenges and opportunities of the new millennium.

Robert K. Avery
University of Utah

Alan G. Stavitsky
University of Oregon

Key documents accessible online

**PB
PB**
Marginal notes indicate that there are related documents online.

To supplement this volume, *Current* and the National Public Broadcasting Archives at the University of Maryland have begun compiling a new web site for students and teachers of media policy, **Public Broadcasting PolicyBase** at the web address below.

The site will include new as well as old legislation, pertinent court decisions, organizational charters, Carnegie Commission documents and other signficant texts and articles.

We will continue to add to the site, and welcome your suggestions and submission of suitable texts.

**Public Broadcasting PolicyBase:
www.current.org/pbpb/**

Tribal Memories

By John Witherspoon and Roselle Kovitz

With just one vacuum tube in its engineering lab, the University of Illinois signed on its radio station in 1922. (Technicians frequently interrupted broadcasts to let the tube cool off.) The first program reported the news and sports and included a lecture on "Turning Cream into Gold." That fall, WRM (later renamed WILL) aired its first live football game. At left: **Chief Engineer W.E. (Ted) Phillips** at WILL's controls in the 1930s. (Photo: WILL.)

The first half century

*Government and education find their roles in broadcasting —
and eventually back reserved channels*

Public broadcasting began in education. Its first stations were
licensed to educational institutions; eventually, the government
reserved channels for a new category of "noncommercial educational" stations; and when local, state and federal tax support began,
authorizing laws typically mandated an educational mission.

"Education" in American broadcasting has never meant just
instruction. Rather, public broadcasting's programming mission traditionally has centered on alternative programming: programs that
probably could not survive in the ratings-oriented commercial system, but are perceived to be of value to particular audiences. Even
stations that carry little or no formal instruction are seen as educational, just as museums, libraries or theater groups often are considered broadly as educational community resources.

Educational institutions customarily are supported by personal,
foundation or corporate philanthropy, and by the public purse.
Whether they are supported mostly by taxes, like public schools, or
mostly by philanthropy, like symphony orchestras or art museums,
they stand apart from conventional business. Schools, museums,
libraries, orchestras—and
public broadcasting sta-
tions—are considered
cultural assets; one can-
not measure their suc-
cess simply by the stan-
dards of the marketplace.

Public schools and
libraries clearly are the
responsibility of the
body politic; they pro-
vide public services paid

At the University of
Wisconsin, **Prof.
Earle Terry** and stu-
dents built a "wire-
less telephone" trans-
mitter and experi-
mented under the call
letters 9XM in 1917.
(At left: Terry in 1923.)
By the early 1930s,
the Wisconsin School
of the Air aired a full
schedule of lectures.
The university
changed the call let-
ters of its Madison
station to WHA in
1922 and still oper-
ates the major pro-
duction center for
Wisconsin Public
Radio and Wisconsin
Public Television.

for by taxes. In contrast, commercial broadcasting lives in a turbu-
lent marketplace; its programs and revenues are clearly linked.
Public broadcasting lies somewhere between, and eight decades after
9XM took to the air on the campus of the University of Wisconsin,
there still has not been a satisfactory public policy decision about
how to support "noncommercial educational" broadcasting.
Arguments over advertising began in 1934. They continue today.
President Lyndon Johnson promised to propose a financial plan in
1968, but it was not to be. Public broadcasting today lives on an
uneasy mix of audience subscriptions; local, state, and federal tax
support; traditional philanthropy; sale of services and program-related products, and the increasingly enhanced underwriting that represents the system's compromise with advertising. This combination
may be America's *de facto* decision about support, but there is no
sign that the discussion is ending.

Public broadcasting's missions, mandates and assumptions are reflected in a few closely intertwined facts and themes:

■ Its roots are in education. This is more than an historical arti-fact; it's a matter of law.

■ It has unique programming responsibilities. These go beyond conventional education and are intended to provide Americans with programming not feasible in a commercial system.

■ By law it has responsibilities to specific audience groups, pro-ducers, and those traditionally unable to achieve equity in employ-ment.

■ Its long-range financing problems have not been solved, which affects its program output.

■ It is the world's most decentralized national broadcast system.

Foundations of the field

In its first half century, public service radio and television devel-oped in spite of the Great Depression, some educators' reluctance to try new ideas, the country's orientation toward a commercial sys-tem, and a pervasive doubt that educational broadcasting could ever amount to much. The difficulties were so great, progress seemed so slow, and public attention was then so slight, that it's easy to assume that the world began with the Carnegie Commission in 1966.

But this would ignore the accomplishments that laid the founda-tions for public broadcasting. These included:

■ establishing many of the nation's first radio stations, dating from 9XM (now WHA), in Madison, Wisconsin, in 1917;

■ establishing the principle of reserved channels, on a limited basis in 1938, and fully with the reservation of FM frequencies in 1940 and 1945;

■ establishing the principle of audience-supported broadcasting (by the Pacifica stations in 1949);

■ establishing television channel reservations in 1952;

■ developing a prototype national program service by the National Association of Educational Broadcasters (NAEB);

■ developing early "noncommercial educational" television sta-tions, supported mostly by the Ford Foundation, educational insti-tutions and community groups;

■ establishing National Educational Television, public TV's first major national program service;

■ establishing the principle of federal support with the Educational Television Facilities Program in 1962;

■ establishing the first regular interconnection system for public broadcasting (by the Eastern Educational Network in 1960).

A spectrum free-for-all

Not long after Guglielmo Marconi developed wireless telegraphy in 1895, and Reginald Fessenden succeeded in transmitting voice messages in 1906, amateur radio enthusiasts began crowding the airwaves. A spectrum free-for-all ensued. In his 1950 history of broadcasting, *Radio, Television, and Society*, Charles Siepmann noted:

"All the virtues and defects of unfettered enterprise were exemplified in the mad rush to develop the new market—rapid expansion, ingenious improvisation, reckless and often unscrupulous competition, in which the interests of the consumer (and, in the long run, of the producer also) were lost from sight."

Radio's capability of reaching large audiences, coupled with the inherent scarcity of channels and many competing interests thrust the new communications miracle into the center of an unpleasant "custody" battle involving the U.S. Navy.

In response, the federal government made several attempts to regulate radio communication in its early years, including the Radio Act of 1912, which required radio operators to obtain a license from the Secretary of Commerce.

Early radio was mostly a way for ships at sea to communicate: The S-O-S from the Titanic in 1912 was an example. Consequently, the government banished amateur radio operators from the air during World War I, sealed their equipment, and gave the military control of the airwaves. During the war, the Navy, in the industry's first coordinated effort, advanced radio to an extent not possible during the earlier years of chaos. At the war's end in 1917, the Navy touted its war-time technical advances and proposed that Congress leave it to control radio. Legislation to do this was introduced in Congress in the fall of 1918.

The legislation's advocates and opponents went to work. The State Department and the Army supported the bill. Amateur radio enthusiasts, headed by Hiram Percy Maxim, president of the American Radio Relay League, opposed it. The bill's supporters pointed to the Navy's recent achievements as reasons it should maintain control over the industry. Maxim argued that the Navy's proud technical achievements came largely from the amateurs he represented. Most of these were once again civilians. So a Navy monopoly, Maxim maintained, would prove a disaster.

But it was Rep. William S. Greene who added the crowning blow on behalf of the Navy's opponents. Greene said he had "never heard before that it was necessary for one person to own all the air in order to breathe" and warned that, "having just won a fight against autocracy, we would start an autocratic movement with this bill." The Navy's bill died in committee.

Disappointed but undaunted, the Navy pursued another avenue: creating a private monopoly sympathetic to its interests. It began closed-door discussions with General Electric. Within a year GE gave birth to the Radio Corporation of America. RCA immediately achieved the dominant role in international communications. No wonder. Its owners included not only GE, but also Westinghouse, American Telephone & Telegraph, and United Fruit. And the new radio corporation owned some 2,000 electronic patents. It is also no surprise that in 1924 RCA, AT&T, GE, Westinghouse and United Fruit became the targets of antitrust allegations and Federal Trade Commission investigations.

The possibility of FTC hearings made these companies especially interested in settling matters themselves, so, despite bickering over pieces of the radio pie, the companies already had begun secret negotiations. When the dust settled, AT&T was in the telephone and telegraph business. GE, Westinghouse, United Fruit and RCA

When radio was booming as a novelty hobby in the early and mid-1920s (with radio sets like the $25 **Westinghouse Aeriola Jr.**, above), few broadcasters thought it would become a medium driven by advertising, writes historian Robert W. McChesney. AT&T tried selling listener subscriptions. RCA's David Sarnoff thought radio manufacturers would support broadcasting. Herbert Hoover, then secretary of commerce, proposed a receiver tax to subsidize programs in 1924. Only a quarter of stations sold airtime in 1926. But within a few years after the founding of NBC in 1926 and CBS in 1927, ad-supported network radio became a hit. Radio ad sales hit $100 million in 1930. Federal Radio Commission member Orestes Caldwell observed: "there seems to be no other way to finance these wonderful programs."

remained radio broadcasters, manufacturers and equipment distributors. In 1926, RCA formed the first network, the National Broadcasting Company.

"The public interest, convenience and necessity"

While the industry still lacked significant regulation, the government's decision not to grant the Navy, or any other government arm, control of the medium was a fundamental decision in the history of U.S. broadcasting that distinguishes it from systems then emerging in virtually every other developed nation.

Under the U.S. system in the 1920s, the Secretary of Commerce, then Herbert Hoover, was the radio industry's sole licensing authority. President Warren Harding, seeing the chaos in radio communications, directed Hoover to call a radio conference in Washington to advise the secretary about the limits of the government's power and help develop proposals for regulatory legislation. The professionals who attended the conference had lots of ideas, but failed to agree on what form regulation should take. Hoover called three more such conferences in a futile attempt to reach consensus on the kind of legislation necessary.

In 1923 Hoover made a desperate attempt to impose order over the airwaves by reassigning most stations' frequencies. Broadcasters challenged Hoover's authority on the grounds he had exceeded his statutory powers, and in 1926 the courts forced Hoover to stop. The industry was now hopelessly out of control and begged for legislation to relieve the chaos that threatened to destroy this young but potentially powerful medium.

Help came the following year. On Feb. 23, 1927, Congress approved the Dill-White Radio Act of 1927, giving the government discretion over granting frequency licenses based on a standard of "public interest, convenience and necessity." The act created the Federal Radio Commission as the temporary, but sole, licensing authority for the industry. The 1927 legislation also forbade monopolies and established a precedent, based on the First Amendment, of prohibiting government intrusion into programming. But the Radio Act of 1927 did more than provide immediate relief for an industry in distress; it set the stage for the legislation that still governs the broadcasting industry today: the Communications Act of 1934.

By the time Franklin D. Roosevelt took office in 1933, the Federal Radio Commission—originally expected to last a single year—had existed for six years. Roosevelt quickly established an interdepartmental committee under the direction of Secretary of Commerce Daniel C. Roper to study the entire communications industry. The commission's task was to suggest legislation to replace state regulations for the radio, telephone and telegraph industries with national rules enforced by a single, permanent regulatory commission. The committee's report gave Roosevelt the ammunition he needed to go before Congress on Feb. 26, 1934 and recommend consolidating the Federal Radio Commission and the communications interests of the Interstate Commerce Commission under a new agency, the Federal Communications Commission. Sen. Clarence Dill (D-Wash.), who sponsored the 1927 act, and Rep. Sam T. Rayburn (D-Tex.) introduced bills that became the Communications Act of 1934.

Broadcast reform v. Cooperation

Will commercial radio bring education to the people, or should educators do it on their own stations? Two rival groups, both founded in 1930, represented the opposing views on that pivotal question:

■ The National Advisory Council on Radio in Education (NACRE), imbued with faith in enlightened capitalism and backed by NBC and the Carnegie Corporation, promoted a doctrine of "Cooperation" between educators and commercial broadcasters.

■ The National Committee on Education by Radio (NCER), driven by the broadcast reform movement, with its Midwestern public-education values and a populist distrust of big business, and backed by the Payne Fund, pushed for reserved channels for educators in 1931. (For more on the groups, see pages 7-8.)

Working with broadcasters, NACRE helped foreclose channel reservations by stimulating a wave of educational roundtables and lectures on commercial stations, with more than a dozen educational series on the networks in 1932, writes historian Eugene Leach. But they drew "pitifully small audiences," disappointed NACRE executive director Levering Tyson said in 1934, and networks cut their airtime. NACRE had folded by 1938, as the FCC began reserving channels for education. The Cooperation doctrine survived, however, and can be heard in arguments that cable TV can serve all audience needs. —Steve Behrens

The act was controversial. Many critics expressed concern over the growing commercialization of the airwaves. Educational institutions operated many early stations, and radio's potential to extend and enhance education had been widely recognized. But in the late '20s and early '30s the Great Depression and the growing pressure for commercial development of the radio spectrum reduced the number of educational stations. It appeared that without reserved frequencies, educational radio might die. Educators, churchmen, and labor leaders came forward, stressing radio's educational and cultural potential. The debate reached the floor of the Senate when Sen. Robert F. Wagner (D-N.Y.) introduced an amendment requiring the commission to reserve and allocate one-fourth of all radio broadcasting facilities to nonprofit stations.

The first advertising debate

The amendment called for withdrawing all existing broadcast licenses, and reallocating frequencies, power and operating hours for all stations within 90 days. It also required the FCC to allocate comparable frequencies to commercial and nonprofit stations and ensure that the facilities reserved for nonprofit stations would "reasonably make possible the operation of such stations on a self-sustaining basis, and to that end the licensee may sell such part of the allotted time as will make the station self-supporting." The amendment sparked heated debate.

Its authors strongly advocated the need for educational, religious, agricultural, labor and other nonprofit organizations in the radio industry. Opponents said the amendment was unreasonable. They argued that reallocating frequencies was a monumental task which could not be accomplished in 90 days, or even six months. During the debate over the amendment, Wagner agreed. But the clause authorizing noncommercial stations to sell time to cover expenses came under the heaviest fire, and most likely sealed the amendment's fate. In the final vote, Wagner's proposal was defeated 42 to 23. But in a conciliatory gesture, Congress included a section in the Act requiring the FCC to study assigning channels to nonprofit

Heads of the lobbies: NCER's **Joy Elmer Morgan** (upper photo, courtesy of National Education Association) and NACRE's **Levering Tyson** (lower photo, courtesy of Columbia University).

PB
PB

See online: *Tuning Out Education: The Cooperation Doctrine, 1922-38* by Eugene Leach organizations.

On June 19, 1934, the Communications Act of 1934 became law. In its final form, the act established the Federal Communications Commission as a permanent federal agency to regulate interstate and international communications by wire and radio. The act called for the FCC to be a bipartisan commission of seven commissioners serving seven-year terms. The FCC would issue and revoke licenses, allocate frequencies for broadcast and experimentation, and study new uses for radio. It also established conditions for license applicants.

With the FCC in place and a coherent piece of legislation now governing the industry, broadcasting enjoyed more orderly development, benefiting both broadcasters and listeners. But education's role remained uncertain.

Above: **UM's program director Lee Seymour** (above), when the station (then WLB-9XI) was located in the electrical engineering building. (Photo: National Public Broadcasting Archives.)

Educators begin using radio

Radio was the new technology of the early 20th century, and experimentation dominated its early days. Much of the experimental work in wireless communication in the late 1800s and early 1900s occurred at colleges and universities, and by 1923 educational institutions owned more than 10 percent of all broadcast stations.

One of these was 9XM, which began broadcasting from the University of Wisconsin in 1917 under an experimental license. Four years later the Latter Day Saints' University in Salt Lake City, Utah, began operating as the first educational institution granted an official license.

But education's strong involvement in broadcasting did not last long. Some institutions lost interest after the technology's most challenging engineering issues had been resolved. And many colleges and universities were not committed to applying the new technology to education.

Meanwhile, strong commercial interests developed, putting educators under pressure to relinquish their frequencies. It was argued that educational broadcasters should stay on the periphery of the industry and use their commercial counterparts to transmit educational programming.

From 1921 to 1936, educational institutions obtained 202 licenses. But by 1937, 164 of those licenses had either expired or been transferred to commercial interests. What accounted for this dramatic drop? Many educators decided that this new medium didn't do what they had hoped it would. Enrollment at institutions using radio did not increase because of it. Educational radio was not paying off as a publicity tool, nor was it attracting lots of listeners, as its commercial counterparts did. Educators largely lacked expertise in broadcasting and the time necessary to develop radio as a teaching tool. Most of all, the Great Depression meant educational institutions didn't have enough money to support radio stations. Besides, they could raise needed cash by selling their radio operations to commercial interests.

In 1927 the National Broadcasting Company created the "Red" and "Blue" networks. The Columbia Broadcasting System also began

See Chapters 7 and 8: Public broadcasting's many purposes and audiences.

Key organizations in public broadcasting's early days

From the beginning, public broadcasting has advanced through the work of committees and agencies known by their acronyms.

Association of College and University Broadcasting Stations (ACUBS)

Recognizing the unique position of educational broadcasters and the need to organize to further their cause, representatives from college- and university-owned radio stations, meeting at the fourth Washington Radio Conference, formed the Association of College and University Broadcasting Stations in 1925.

Membership in the early years was low, and the association suffered from economic woes. Despite these difficulties, ACUBS held its first annual convention in 1930. There it identified three goals: to seek official channel reservations for educational use; to establish a national headquarters (preferably in Washington, D.C.); and, to develop a mechanism for program exchange. The goals were designed to establish a place for educational broadcasting in an industry dominated by commercial stations and to begin building a foundation for enhancing programming.

As a step toward its first goal, ACUBS approached the annual State Governor's Conference and urged the governors to support congressional legislation that would reserve radio channels for state-, college- and university-operated stations.

Neither this, nor any of ACUBS' other goals, seemed within reach in the early '30's. The prospects for edu-

cational broadcasting looked bleak. As Donald Wood and Donald Wylie wrote in their 1977 book, *Educational Telecommunications*, "Money problems were increasing, membership was decreasing, the Federal Radio Commission did nothing to encourage noncommercial radio, and educators themselves were turning more frequently to commercial broadcasters for the opportunity to present their programs over adequate facilities."

In 1934, ACUBS regrouped and changed its name to the National Association of Educational Broadcasters.

Advisory Committee on Education by Radio (ACER)

The Advisory Committee on Education by Radio was formed in 1929 and disbanded only a year later. Nevertheless, it has a significant impact on educational radio. Secretary of the Interior Ray Lyman Wilbur appointed the committee in June 1929 to conduct a national survey on the potential of instructional radio. With funding from the Payne Study and Experiment Fund and the Carnegie Corporation, the committee was comprised of representatives from education, broadcasting, manufacturing, government and the public.

The following year the committee forwarded a report to Secretary Wilbur recommending the reservation of "air channels" for educational use. ACER also recommended establishing an educational radio division in the Interior Department's Office of Education; establishing an advisory commit-

tee of educators, commercial broadcasters, and the public; securing funding for educational programs; and alerting the President and the Federal Radio Commission of the importance of educational programming to the American public.

But it was the recommendation of reserved channels for educational use that stirred the interest of ACUBS, which requested channel reservations that same year.

National Advisory Council on Radio in Education (NACRE)

The council was one of the more controversial organizations in the development of educational radio. It was established as a result of recommendations by ACER (see above) on the need for an advisory committee representing a variety of interests to help educational radio establish consistent funding for developing educational broadcasts with support from the Secretary of the Interior and the Commissioner of Education.

With financing from the Rockefeller Foundation, NACRE was organized in July 1930 and lasted for eight years, during a time when college and university broadcasters were struggling to find their place in the broadcasting industry. But NACRE included commercial broadcasters as well as educators, and was largely concerned with getting educational programs on commercial stations rather than encouraging the development of educational stations. Many educators objected to this, say-

Continued on next page

ing the commercial sector was co-opting them. The educational broadcasters found it increasingly difficult to survive on their own.

NACRE conducted research, convened conferences, and supported the development and airing of educational programs. It also attempted to unify educational broadcasting by identifying common goals. One of its most notable accomplishments was arranging for NBC to carry a series of educational broadcasts over its networks. NACRE folded in 1938 when the Rockefeller Foundation stopped funding it.

National Committee on Education by Radio (NCER)

The National Committee on Education by Radio came about in 1931 at least partly because of the distrust some educators had for the mingling of commercial and educational interests in NACRE (above). Although NCER did not oppose cooperating with commercial stations, it was more committed to seeing educational broadcasting grow as its own entity. Its members were committed to helping existing educational radio stations survive, and encouraging the construction of others. The committee advocated legislation to reserve 15 percent of the radio channels for education. Sen. Simeon D. Fess introduced a bill based on this recommendation in three consecutive years. The bill never left committee.

Financed by a grant from the Payne Fund, NCER was "organization of organizations" with representatives from many national educa-

tion associations as members. In this way, it was a precursor to the Joint Committee on Educational Television, which was instrumental in achieving television channel reservations 20 years later. Before its demise in 1940, NCER succeeded in focusing educators on a common goal: safeguarding a place for education in radio.

Institute for Education by Radio (IER)

The Institute for Education by Radio—which later added "and Television" to its name —held annual conferences, sponsored by Ohio State University, from 1930 to 1953. The record of its conferences provide probably the most comprehensive record of educational radio and TV's early development. The conferences served as forums for educators, commercial broadcasters and others to discuss the current status and future possibilities for educational broadcasting.

National Association of Education Broadcasters (NAEB)

From meager beginnings as ACUBS, NAEB became the most significant association in the overall development of educational broadcasting. The courage, stamina and sheer fight of many of its leaders and members over the years made it for more than 50 years one of the toughest and most effective organizations in the industry.

In an effort to gain new members, NAEB broadened its membership requirements and rewrote the old ACUBS constitution. Critics of educational broadcasting continued their complaints, among

them that even if the government reserved radio channels for educators, the educational community lacked the wherewithal to activate them. Still, the NAEB trudged on. In 1938, it achieved its first big victory when five channels were set aside for noncommercial educational radio. By 1945, the FCC had allocated a total of 20 radio frequencies for educational use. In 1952, the NAEB mobilized the educational community and convinced the FCC to allocate television channels for noncommercial educational TV stations.

But educational stations still suffered from a lack of programming resources. In 1950, with funding from the Kellogg Foundation, NAEB realized its third goal and inaugurated a national, noncommercial tape network. It was called a bicycle network because program tapes were "bicycled"—shipped from station to station. The new network brought domestic and foreign educational programming to more than 50 NAEB member stations from coast to coast.

Federal Radio Education Committee (FREC)

In 1935, the FCC appointed the Federal Radio Education Committee, chaired by Commissioner of Education John W. Studebaker, as another attempt to unite educational and commercial broadcasters. During its brief existence, the committee—which included both educational and commercial broadcasters—launched research projects, compiled reports, distributed newsletters, and held conferences. It faded from existence in the early 1940s without accomplishing any tangible compromise between the two camps.

Joint Committee on Educational Television (JCET)

The ad hoc Joint Committee on Educational Television, like the NCER, included representatives from prominent educational organizations and associations including the American Council on Education, NAEB, the National Education Association, and the National Council of Chief State School Officers. The committee selected as its chairman I. Keith Tyler, director of the Institute for Education by Radio-Television.

JCET resolved basic differences within the educational community, raised funds for coordinating the testimony of over 70 educators, cosponsoring a commercial television monitoring study that bolstered the educational community's testimony, and providing the cohesion and force that the educational community needed in order to make an effective argument for channel reservations before the FCC.

The committee disbanded when the FCC's hearings ended, but the Fund for Adult Education renewed it with a $90,000 grant to advise stations in both legal and technical areas and represent educational television before the FCC.

Fund for Adult Education (the Fund)

C. Scott Fletcher, an Australian-born businessman and recent director of Encyclopedia Britannica Films, headed the Ford Foundation's Fund for Adult Education. It adopted three major goals: to persuade the FCC to reserve channels for educational television, to encourage educators to develop and operate them, and to create a "national educational television center for the exchange of programs, ideas, information and the providing of services." The strategies for accomplishing these goals were threefold: first, the Fund would seek out and support existing agencies committed to these goals; second, it would provide monetary support to agencies when needed, and finally, new agencies would be created as needed.

Educational Television and Radio Center

In late 1952 the Fund for Adult Education (above) provided financing to create the Educational Television and Radio Center. The center's first, temporary, president was C. Scott Fletcher, also president of the Fund. The center played a key role for almost 20 years as a national exchange center for educational television, providing programs, services, ideas, and information to educational broadcasters. For much of its early life Harry K. Newburn, a former president of the University of Oregon, ran the center in Ann Arbor, Mich.

In 1958 educational pioneer John F. White, who had become interested in television while vice president of Western Reserve University, was one of the first developers of telecourses for credit and, more recently had been general manager of WQED in Pittsburgh, became president of the Center. Under White, the Center changed its name to the National Educational Television and Radio Center and moved to New York. In 1962 it added instructional TV services. But by 1963 cutbacks forced the center to abandon its radio and instructional services. The center then changed its name to National Educational Television.

operating in 1927. And a fourth network, the Mutual Broadcasting System, took to the air in 1934. The development of networks was a decided gain for commercial stations nationwide. Historian Charles Siepmann credited them with "consolidating the radio industry, of transforming the character and quality of programs, and of securing unprecedented sums of advertising revenue." Educational stations lacked these programming resources. With neither resources nor expertise, educational broadcasters' only hope to gain a place in the overwhelmingly commercial radio industry was to organize.

Organizing for reserved channels

When looking at historic trends, it's easy to think of crusaders for a cause as a unified group. But typically, many struggles occur within these groups. Educational broadcasters were no different. They often disagreed on lobbying strategies, and even on what structure educational broadcasting should have. Nevertheless, they did realize the need to organize and created a number of groups to further their cause (see previous pages).

As soon as Congress passed the Communications Act of 1934, the NAEB and other broadcasting organizations began pressuring the FCC to reserve channels for educational broadcasting. Their efforts paid off in January 1938, when the commission established noncommercial educational broadcasting stations that would be licensed to nonprofit education agencies and would operate on a higher frequency than commercial stations. By the end of 1938, the Cleveland City Board of Education had applied for and been granted a construction permit under the new classification. New York City filed an application the same year. Many other agencies and institutions wrote letters to the commission inquiring about the new kind of stations. By 1939, the FCC had granted Cleveland's Board of Education station, WBOE, and New York's WNYE licenses as noncommercial educational stations. In 1940, the FCC designated frequency modulation (FM) as the transmission method for this new class of stations and reserved five channels for noncommercial educational broadcasting.

NAEB, the U.S. Office of Education, and other national educational agencies continued petitioning the FCC for channel reservations during the commission's 1945 hearing on frequency allocation. The FCC allocated 20 FM channels (including the five previously reserved) between 88 and 92 megahertz to noncommercial educational broadcasting. By the end of that fiscal year, the FCC had authorized 12 stations in this classification. Six were on the air.

Although educators now had guaranteed spectrum space, they still faced formidable financial problems. Exacerbating these was the fact that FM broadcasting was developing slowly. There were almost no FM receivers, which vastly reduced educational broadcasters' potential audience.

In 1948 the FCC acknowledged education's financial plight, and proposed rules that would allow noncommercial educational FM stations to operate at 10 watts or less power. This reduced the minimum cost of equipment to a few hundred dollars. Educational broadcasters did not respond much; only one station was operating by June 1948.

In 1950 the Commission further eased the way for low-power stations by reducing the qualifications technicians needed to operate them. Operators applying for this new radiotelephone third-class operator's permit still had to know basic operating practice, but not the theory behind radio systems. By 1951 the number of educational institutions operating low-power stations had increased to about 40 percent of all educational FM stations.

The late 1940s and early '50s were a crucial time for educational broadcasting. Besides winning the battle for radio channel reservations, representatives of educational broadcasting banded together during this period to determine a common mission for their fledgling industry, and pooled their resources to push for television channel reservations.

Some of the first gatherings contributing to this cohesion were the Allerton House Seminars held in Allerton Park, near Urbana, Ill., in 1949. Underwritten by the Rockefeller Foundation, the seminars brought together 30 educational broadcasters from the United States, Canada and Great Britain and provided a meeting ground for some of the day's principal architects of educational broadcasting. These seminars helped establish a new sense of purpose and direction for educational broadcasting and began the planning for what became NAEB's tape distribution network.

Staking a claim in TV

Americans got their first glimpse of television in 1939. World War II slowed TV's development for several years, but by 1948 TV's expansion threatened to exceed the 12 very high frequency (VHF) channels the FCC had allocated it. Moreover, the FCC's existing TV channel allocation scheme was causing technical interference. At this time no educationally owned TV stations existed and only five educational institutions were involved with television.

The FCC was so overwhelmed by requests for television channels in 1948 that it deferred action on all applications so that it could investigate expanding television broadcasting into ultra high frequencies (UHF), adopting a nationwide channel assignment plan for commercial TV and exploring the possibility of color television. The FCC's freeze on television allocations marked a period of intense study, debate and planning at the commission, including TV spectrum allocation hearings that were among the most dynamic in the FCC's history.

During the hearings, educators again advocated reserving channels for education. They had a strong ally in the FCC's first woman commissioner, Frieda B. Hennock. Commissioner Hennock was the sole dissenter in 1949 when the FCC proposed TV allocations that did not reserve spectrum space for noncommercial educational stations. She argued for reserving channels for education despite the educational community's inability to use them. Otherwise, Hennock said, there would be a time when education would be ready, and the channels wouldn't be there. This, she made clear, was not acceptable.

The following year, 1950, Iowa State College's WOI-TV took to the air as the nation's 100th television station—and the world's first non-experimental TV station owned by an educational institution. [The station was not a typical public TV station, however; it always carried advertising, and in 1994 it was sold by the university].

The National Education Association and the U.S. Office of Education both filed petitions seeking VHF and UHF reservations for education. Other groups also began to express interest in reserving channels. But these advocates disagreed among themselves,

See Chapter 4:
Public radio grows
from its roots in
education.
See also Chapter
7: Broadcasters
and policymakers
wrestle with ques-
tions of purpose.

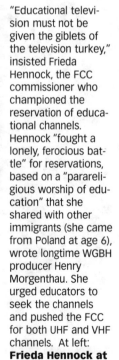

"Educational television must not be given the giblets of the television turkey," insisted Frieda Hennock, the FCC commissioner who championed the reservation of educational channels. Hennock "fought a lonely, ferocious battle" for reservations, based on a "parareligious worship of education" that she shared with other immigrants (she came from Poland at age 6), wrote longtime WGBH producer Henry Morgenthau. She urged educators to seek the channels and pushed the FCC for both UHF and VHF channels. At left: **Frieda Hennock at KUHT's launch** in 1953. (Photo: KUHT.)

some arguing for VHF *and* UHF channels, others only for UHF.

Before educators presented their case to the FCC they saw a need to develop a united front, so in October 1950 the NAEB coordinated a meeting at Commissioner Hennock's home. This was to be the first meeting of the ad hoc Joint Committee on Educational Television, which continued in varying forms until 1982.

About the same time the FCC channel allocation hearings were concluding (in 1951), and the Ford Foundation was holding discussions that soon would make it educational television's single greatest benefactor. Begun as a local philanthropy in Detroit, the Ford Foundation in 1950 broadened its mission to include lofty ideals such as "improving man's conditions and society on a worldwide scale." To do this, and also to decentralize the foundation's projects, it created the Fund for the Advancement of Education (FAE) and the Fund for Adult Education (the Fund). These two projects were instrumental in advancing, respectively, instructional and educational television.

One of the first steps the Fund took to support reserving educational channels was to provide a $90,000 grant to the Joint Committee on Educational Television (JCET) to provide legal assistance to the educational community for the final push toward a place in the television spectrum.

The FCC issued a notice in early 1951, proposing to reserve 209 local channel allocations for noncommercial use. Commissioner Hennock pushed for more. Educators loudly echoed her protests. By the end of the hearings, representatives of educationally related institutions had filed more than 800 formal statements.

When the FCC lifted its freeze in April 1952, and issued its Sixth Report and Order allocating television channels, the commission had put noncommercial reservations on 242 of the 2,053 allocations. The reservations were divided into 162 UHF and 80 VHF reservations. Frieda Hennock's arguments were evident in the Sixth Report and Order's acknowledgement that "a reservation of channels is necessary to insure that such stations come into existence." In 1953 KUHT in Houston, Tex., became the nation's first noncommercial educational television licensee.

Despite this victory, the educational community's work had just begun. Educators knew that the FCC would be watching to see that educators used—and used effectively—the channels the commission had reserved for them. Educators began to build a structure to encourage the development of educational stations, personnel, programming and public support.

In collaboration with the JCET, the Fund created the National Citizen's Committee for Educational Television, to increase public awareness of educators' struggle for a niche in the broadcasting industry, and to foster financial support for these efforts.

In late 1952, the Fund collaborated with the NCCET and the JCET, and financed the Educational Television and Radio Center, which for 20 years played a major role in developing educational television. When John F. White, a pioneer in developing telecourses for credit and recently general manager of WQED in Pittsburgh, became the center's president in 1958, he changed its name to the National Educational Television and Radio Center and moved it to New York. The center later dropped its radio service and changed its name to National Educational Television.

By 1960 the number of local channel allocations reserved for educational television had increased to 257, but the number of stations on the air numbered a mere 49. Although more

than 200 channels remained unused, it was not lack of interest among educators that caused the channels to continue unactivated. It was lack of money. For many years, educational broadcasters had relied on the Ford Foundation, but they knew the foundation could not sustain its support indefinitely. Direct federal funding was tempting, but many feared federal support might result in undue control over programming.

The first direct federal support came not for operations, but for equipment. In May 1962, after a five-year campaign, Congress enacted the Educational Television Facilities Act. The act created a $32 million, five-year program of federal matching grants to construct educational television facilities. [Today's successor to the grant program is the Public Telecommunications Facilities Program in the Department of Commerce.]

Later that same year, the federal All Channel Receiver Act required that all television sets shipped between states have both UHF and VHF tuners. These two laws brightened the picture for educational broadcasting.

Still, educational broadcasting faced its oldest problem: the need for long-term financing. The solution did not seem to be getting closer.

In 1963 the NAEB reorganized, and created a new educational TV stations division. With C. Scott Fletcher and Chalmers Marquis leading, the division tried to:

- develop new educational television stations,
- represent stations before government and private agencies,
- compile data about fundraising activities (but not raise funds),
- facilitate personnel training and placement programs,
- hold regional and national conferences, and
- establish an educational TV program library service.

Fletcher, former head of the Ford Foundation's Fund for Adult Education, concentrated on establishing an educational television program exchange service and exploring long-range financing for educational broadcasting. With a small grant from the U.S. Office of Education and, more significantly, a letter of endorsement from President Johnson, Fletcher launched a national conference that, within three years, led to the first Carnegie Commission and the passage of the Public Broadcasting Act.

Oil money and an ambitious college combined to give the University of Houston the first educational TV station, historian Jim Robertson found. At left: **KUHT staffers** including manager John Schwarzwalder (center), who went on to start KTCA in the Twin Cities, and George Arms (right), who became a prominent programmer in public TV. A technical problem almost marred the first sign-on in 1953: a thick black band was appearing across the picture. Two minutes before airtime, Arms later recalled, the problem was cured by the chief engineer with a swift and intemperate kick to the transmitter. (Photo: KUHT.)

PB PB

See online: text of the Educational Television Facilities Act

CHAPTER 2

Help from the public purse

The first Carnegie Commission and the creation of CPB

It is hard to overstate the importance of the Carnegie Commission on Educational Television. Established in 1965, the commission did not create educational television, but laid the foundations for the field today.

The commission had its roots in the First National Conference on Long-Range Financing of Educational Television Stations, which NAEB and the U.S. Office of Education convened in Washington in December 1964. At the meeting, Ralph Lowell, a longtime supporter of educational radio and television through the Lowell Institute Cooperative Broadcasting Council in Boston, proposed establishing a national commission—perhaps with White House backing—to study educational television's financial needs.

Lowell and NAEB's conference organizer C. Scott Fletcher presented the idea to John W. Gardner, then president of a major foundation, the Carnegie Corporation of New York, and later secretary of the Department of Health, Education and Welfare. The NAEB conference also proposed the commission to President Johnson and obtained his endorsement in November 1965. Gardner committed $500,000 from the Carnegie Corporation, and the commission was created.

Backing from the White House

The White House also backed the effort. In a letter, President Lyndon Johnson wrote:

> "From our beginnings as a nation we have recognized that our security depends upon the enlightenment of our people; that our freedom depends on the communication of many ideas through many channels. I believe that educational television has an important future in the United States and throughout the world . . . I look forward with great interest to the judgments which this commission will offer."

To give momentum to the Public Broadcasting Act, C. Scott Fletcher and NAEB colleagues worked with White House aide S. Douglass Cater, orchestrating an NAEB conference, LBJ's endorsement and the Carnegie Commission recommendations. At right: **LBJ greets Fletcher**. (Photo: National Public Broadcasting Archives.)

The commission's members included prominent leaders in the arts, education, politics and business (see box, next page).

The commission was careful to involve the existing noncommercial stations in its work. In 1965, 124 educational television stations

Carnegie's Commissioners

The first Carnegie Commission's membership offers a case study in the political process. Its chairman was **James R. Killian, Jr.,** chairman of the Massachusetts Institute of Technology and a political independent who had been science adviser to President Eisenhower. Other educators lent both prestige and diversity: **James B. Conant** of Harvard, probably the best-known educator of the day; **Lee A. DuBridge**, president of the California Institute of Technology and a major force at Los Angeles public TV station KCET;

David D. Henry, president of the University of Illinois; and **Franklin Patterson**, president of Hampshire College.

Oveta Culp Hobby, a well-known Houston publisher, had served the nation with distinction during World War II as head of the Women's Army Corps. Another Texan, **J.C. Kellam**, was a principal of broadcasting interests close to the president's family.

Edwin H. Land and **Joseph H. McConnell** were major figures in American business, and **Leonard Woodcock** of the United

Auto Workers represented labor. **John S. Hayes**, a commercial broadcaster, was appointed ambassador to Switzerland during the commission's work, and **Terry Sanford** had been governor of North Carolina.

Representing the arts were: pianist **Rudolf Serkin**; television producer **Robert Saudek**; and the best-known black author of the day, **Ralph Ellison**.

The commission's executive secretary was **Hyman H. Goldin**, an economist who had recently completed a 22-year career with the FCC.

---

were on the air. The commission contacted all of them and visited 92; its report provided the first comprehensive database ever compiled about educational television in the United States.

The commission's 12 primary recommendations focused on two ideas: greatly enlarged federal support, and establishment of a Corporation for Public Television. Major operating functions—particularly programming and interconnection—were built on this core.

The commission gave prominence to the term "public television." It did not, however, adopt "public television" as a replacement for "educational television," but as a subdivision of it. In the mid-1960s, typical educational stations devoted a large part of their schedule to formal instruction. The commission was concerned with the rest of the schedule, intended for general audiences: "Public television, to which the commission has devoted its major attention, includes all that is of human interest and importance which is not at the moment appropriate or available for support by advertising, and which is not arranged for formal instruction."

This distinction evolved during the commission's life. At the group's first meeting, several commissioners noted the importance of instruction and its central role in the development of educational television. The commission's executive secretary, Dr. Hyman Goldin, later remarked, "I felt that from a political standpoint, if we came out without having dealt with the instructional broadcasting part, I was fearful that we wouldn't be able to sell the rest of it. And I argued strenuously. But I was overruled on that."

As the commission defined it, the Corporation for Public Television would have limited its work essentially to acquiring programs and interconnecting stations, plus some recruiting, training and research and development efforts. General station support grants, which now account for a major portion of the corporation's

Bostonians were leaders on the ramp up to federal aid. **Ralph Lowell** (above) gave President Johnson the 1964 proposal for a citizen's commission; WGBH manager Hartford Gunn had drafted it; MIT chairman James Killian was to head the commission. Lowell, a textiles heir whose family had backed the Lowell Institute lecture series since 1836, allied with area colleges to put lectures on local commercial radio stations in 1946 and then get their own licenses, starting WGBH-FM in 1951 and WGBH-TV in 1955. (Photo of portrait: David Binder.)

"Unless you really promote and explain and engage the interest of the people who make decisions, a commission of this kind doesn't get very far," said Carnegie I Chairman **James Killian** in an oral history interview with Jim Robertson. Carnegie members didn't sit back. They visited key chairmen in Congress—Edward Kennedy hosted a meeting with 22 senators—and called on David Sarnoff of RCA and Frank Stanton of CBS. Stanton volunteered a million-dollar contribution from CBS. Within 11 months after announcing Carnegie findings, Congress had passed the act creating CPB, and President Johnson had signed it into law. Killian became vice chairman of CPB and then its second chairman.

The 12 commandments of Carnegie I

1. We recommend concerted efforts at the federal, state and local levels to improve the facilities and to provide for the adequate support of the individual educational television stations and to increase their number.

2. We recommend that the Congress act promptly to authorize and to establish a federally chartered, nonprofit, nongovernmental corporation, to be known as the "Corporation for Public Television." The corporation should be empowered to receive and disburse governmental and private funds in order to extend and improve public television programming. The commission considers the creation of the corporation fundamental to its proposal and would be most reluctant to recommend the other parts of its plan unless the corporate entity is brought into being.

3. We recommend that the corporation support at least two national production centers, and that it be free to contract with independent producers to prepare public television programs for educational television stations.

4. We recommend that the corporation support, by appropriate grants and contracts, the production of public television programs by stations for more-than-local use.

5. We recommend that the corporation on appropriate occasions help support local programming by local stations.

6. We recommend that the corporation provide the educational television system as expeditiously as possible with facilities for live interconnection by conventional means, and that it be enabled to benefit from advances in technology as domestic communications satellites are brought into being. The commission further recommends that Congress act to permit the granting of preferential rates for educational television for the use of interconnection facilities, or to permit their free use, to the extent that this may not be possible under existing law.

7. We recommend that the corporation encourage and support research and development leading to the improvement of programming and program production.

8. We recommend that the corporation support technical experimentation designed to improve the present television technology.

9. We recommend that the corporation undertake to provide means by which technical, artistic and specialized personnel may be recruited and trained.

10. We recommend that the Congress provide the federal funds required by the corporation through a manufacturer's excise tax on television sets (beginning at 2 percent and rising to a ceiling of 5 percent). The revenues should be made available to the corporation through a trust fund.

11. We recommend new legislation to enable the Department of Health, Education and Welfare to provide adequate facilities for stations now in existence, to assist in increasing the number of stations to achieve nationwide coverage, to help support the basic operations of all stations, and to enlarge the support of instructional television programming.

12. We recommend that federal, state, local and private educational agencies sponsor extensive and innovative studies intended to develop better insights into the use of television in formal and informal education.

budget as community service grants (CSGs), would have come from the Department of Health, Education and Welfare (HEW, precursor of today's Department of Education), appended to the facilities program which already was supplying stations with money for capital improvements. The corporation would not have been concerned with radio, or formal education.

The commission was sensitive to the potential for federal interference in public broadcasting programming, and so proposed two ways to insulate the industry from government pressure. First, public broadcasting would obtain its federal dollars from an excise tax on the sales of new television sets, rather than from direct federal appropriations. Proceeds from the tax were to be held in a trust fund until drawn by the corporation. Second, the corporation's board was to be composed of 12 members, six appointed by the President with the advice and consent of the Senate, the other six chosen by the appointees.

Both ideas were political non-starters. Legislators dislike excise taxes because they are hard to control; economists dislike them because there may not be a connection between the amount of money raised and the amount needed. And appointments are a traditional and highly valued prerogative of the executive branch.

The commission seemed less concerned about the prospect of pressure applied directly to the stations, and recommended that stations' general support grants come straight from the government. The resulting legislation, however, did not contain that provision.

The commission deliberated for just over a year. Members and the commission staff pored over research papers, articles and memoranda; visited stations; commissioned studies; and conducted interviews. In January 1967, the commission released its report, *Public Television: A Program for Action*.

In the report, the commissioners made 12 recommendations to help develop what they now called "public television" (see box on previous page). The report—addressed to "the American people" but aimed squarely at Congress and the Administration—was released early in 1967. In February a bill based on the report was introduced.

PB PB
See online: portions of the Carnegie reports.

The journey through Congress

The bill went to Congress with President Johnson's Feb. 28 "Message on Education and Health in America." In urging support for public broadcasting, the president returned to the system's roots, recalling that when the Federal Communications Commission reserved television channels for education 15 years earlier, it declared, "The public interest will be clearly served if these stations contribute significantly to the educational process of the nation."

The president recommended passage of a "Public Television Act," which would create a "Corporation for Public Television" with a 15-member board to be appointed by the president and confirmed by the Senate. Johnson proposed federal support for both television and radio at triple the level for facilities, plus $9 million in initial funding for the corporation. Johnson said he would make further proposals for the corporation's long-term financing after a year. In his speech, Johnson also emphasized the potential value of satellite interconnection and directed the administrator of the National

Aeronautics and Space Administration (NASA), the secretary of HEW and other government and private organizations to begin experimenting on a satellite distribution system for public and instructional television.

Congress held hearings on the proposals, during which it debated fundamental issues such as the relationship between government and the broadcasting it helps finance. No issue was more sensitive than the prospect of a partisan political tilt in public broadcasting programs. Critics had complained that numerous programs produced by National Educational Television reflected a liberal bias and several members of Congress were determined that any future system should be rigidly neutral.

Republican Rep. William L. Springer of Illinois expressed this view during testimony by Dr. James R. Killian, Jr., the commission's chairman. "One of the things that is very disturbing and I think the biggest issue this committee is faced with, after talking with my colleagues on both sides of the aisle, is whether or not there will be any federal control in this whole thing," Springer said. Killian said the commission's proposed method for appointing the corporation's board members would help prevent federal interference. He also expressed hope that the Senate would "be much tougher and more careful in the confirmation procedures, in looking at people for this kind of a corporate entity than it might normally be."

Springer emphasized that even the choice of topics sometimes reflected political points of view: "You understand that you can even take certain issues and discuss them which are interesting to one party and not interesting to another party . . . the issues you pick out to discuss may have a political connotation . . . I don't know what we will do on this question, or what anyone else can do about this. But we realize that here is the nub and we will have to live with it for a long time." Killian replied:

> "The Carnegie Commission gave more attention and thought to this problem of insulation and independence than anything else. We are heart and soul committed to an independent and free system . . . Unless we can get that freedom and independence, we are in trouble."

The radio issue

Perhaps the most divisive issue of 1967 for public broadcasters was whether to include radio in the act. For a decade, public broadcasters had focused their efforts to secure federal support on television. The facilities program established in 1962 was the Educational *Television* Facilities Program. The NAEB conference that spawned the Carnegie Commission was specifically concerned with the long-range financing for educational *television*. The resulting commission recommended a structure only for public *television*. By the time the bill was introduced, Johnson was recommending support also for radio—to be administered by a Corporation for Public *Television*.

Jerrold Sandler, executive director of NAEB's National Educational Radio division, spearheaded the effort to add radio, despite the NAEB's decision not to pursue support for both. Sandler began to develop arguments that would parallel the Carnegie Commission's.

In NAEB, with its deep split between radio and television stations, TV leaders had been working toward federal funding for years, and radio was left out. The head of NAEB's radio division, **Jerrold Sandler** (pictured below), gambled by spending much of his budget on a quick report, *The Hidden Medium*, said report author Herman Land. After the Senate hearing on the Public Broadcasting Act, Land recalled, Sen. John Pastore said it was the first time he'd heard the radio story.

PB
PB
See online: summary of *The Hidden Medium* report, 1967.

Members of the first CPB board meet with President Johnson in April 1968, five months after enactment of the Public Broadcasting Act. He's signing CPB's first reauthorization bill, the beginning of an annual authorization-and-appropriation cycle involving at least a dozen separate congressional votes each year. For CPB's second year, Congress authorized $9 million and later appropriated $5 million. (Photo: CPB.)

A conference held in September 1966 at the Johnson Foundation's Wingspread Center in Racine, Wis., helped mobilize support. Central to the campaign was a hastily written report called *The Hidden Medium,* by Herman W. Land Associates, which outlined the history, status and potential of educational radio. Public radio advocates distributed the report in April 1967, more than a month after the original public television bill was introduced in Congress. *The Hidden Medium* proved to be a persuasive instrument in Congress and the Administration.

Still, opponents argued that the educational radio system's long history of weakness would drag the entire Carnegie effort into oblivion. Some also complained that financing radio would dilute already limited prospective federal support.

But others recognized that this might be a now-or-never opportunity to develop noncommercial radio in the United States. Public radio champions launched a hard sell in Congress.

A campaign for congressional action is nearly always more effective if the interested parties have agreed in advance. In this case they hadn't, although both sides tried to maintain a comradely facade. There were frantic behind-the-scenes maneuvers on all sides until dangerously close to the final vote on the bill. In the end, the radio forces won: the bill became the Public *Broadcasting* Act instead of the Public *Television* Act, and Congress instructed the new Corporation for Public Broadcasting (CPB) to aid the development of both media. In this and several other ways the 1967 Act was different from what the Carnegie Commission recommended.

Killian later recalled how, when CPB began to organize the radio system, "PBS was very troubled by a diversion of funds necessary to get the radio system going. I remember one very difficult session when they were urging that we greatly reduce the funds that we had planned to appropriate for public radio. But public radio has turned out to be a great success."

The bill set something of a record for quick passage, clearing the Congress in seven months. President Johnson signed the Public Broadcasting Act of 1967 on Nov. 7, in a full-dress ceremony that

PB PB

See online: text of the Public Broadcasting Act.

What is CPB supposed to do?

Excerpts and paraphrases from CPB's authorizing law, as amended into the 1990s:

■ "facilitate the full development of public telecommunications in which programs of high quality, diversity, creativity, excellence and innovation, which are obtained from diverse sources, will be made available to public telecommunications entities, with strict adherence to objectivity and balance in all programs or series of programs of a controversial nature;"

■ "assist in the establishment and development of one or more interconnection systems to be used for the distribution of public telecommunications services . . .";

■ "assist in the establishment and development of one or more systems of public telecommunications entities throughout the United States;"

■ "carry out its purposes and functions and engage in its activities in ways that will most effectively assure the maximum freedom of the public telecommunications entities and systems from interference with, or control of, program content or other activities."

The law also prohibits CPB from:

■ "owning or operating any television or radio broadcast station, system or network, community antenna television system, interconnection system or facility, program production facility, or any public telecommunications entity, system or network;"

■ "producing programs, scheduling programs for dissemination, or disseminating programs to the public."

A provision dating back to a 1988 amendment led to the creation of the CPB-funded Independent Television Service (see Chapter 10):

■ CPB shall "provide adequate funds for an independent production service" . . . "separate from the Corporation," "for the expenditure of funds for the production of public television programs by independent producers and independent production entities." Its funds "shall be used exclusively in pursuit of the Corporation's obligation to expand the diversity and innovativeness of programming available to public broadcasting."

took place in Washington while the NAEB convention was under way in Denver. A contingent of broadcasters invited to the signing ceremony flew to Washington and returned to the convention later in the day.

The Public Broadcasting Act

The act addressed the critical tension between political program content and broadcasters' independence. All stations, both public and commercial, were required to observe the Fairness Doctrine and equal time requirements of the FCC. But the act held public stations to a more rigorous standard of objectivity than commercial stations. It prohibited public stations from editorializing, and gave them an additional mandate for objectivity and balance. Though the courts struck down the prohibition against editorializing in 1982 as a violation of the First Amendment, the "objectivity and balance" requirement remains in the amended version of the Public Broadcasting Act.

In the corporation's charter, Congress assigned CPB to help develop an educational broadcasting system "in which programs of high quality, obtained from diverse sources, will be made available to noncommercial educational television or radio broadcast stations, with strict adherence to objectivity and balance in all programs or series of programs of a controversial nature."

Congress tried to ensure CPB's role as the protector of the educational broadcasting system's independence, calling on the corporation "to afford maximum protection to such broadcasting from extraneous interference and control," and, in another section directing the corporation to "carry out its purposes and functions and engage in its activities in ways that will most effectively assure the maximum freedom of the noncommercial educational television or radio broadcast systems and local stations from interference with or control of program content or other activities."

The 1967 act included a "Congressional Declaration of Policy," with six key points: that noncommercial radio and television, including instructional television, were in the public interest and that freedom, imagination and initiative on the local and national levels are necessary to develop diverse programming on public broadcasting; that federal support for public broadcasting was appropriate; that encouraging diverse programming on public broadcasting that is responsive to local and national populations "furthers the general welfare"; that the federal government should help make public broadcasting available to all U.S. citizens; and that the government should create a private corporation to help develop public broadcasting and "to afford maximum protection to such broadcasting from extraneous interference and control."

With the bill, Congress established CPB—"which will not be an agency or establishment of the United States Government"—to help develop programming, establish an interconnection system, and help develop and support public TV and radio stations, and do all of this in ways that assured public broadcasting maximum freedom.

Subsequent modifications in the language of these "purposes and activities, have not changed their spirit. One changed "noncommercial educational radio and television stations" to "public telecommunications entities." The section requiring "programs of high quality" has become ". . . programs of high quality, diversity, creativity, excellence and innovation . . ."

During the corporation's early years, its board decided how to spend the money it received, within the broad limits in the act's statement of purposes and activities. Congress gradually has reduced the corporation's discretion through legislated formulas that prescribe the percentages of appropriations to be applied to major budget items. The largest of these fund stations through community service grants.

The Public Broadcasting Act of 1967 put in place the cornerstone for future development. The creation of the organizations that became the Public Broadcasting Service and National Public Radio was implied but not prescribed.

Major difficulties remained. The Public Broadcasting Act did not solve the problem of long-range financing, and initial appropriations were barely enough to get started. There were no plans for developing a structure for programming, or for executive training. Nevertheless, public broadcasters had won a fundamental victory. After half a century, noncommercial broadcasting's goals seemed within reach.

See Chapters 6, 9 and 11: The matter of funding sources, not resolved in 1967, will return as an issue in the 1980s and '90s.

The institutions take shape

From local stations, public television develops a national structure

National Educational Television, the predecessor of PBS, grew out of public TV's Foundation Years, historian Ralph Engelman points out. The Ford Foundation not only promoted and created local stations but also created NET's predecessor, the Educational Television and Radio Center in 1952, before any of the stations were on the air, to provide programs for them. Pictured: **NET producer Nazaret "Chic" Cherkezian** in the studio. (Photo: NPBA.)

The first verse of a public broadcasting testament would read, "In the beginning was the station." The key to understanding the sometimes Byzantine organization of public broadcasting is to start there, with the individual broadcast outlet. In all their variety, complexity and occasional contrariness, stations are the heart of the industry; the fundamental conversation in public broadcasting is between stations and their audiences.

This focus is not merely rhetorical. By tradition and, since 1967, by law, the U.S. public broadcasting system is the least centralized national broadcasting structure—anywhere.

In most broadcasting systems around the world, the local station is largely incidental, a necessary step in the transmission chain that begins in a national network studio and ends with the viewer or listener. In the United States, the Communications Act of 1934 assumes the primacy of the local station; although the Federal Communications Commission has devoted considerable time and study to issues related to networks, the commission actually regulates licensees that operate individual stations. Under the law, the station is the primary element of U.S. broadcasting. In the "Definitions" section of the Communications Act, there is no entry for "network."

"Network" has a very different meaning in commercial broadcasting. There, affiliates are bound to their networks by basic business arrangements: the networks pay the stations to carry programs, and to carry them at specific times. Although the stations are independent in a regulatory sense, and value the time they program locally, the strong commercial network system has centralized decision-making in American commercial broadcasting.

This conventional pyramid organization, with authority at the top, is anathema to public broadcasting, which began as a small band of individual stations scattered across the country. While commercial and foreign radio formed national services in the mid-1920s, when NBC, CBS and Britain's BBC were created, interconnection was far beyond the means of poverty-stricken educational radio. Stations had to survive on their own, with neither the central programming nor the financing that networks permitted. The advent of National Educational Television did little to change this; NET provided only a few hours of programs a week, and these came not by interconnection but by mail. Programs were shipped to sequences of stations, initially on kinescope film and then on videotape. While NET encouraged stations to help national promotion by broadcasting a given series on a given day (although different sets of stations would of course have different episodes), the local schedule was paramount. Indeed, even NET's modest attempt at consistent primetime scheduling raised storms of protest.

Stations' varied interests

The fierce independence of local stations also is due partly to their varied institutional and financial arrangements. Commercial stations large and small share basic economic purposes and strategies, but the manager of a public station licensed to a college or state commission may face assumptions and pressures very different from those confronting the manager of a metropolitan station licensed to a nonprofit community corporation. One example: Jack McBride, who has headed Nebraska Educational Television since its inception, says his system consciously has avoided changing its name to the Nebraska Public Television Network in order to maintain a clear identification with education.

Part of stations' independence and individuality derives from the fact that each began not as a business investment, but as a commitment to render a service. Although an educational institution, state commission, or community nonprofit corporation makes the commitment, it typically begins as the mission of a determined individual who can engage the community's support. Investment financing is not available, and until 1962 there was no federal program to help buy hardware. Even in the mid-1980s, grants from the federal Public Telecommunications Facilities Program covered about half the cost of equipment, and direct station support through CPB's congressionally mandated Community Service Grants amounted to about 15 percent of most stations' operating budgets. Stations are coaxed—virtually levitated—into operation. It's no wonder, then, that a kind of frontier independence comes easily.

Public broadcasting traditionally has obtained programs from many sources. Early program services exchanged programs that stations produced. NET initially commissioned stations to produce programs instead of making them itself. Later, NET began to produce its own shows, but the stations also remained important producers.

In proposing the concept that became the Corporation for Public Broadcasting, the Carnegie Commission envisioned an agency that was concerned principally with programs, but that commissioned national program producers and exceptional local stations to produce them. The resulting federal law prohibits the corporation from owning or operating any broadcast or cable organization, interconnection system or facility, program production house or public telecommunications organization. The law further prohibits CPB from producing, scheduling or distributing programs to the public.

When the Public Broadcasting Service was formed, its articles of incorporation were broad. But on one point they were quite specific: they prohibited PBS from producing or broadcasting programs and from owning or operating any station.

National Public Radio is an exception to that rule. When it was created, both CPB and the stations recognized that contemporary public radio required a producing network; in fact, the program that became *All Things Considered* already was partly planned. So from the beginning, NPR was intended to produce programs—in collaboration with stations.

But stations' central role does not mean that they are solitary or isolated. On the contrary. James Day, one of the earliest and most respected public television managers, once called public broadcast-

A generation of general managers built distinctive local institutions, including the hyper-energetic **Jack McBride** (above), who built a statewide network from a station donated to the University of Nebraska, and then added a national instructional video distributor (GPN), an interactive videodisc production house, live satellite hookups for university courses, an agricultural satellite service and, finally, a radio network. McBride retired in 1996 after more than 40 years on the jobs.

Regional public TV and radio networks

In 1959-60, WGBH President Hartford Gunn initiated public television's first regional network. Gunn later said he founded the **Eastern Educational Network** (EEN) to have a way to distribute programs instantly and to encourage the growth of other stations in the Northeast by increasing their program supply. Gunn also wanted to supplement the programs available from NET, exchange instructional programming (which was largely outside the scope of NET) and, finally, to provide a structural backup in the event NET failed.

In an 1981 interview, Gunn described the frustration of missed opportunities during an era without a modern program distribution system. "I knew that if we were to survive, there had to be more going on in this field in the Northeast, so that people were talking about it, people were writing about it. And that stations couldn't go on the air— there couldn't be a station in New Hampshire and Maine and Vermont and elsewhere in the Northeast—unless there was more programming than NET could supply. And we had some programming that we could offer . . . Then also, I had a feeling that if NET—which was totally and solely dependent on the Ford Foundation—went down, we would be left with a hole in our schedule that would leave the audience wanting, and then station funding would dis-

appear."

EEN became the major alternative to PBS as a national program source. [Its Interregional Program Service was renamed the American Program Service in 1992 and American Public Television in 1999.] Except for EEN's programming successes— it, not NET, introduced Julia Child to national acclaim— regional networks have not served primarily as program agencies. Instead, they became intra-system forums and political organizations, bringing together station leaders in natural regional groupings. In addition, each of the four regional public television organizations gradually took on specific roles.

EEN concentrated on its program service. The **Southern Educational Communications Association** (SECA) concentrated on developing educational services [and its meeting services, going national in 1998 as the National Educational Telecommunications Association, winning many western and northern stations as members]. The **Central Educational Network** (CEN) also led the way in applying new technology to education and public broadcasting. [In 1999, it made its national scope explicit by creating a new umbrella organization for itself, the American Telecommunications Group.] The **Pacific Mountain Network** grew to represent a vast area from Denver to Guam [and voluntarily ceased

most operations in 1997].

Independently valuable as these functions are, John Porter, longtime head of EEN [and then APS], probably spoke for many when he observed that the regional organizations' viability was based on their collegiality and their natural political alliances.

Radio's regionals

Although radio managers had organized themselves before television was invented, regional groups had little significance until the national public radio system was well established. **Eastern Public Radio Network**, the radio counterpart of EEN, was the sole exception. As the Educational Radio Network, it achieved regional interconnection about the same time EEN did. The network carried *Kaleidescope*, a daily newsmagazine that originated in Boston, New York, Philadelphia and Washington. But a lack of funds killed, for then, public radio's dream of permanent interconnection.

SECA added a radio division as public radio developed nationally in the 1970s [and then spun off the separate **Southern Public Radio** in the 1990s]. **Public Radio in Mid-America** (PRIMA) took a strong role in national affairs. Farther west, stations organized **Rocky Mountain Public Radio** and **West Coast Public Radio**.

ing "a long series of meetings occasionally interrupted by a program." The early stations joined to share programs, fight political battles, attract attention and support from their audience, seek channel reservations, encourage education to use the media, and secure financing from philanthropies and government. Organizations of stations and their people—most prominently the National Association of Educational Broadcasters—were the working core of the movement that became public broadcasting.

The death of NAEB

For nearly 60 years, the National Association of Educational Broadcasters was public broadcasting's primary forum and voice. NAEB was open to all licensed public stations. It was the initial rallying point for channel reservations for radio and television. It hosted the meeting that launched the Carnegie Commission. Its publications provided extensive information about the field and served as the medium for a continuing national conversation among public broadcasters.

NAEB began as the Association of College and University Broadcasting Stations in 1925, representing a few small stations. When it folded more than half a century later, 80 percent of American homes had full schedules of public radio and television programs on their dials.

The association was in many ways a victim of its own success. At its peak, NAEB was a forum, program service, research and development unit, information source, national voice and rallying point. As the field grew, newer, more specialized institutions performed many of these functions. At its end, NAEB remained the only grassroots-based organization attempting to embrace the entire public broadcasting industry, but it lost its base of stations' support as their resources were redirected to support functions now conducted elsewhere. The historic standard-bearer of public broadcasting was no longer viable and, late in 1981, it was dissolved.

"When NAEB died our national, interregional forum died," said Virginia Fox, who served as one of NAEB's last chairmen. Regional organizations, America's Public Television Stations (APTS) and NPR's representation division have taken over many of the NAEB's functions, Fox said.

The stations shifted to the present regional-national representation structure soon after CPB was born in 1968. By prohibiting the corporation from operating interconnection systems, the Public Broadcasting Act created the need for PBS and NPR. Both are nonprofit corporations with station members.

The roles of NPR and PBS

National Public Radio was incorporated in March 1970, and went on the air 13 months later—operating public radio's first full-time, national, live interconnection system—with a live broadcast of the Senate Foreign Relations Committee hearings on ending the Vietnam War. Two weeks later came the debut of *All Things Considered*. Within two months, NAEB's radio program service, the National Educational Radio Network, merged with NPR. For a time, NAEB continued to represent radio stations, but in 1973 public radio broadcasters created the Association of Public Radio Stations (APRS) to represent public radio stations. NPR, run by a board of mostly station managers, produced national programs and operated the network. APRS was the stations' Washington lobbying and public relations organization.

But within several years the stations decided APRS was too expensive to support, and that having two organizations made it difficult for public radio to speak with one voice, so in 1977 APRS merged

Between 1960 and 1975, **William G. Harley** was the cement that held NAEB together—a confederation that ranged from tiny college radio stations to ambitious big-city TV stations, said colleague Chalmers Marquis. In 1960, he left Madison, where he was the first manager of WHA-TV, to open NAEB's D.C. office. He threw the association's support behind the campaign for federal aid, working with NAEB counsel Leonard Marks and consultant C. Scott Fletcher, and later recruited Ralph Rogers to work with other local station leaders to help defend the field during the Nixon Administration. Harley left NAEB in 1975 to work on international issues and died in November 1998 at the age of 87.

with NPR. There have since been periodic attempts to divide the functions again.

Public television stations eventually took almost the opposite approach. After PBS was formed in 1969, NAEB continued as the stations' representation agency and continued operating the Educational Television Stations Program Service. In 1973, PBS absorbed NAEB's Educational Television Stations division when the network was reorganized; until 1979, PBS programmed the network and attempted to represent stations' national interests. Gradually, public TV leaders decided that programming and operating the interconnection system were not always compatible with stations' interests regarding legislation, CPB budget policy, and FCC regulatory issues. Early in 1979, stations created the National Association of Public Television Stations (NAPTS), later renamed the Association of America's Public Television Stations (APTS). APTS emerged as one of the most respected institutions of public TV.

Since they began operating in 1970-71, PBS and NPR have become fundamental building blocks in the structure of public broadcasting. Both are membership corporations with boards of directors composed of representatives from stations and the public. While stations acquire national programs from many distributors, NPR and PBS constitute their members' basic, most important sources of national material through the public radio and TV satellite interconnection systems.

But many other organizations long have been part of public broadcasting. Some, such as the longstanding Agency for Instructional Technology or the Great Plains National Instructional Television Library, are educational program services. Others, such as Native American Public Telecommunications, represent special groups of citizens. Some are specialized production companies, such as the Children's Television Workshop (*Sesame Street*) and Family Communications, Inc. (*Mister Rogers' Neighborhood*). And a number, such as the National Captioning Institute and organizations devoted to research, provide specialized technical and support services. The National Federation of Community Broadcasters serves a major constituency of community radio stations, and for many years the Broadcasting Foundation of America specialized in distributing radio programs from international sources.

CPB's ambiguous, unique role

CPB's place in this system structure remains one of public broadcasting's ambiguities. Is CPB an integral part of public broadcasting, or must it stand apart? Public broadcasting stations and systems (and to some extent their recent relatives in the broader field of public telecommunications) are the reason the corporation exists.

The corporation's policy decisions are significant to all of public broadcasting. As the recipient of appropriated funds, the corporation is the natural contact point for issues Congress or the Administration is concerned about, particularly since the President appoints CPB's directors and the Senate must confirm them.

As a funding agency, the corporation is directly linked to other parts of public broadcasting. But as the system's major device for insulation from "extraneous interference and control," the corporation must itself maintain a discreet distance from day-to-day activities.

So if one were to devise an organization chart of public broadcasting, where would the corporation be? Certainly not at the top of a pyramid: in this decentralized system, the pyramid doesn't exist. The corporation's role may be unique in world broadcasting. Positioned between the rest of public broadcasting and the federal government, it is at once a link and an insulator. Its policy decisions are critical, but it must undertake its major responsibilities without engaging in system operations. Leadership is expected, but leverage is limited. Despite occasional calls for abolishing, replacing or restructuring it, the corporation is generally considered to be an essential—if not entirely comfortable—mechanism.

How to interconnect the stations?

The pioneering networks were regional: television's Eastern Educational Network and its counterpart, the Educational Radio Network. The goal, however, was national.

For a time it appeared that ERN would be the prototype. In 1962 the interconnected regional network became part of NET, and demonstrated networking's potential. Donald R. Quayle, of WGBH in Boston, joined the staff of NET as director of radio. Within several months, however, the Ford Foundation decided to focus its grants on a few NET activities; the radio network's last live broadcast covered Martin Luther King's march on Washington in August 1963.

Radio broadcasters pursued interconnection by establishing a system designed to be shared with other educational telecommunication services. A planning study, funded by the U.S. Office of Education, focused on three different models: a regional university group based on the Committee on Institutional Cooperation (the Big Ten Universities and the University of Chicago); a single-state system, in Oregon; and a diverse regional group in the Northeast, essentially ERN members. The national educational radio division of the NAEB conducted the study, which resulted in plans for a prototype multipurpose telecommunications system for education. But there were no funds to pursue the plan, and interconnection had to await the creation of CPB. As it turned out, the corporation's arrival was imminent.

Several weeks after CPB's incorporation, its board established an interconnection committee and began to consult with public TV leaders and AT&T.

How should the interconnection be managed? Although the Carnegie Commission had recommended that the corporation manage the interconnection system, the idea met stiff opposition in the subsequent congressional hearings, and public broadcasters, CPB itself, and the Ford Foundation (then the major funder of public television) agreed that a separate arrangement would be necessary.

The NET affiliates council had proposed that it operate the interconnection system. NET was the primary source of national programming and had the most obvious administrative mechanism to manage the forthcoming system. On the other hand, the most cursory reading of the Carnegie Commission's report and the legislative history of the Public Broadcasting Act revealed that the corporation's mandate was to diversify the system, and specifically to reduce the relative power of NET.

The CPB committee considered stitching together the existing state networks, EEN, and other regional systems that seemed imminent. AT&T suggested a network based on off-hours use of its facilities (2 a.m. to noon), an idea which attracted little interest. On one point there was no dispute: the stations themselves would have a primary role in managing the interconnection system. Michael Gammino, chairman of the CPB board's interconnection committee, concluded a July 1968 meeting saying CPB should be "a servant to the communities, states and regions," adding that they should have "a great deal of independence."

In September 1968 Ward B. Chamberlin, Jr., and Robert D.B. Carlisle of the CPB staff advised Chairman Frank Pace that "interconnection management is not logically something which should be in NET's portfolio." In a memo to Pace, they explained: "It doesn't make good sense to have the primary program producer control what goes out over the network. CPB should support NET as a—not the—national production center." Chamberlin and Carlisle concluded that "there should be a new, quasi-independent mechanism to operate the public TV network." That agency would then respond both to the stations and to the national producer-distributor.

PB PB

See online: Chamberlin and Carlisle's 1968 proposal for a Public Television Network.

Meanwhile, NET and its affiliates council were pressing hard to manage the network. CPB, while actively negotiating with AT&T and with agreement clearly imminent, didn't have an alternative in place. But the corporation, the Ford Foundation (NET's funder), and others agreed that NET should not be designated.

An independent network: PBS

Under Chamberlin's guidance, CPB and the Ford Foundation began developing a plan for an independent network. They proposed a separate corporation with an 11-person board composed of five station representatives; two NET representatives; two public members; one regional network representative, and one CPB representative. "This plan would give representation to the important elements in public TV, at the same time leaving the dominant voice in the stations," Chamberlin wrote. He noted that the station managers of the "big eight" stations (New York City, Boston, Pittsburgh, Washington, Chicago, San Francisco, Los Angeles and Philadelphia) had developed a very similar plan. But even among the eight, there were disagreements. Gunn from WGBH in Boston, John Kiermaier from WNDT in New York, and James Loper from KCET in Los Angeles advocated an independent network, while Donald Taverner from WQED in Pittsburgh and James Day from KQED in San Francisco were involved in preparing the NET affiliates plan and were committed to it.

To launch the trial system, the corporation delayed long-range agreements and assembled an interim interconnection management group, with representatives from NET, the Public Broadcasting Laboratory, stations, regional networks and CPB. Donald Quayle, who had temporarily left his post as executive director of EEN to join CPB, chaired the group, which later provided short-term oversight while NET handled the system's technical operation until a new, permanent, organization could be created. Chamberlin, a long-time associate of Pace who later became one of CPB's first principal staff members, represented the CPB chairman at the first meeting. Chamberlin told the group that they should be "an 'interim' committee acting only until there has been established a long-range entity to manage the interconnected system." Chamberlin said he hoped that CPB and the public television system could reach agreement in a few months on permanent management of the system.

There were several proposals, all of which put stations in control of the system. The NET affiliates council plan envisioned having only stations; another plan proposed that producers and others be represented, with the stations having majority control. "Since this fundamental is agreed upon, it should not be difficult to agree on one plan," Chamberlin commented. "Clearly even this will not be fixed forever; hopefully experience will cause us to change as we move along."

Interconnection begins, two hours a night

On Nov. 11, 1968, the Ford Foundation and the fledgling CPB (it didn't even have a president yet) simultaneously announced grants of $250,000 each to launch primetime interconnection of 150 public television stations.

The arrangement CPB worked out with AT&T provided for a six-month trial of preemptible interconnection service for two hours a night, Sunday through Thursday, beginning Jan. 5, 1969. More than half the programming would come from NET. But there also would be regular offerings from the Public Broadcasting Laboratory (PBL), which was established by the Ford Foundation and focused on TV journalism, NAEB's Educational Television Stations Program Service, and the six regional public TV organizations then in operation. NAEB, incidentally, provided the only program still in public TV's national schedule: *Washington Week in Review*.

Once the trial interconnection launched its five-day-per-week schedule in January 1969 (a limited version had begun earlier), work proceeded on two fronts simultaneously: operating the system and developing long-term management arrangements. Serious operational problems arose immediately: AT&T began frequently preempting television transmissions. By the end of January, Chamberlin had informed the chief of the FCC's Common Carrier Bureau that AT&T's service was unsatisfactory. In a January 30 letter, Chamberlin wrote, "In the 31 nights of broadcasting from December 1 through January 30, there have been a total of 39 AT&T point preemptions and a total of 84 public television station preemptions. In the 19 nights of interconnected broadcasting in January, on all but five nights one or more stations have been preempted. With few exceptions, these preemptions have been made on less than 12 hours notice."

Planning for a permanent, independent organization proceeded. NET continued to press its case. During the spring and summer of 1969, CPB and a six-member group equally representing the NET affiliates council and the board of NAEB's TV division continued negotiations. Early in June, this joint committee of six, quickly nicknamed "the six-pack," reported to its constituency that they

The first president of PBS, **Hartford N. Gunn, Jr.,** was a key strategist for federal funding and a visionary who established public TV's first landline interconnection in the Northeast and later led PBS into the satellite age. During his decade as president of PBS, Gunn devised the Station Program Cooperative that protected PBS programming from CPB control. Later, after leaving the presidency, his System Planning Project in 1979 urged public TV to begin distributing multiple channels. But Gunn was not decisive in all matters—referring major program decisions on "Banks and the Poor" and the Watergate hearings to his board. Chairman Ralph Rogers, who admired quick decision-making, moved Gunn into a planning role as vice chairman, hiring Lawrence Grossman as president in 1975. His System Planning Project was before its time in proposing that PBS distribute specialized program services. He later held the No. 2 job at KCET in Los Angeles and then headed Comsat's planning for an early DBS project. In 1986, he died of cancer at the age of 59. (Photo: Fabian Bachrach.)

had reached consensus on several points, including the following:

■ A new, independent corporation governed by a board of directors, which would determine policy and hire staff, would operate the interconnection facility.

■ CPB would fund the new corporation with annual grants and avoid involvement in day-by-day discussion of interconnection costs.

■ The interconnection facility would make scheduling decisions independent from conditions of CPB program grants.

■ The interconnection corporation would not own, commission, create, or otherwise be involved in producing programs.

■ The interconnection facility would allocate time to national and regional public broadcasting agencies by block for substantial periods of time, as determined by the corporation's board of directors.

■ The interconnection facility would deal with national and regional public broadcasting program agencies. Individual stations, producers or others would seek access to interconnection through these existing agencies, or if necessary, there would be some provision for access directly to the facility's staff or board.

Day for White

Meanwhile, John F. White resigned as president of NET and was succeeded by James Day, who had headed San Francisco's KQED for 15 years. Day immediately sought a 60-day moratorium on the development of the new organization—then referred to as the Public Broadcasting Network—so that he could assess the situation and propose an alternative course. The corporation and the committee of six agreed, but ultimately the die was cast.

On Oct. 1, CPB sent to the stations a memorandum describing the proposed Public Broadcasting Service. It would be a membership corporation "organized specifically to provide national interconnection services for its station members." A second class of "general" members would consist of national program production agencies admitted to membership by a vote of at least two-thirds of the station members. The memo noted: "At present, of course, there would be only one such member: NET."

The board was to consist of nine directors, five representing stations, one representing national program centers, one representing CPB, and two representing the public at large.

On Oct. 6, Robert F. Schenkkan, chairman of the NET affiliates council, and Hartford N. Gunn, Jr., chairman of the NAEB ETS board, jointly sent a letter to station managers advising them that both boards had unanimously endorsed the plan.

On Nov. 7, 1969, PBS was incorporated. Its articles of incorporation and initial by-laws closely followed CPB's plan. NET and CPB were "general members." During the next few months, Hartford Gunn became PBS's first president, hired an initial staff, and assumed responsibility for interconnection management. Work then began on a long-range working agreement between PBS and CPB.

PB
PB
See online: PBS by-laws from 1969.

See Chapter 5:
CPB clashes with the Nixon Administration, resulting in a reorganization of PBS.

A new day for radio

The older medium asserts itself

By the time the Public Broadcasting Act of 1967 was passed, educational radio had been broadcasting for half a century. Berkeley's KPFA, the first of the Pacifica stations, had pioneered the concept of broadcasting supported by contributions from its audience. A number of stations, particularly a few licensed to the Big Ten universities and a handful in the Northeast, were rendering consistently fine service.

But most stations were not. The majority were licensed to colleges and universities, which intended them as adjuncts to broadcasting curricula or as student activities. In 1969 there were 412 educational radio stations: 384 FM and 28 AM facilities. About half the FM stations were in the low-power, Class D category, which had not grown into higher-power stations as the FCC had intended. Most of the rest were too weak to be heard in much of their intended service areas. Even excluding the Class D stations (which often had virtually no budget), more than half had operating budgets of less than $25,000. Many stations did not broadcast on weekends or during summers and university holidays. Even though there were more than twice as many noncommercial radio stations as television stations, they reached much less of the population.

Although educational television had been chronically underfunded from its inception, it nevertheless had received virtually all the national support available from the Ford Foundation and the 1962 Educational Television Facilities Program, and all the attention in the Carnegie Commission's report. Until Jerrold Sandler and his colleagues managed to convert the Public Television Act into the Public Broadcasting Act in 1967 (see Chapter 2), television benefited from virtually all of the limited support that was available.

The technique is fast becoming obsolete as radio producers increasingly do their audio editing on computers, but for years public radio's tape cutters used single-edged razor blades to trim excess moments as short as an "um" from countless interviews. Above, **Marika Partridge cuts tape at NPR** in 1987. In January 1998, NPR began switching to computers for editing part of its daily news programming, the hourly newscasts. (Photo: NPR.)

Which stations to aid?

Most of the 412 stations were virtually inaudible and very few had enough financial support to sustain hope. Managers strove for adequacy; excellence was clearly impossible. Only the most rudimentary sort of national program service was offered on tape via the National Educational Radio (NER) network.

This was the situation facing the new Corporation for Public Broadcasting, with its mandate to "assist in the establishment and development of one or more systems of noncommercial educational . . . radio broadcast stations throughout the United States."

And the funding shortfall was becoming worse. The number of stations continued to rise: by September 1970, 412 had become 427, and the FCC had authorized 30 more stations expected on the air soon. An early CPB survey yielded returns from 368 stations; half had annual budgets of less than $10,000, and 72 percent reported budgets of less than $25,000. Approximately 180 had no full-time

Before landlines, satellites and fiber optics, educational radio shared programs by "bicycling" tapes among the stations. At left: NAEB leaders Allen Miller, Burton Paulu and Richard Hull examine one of the association's **tape duplicating machines** in the mid-1950s. (Photo: National Public Broadcasting Archives.)

PB PB

See online: recommendations of Sam Holt's Public Radio Study.

paid professional staff, and many did not have a single person who devoted at least half time to the station. Nearly 60 percent were on the air less than 48 hours per week.

Furthermore, it was painfully clear that if the corporation's available resources were spread among all the stations, each would receive so little that the ultimate effect would be to perpetuate the status quo. Samuel C.O. Holt's Public Radio Study pointed up public radio's difficult prospects. The NER board, a radio advisory council composed of 12 managers, and the CPB board's radio committee discussed how to distribute the new federal money. In September 1969 the corporation announced a six-year plan that provided increasingly stiff criteria for stations to qualify for federal funding. The criteria set minimum levels of programming, power, staffing, hours of broadcasting, and local production facilities.

The programming criterion required stations to direct their programming toward the general public rather than a narrow or specialized group. The initial criterion for broadcast hours required stations to be on air at least 48 weeks a year, six days a week, eight hours a day. The power requirements tried to assure that most of a station's community could in fact receive its signal. The first staffing requirement called for one full-time and four half-time staff members. The standards described local production facilities as "an adequately equipped control room and studio . . . for program production and origination." Minimum budget levels were imposed as the system developed.

CPB increased the standards over the six years; by fiscal 1976, stations had to have at least five full-time staff members and broadcast at least 18 hours a day, 365 days a year to qualify for funding. CPB encouraged stations to reach the final criteria ahead of schedule by providing extra money to those meeting the more stringent standards. The corporation devised a parallel grant program to help promising, but non-qualifying, stations meet the criteria.

While most public radio broadcasters today would smile at a requirement for only 48 weeks of broadcasting, eight hours a day and six days a week, in fact only 73 stations "qualified" in 1970. And only 103 out of 501 noncommercial stations then operating qualified for support in fiscal 1971. By 1986, 297 stations had qualified; they broadcast an average of 19 hours per day, 365 days a year.

Reasonable as this approach may appear in retrospect, radio managers protested vehemently when the standards were initiated. And although CPB has made an occasional exception, the qualification criteria have been a consistent part of the corporation's radio policy since 1970. It is probably not too much to say that this policy more than any other has helped build a strong public radio system for the United States. Its principal architect and first administrator was Albert L. Hulsen, the corporation's first director of radio activities. If Jerry Sandler was the individual who did most to launch public radio by hammering it into the Public Broadcasting Act, it was Al Hulsen who patiently and stubbornly created a public radio system capable of being consequential.

National Public Radio

The creation of National Public Radio was attended by little of the controversy surrounding the decision to proceed with the Public Broadcasting Service. Indeed, the PBS decision suggested a structural pattern. The radio stations could not properly be called a system: they were diverse, weak and fragmented; there was no major force (or support base) to parallel the Ford Foundation; NAEB's National Educational Radio network performed long and useful service, but only by the most charitable definition would it have been called a radio version of NET. While radio stations valued local and regional programming, they recognized a need for truly national and timely production as they moved toward interconnection.

Late in 1969, a group of station managers—most long active in NAEB—began a series of meetings under CPB auspices that culminated in establishing NPR. The group sketched the network's outlines at its second meeting, held in January 1970 at San Diego. Also at the meeting, William H. Siemering described the concept for what became *All Things Considered*.

NPR was incorporated little more than a month later. Its directors held their organizational meeting March 3. The board's structure generally paralleled that of PBS: there were to be 14 directors, nine representing stations, two representing CPB and NPR, and three from the general public.

But NPR was different in one major way from PBS: it produced programs. While PBS bylaws specifically prohibited it from producing programs, the first of the purposes for which NPR was organized was, "To propose, plan and develop, to acquire, purchase and lease, to prepare, produce and record, and to distribute, license and otherwise make available radio programs to be broadcast over noncommercial educational radio broadcast stations, networks and systems."

NPR's first offering to stations was tapes of 20 concerts by the Los Angeles Philharmonic; its first live programming was the April 1971 Senate Foreign Relations Committee hearings on ending the Vietnam War. The board appointed Donald Quayle, formerly of WGBH in Boston and National Educational Television in New York, as NPR's first president. Siemering was hired as program director.

A month later, on May 3, 1971, 104 member stations in 34 states and Puerto Rico carried the first broadcast of *All Things Considered*.

Later that week, CPB, NPR and NAEB's National Educational Radio division sponsored the first annual Public Radio Conference in Washington. The radio managers attending agreed to focus on

Some listeners wondered whether *All Things Considered* could survive when co-host **Susan Stamberg** left the program after its first 15 years, in 1986, because her voice and personality had made such an enduring impression. With *ATC*, Stamberg became the first woman to anchor a daily national broadcast, and the first female star among many who have reported for public radio. She moved to a new Sunday *Weekend Edition* and later settled in as an NPR arts correspondent.

PB
PB

See online: Bill Siemering's "National Public Radio Purposes" station development and fundraising, station management and community service, and programming.

Association of Public Radio Stations

NAEB long had been public broadcasting's primary national organization. But as federal funding, authorized by the Public Broadcasting Act, began to have an impact, NAEB's functions narrowed. PBS already had assumed many of NAEB's former responsibilities for public TV, including representation. NAEB's radio division, which had a similar function for radio stations, also was soon dissolved. But instead of moving representation functions to their network, the CPB-qualified public radio stations created a new, separate organization: the Association of Public Radio Stations.

The radio managers felt that NPR necessarily had its own agenda as a producer and distributor of programs. APRS, alternately, would represent in Washington the broad range of station interests. After a considerable search, Matthew B. Coffey, formerly assistant to CPB President John W. Macy, Jr., was named president of APRS.

But what seemed logical in theory was less so in practice. Both NPR and APRS were membership organizations. Stations had to pay more for APRS, however, because it was a freestanding, station-supported agency, unlike NPR, which received almost all of its funding not from stations, but from CPB. Because of this, no more that 60 percent of the eligible stations ever belonged to APRS. Also, institutional roles and relationships turned out to be more difficult to separate than anticipated. Furthermore, radio stations felt that they were losing some skirmishes to television interests, partly because the television stations presented a united front via PBS.

In May 1977, APRS was merged into NPR, which in turn was reorganized into two major divisions: programming/distribution and representation. The former presidents of NPR and APRS, Lee Frischknecht and Matthew Coffey respectively, became senior vice presidents of the new organization. Meanwhile, NPR's board had been looking for a permanent president. In August 1977, Frank Mankiewicz was named president of the new NPR.

American Public Radio/Public Radio International

A system that emphasizes diverse programming sources inevitably leads to tension between its major producer—particularly one as prominent as NPR, which also operates the interconnection system—and other producers, actual or potential. In their design deliberations the board of the nascent NPR agreed that "it should reflect regionalism and that it should provide for as much production participation by member stations as possible."

But from the beginning, stations have questioned NPR's adherence to this principle. This, coupled with the entrepreneurial spirit of a group of station managers led by William H. Kling, president of Minnesota Public Radio (and a member of NPR's founding board), led to the formation in 1981 of American Public Radio [now Public Radio International]. The organization, closely related to Minnesota Public Radio when first incorporated, initially was built around Garrison Keillor's *A Prairie Home Companion*, which made its nation-

Public radio's top entrepreneur, Minnesota Public Radio President **William Kling**, founded APR, creating a competitive marketplace in national programming. Starting with the MPR hit, *A Prairie Home Companion*, APR grew to become public radio's second major network, renamed Public Radio International in 1994. In Minnesota, Kling built public radio's largest chain, with the field's most advanced revenue-generating ventures and fundraising. In its third decade, MPR operates 32 stations carrying separate classical music and news/information networks.

al debut in May 1980. Within a few years, APR was providing more programming hours per week than NPR. While much of its programming is music, its public affairs offerings are growing. Among APR's offerings were Canadian Broadcasting Corporation programs; *Monitor Radio* newsmagazines produced [until 1997] by the *Christian Science Monitor*; and a business news program initially produced by CBS that became *Marketplace*. American Public Radio, unlike NPR, did not produce programs—it distributed them.

A Prairie Home Companion—a regional Minnesota Public Radio variety series rejected for national syndication by NPR—became the foundation of today's PRI network. At left: one-time MPR deejay **Garrison Keillor** performs with Ivy Austin and sound effects man Tom Keith during the period of Keillor's self-exile in Manhattan, when he hosted and wrote a similar show called *American Radio Company of the Air*. (Photo: Frederic Petters.)

NPR's time of crisis

In 1982, with federal support for public broadcasting in question and with the administration emphasizing the private sector, NPR undertook an ambitious program intended to eliminate its direct dependence on CPB. A board resolution stated that "NPR management has developed a financial plan of action which could reduce and ultimately eliminate dependency upon federal financial support within five years . . ." The board resolved to raise money from sources other than CPB so that by fiscal 1988 all CPB's funding for radio would come in the form of unrestricted Community Service Grants from CPB to qualified stations.

The plan envisioned greatly increasing underwriting for NPR programs, establishing a profit-making subsidiary and participating in technology-related ventures, and further developing NPR program services.

Almost immediately, however, troubling financial questions surfaced. In early 1983 there were reports of a crisis, but its extent was not yet known. At NPR's annual membership meeting in Minneapolis that April, NPR Chairman Myron Jones brought a message from CPB President Edward Pfister saying that Pfister would recommend to his board that CPB encourage NPR to take steps to restore the radio network's financial stability.

On the surface the situation seemed awkward but not dangerous. The treasurer reported that the finance and development committee would work with NPR's auditing firm to examine the organization's fiscal controls. The treasurer then presented the results of the previous year's audit, which showed that the year ended with a slight cash surplus, an increase in assets, a reduction in debt, an increase in the fund balance and an increase in revenues.

The true picture was not nearly so bright. A major deficit, first estimated at $3 million, emerged. Less than a month later, Mankiewicz resigned. Ronald Bornstein, a veteran public broadcaster who had served as vice president of CPB, took a partial leave from his post at the University of Wisconsin to become interim chief operating officer of NPR.

See online: GAO report on NPR crisis, 1984.

See Chapter 9: Public broadcasting institutions evolve in the 1990s.

In May, Bornstein projected a deficit of $5.8 million for the year. On May 19, CPB made an interim interest-free loan to NPR in order to permit operations to continue. A few days later, Bornstein announced the firing of 84 persons. On June 15, a preliminary audit reported a working capital deficit of $6.5 million. The same report stated that 88 percent of NPR stations had responded favorably to a request to use $1.6 million of their community service grants to assist NPR.

But by now Congress had gotten involved. Congressional inquiries raised disturbing questions about fiscal responsibility in public broadcasting.

The CPB board and NPR directors began intense negotiations for a loan from the corporation, which was to be guaranteed by the member stations. On Aug. 2, 1983, CPB and NPR signed an agreement for a $7 million loan. In addition to the station guarantee, the public radio interconnection system was placed in a trust for three years.

NPR President Douglas Bennet, who joined the network in October 1983, announced early in 1986 that NPR would retire its loan on schedule by September 1986.

NPR's business plan

In February 1985, NPR's board unanimously agreed to recommend to its membership the most far-reaching change since the network's founding. The plan called upon CPB to send all appropriated "radio" funds directly to the stations, rather than providing annual support to NPR. Stations, in turn, would pay NPR through a fee structure to be based on a station's annual revenue. At the same meeting the board voted to dissolve its for-profit subsidiary, NPR Ventures, Inc.

Three months later, in May 1985, the NPR membership overwhelmingly adopted the plan, with one significant modification: not all the radio funds would go to stations' community service grants. The stations asked CPB to maintain a separate $3 million Radio Program Fund "designed to support production of innovative and experimental national radio programming, as well as programming that meets the mandate of public broadcasting to serve minorities and other under-represented groups, and include the work of independent producers."

It appears that the plan's stated intent, to provide increased cohesion and stability to the public radio system, has been realized.

Nixon and public television

The clash tests CPB's accountability to government and its insulating role for broadcasters

The first five years were the hardest. In their earliest days, CPB and PBS had the difficult task of defining their roles while trying to create a complex mechanism for selecting, scheduling, distributing and promoting programs. Almost immediately—and literally before they knew it—they faced their first major test of political involvement in programming.

The Johnson White House had adopted public broadcasting as part of the Great Society. The Nixon Administration, while wary of that legacy, was generally supportive when it came into power at the end of the 1960s. "Although the CPB was established in the Johnson Administration, the Administration will reap the credit or criticism for whatever becomes of public broadcasting over the next decade," the Nixon Administration's chief communications policymaker, Clay T. Whitehead, wrote in August 1969. Whitehead later would be the Administration's key player in a covert attempt to change the basic principles governing public broadcasting.

The Administration then began working on a bill to authorize appropriations to CPB for fiscal years 1971-73. But Nixon and his aides were concerned about the Ford Foundation's dominant position in public television and its relationship with National Educational Television, then public TV's major national production center.

In a meeting kept secret even from the CPB staff, Nixon aide Peter Flanigan in November 1969 told CPB Chairman Frank Pace and CPB director Albert Cole that the Administration would recommend increasing CPB's funding by $5 million—"contingent upon the creation of new program production facilities to replace National Educational Television." Pace replied that phasing down the New York-based production center might take three or four years.

The immediate effects of this meeting were minimal and went largely unnoticed, particularly since the Carnegie Commission and the subsequent Public Broadcasting Act of 1967 that followed it had called for creating additional production centers around the country, and as a result, de-emphasizing NET.

While the act and the commission's report were not the same, the commission's emphasis on the corporation as a programming agency was keenly felt. It meant that the corporation should arrange for programs and serve as a "heat shield" against extraneous interference with or control of the entire public broadcasting system. Under the law, the corporation would be the accountable agency. Both CPB and the stations saw PBS as an interconnection management service that inevitably would have some responsibility for programming.

But the 1967 act created a difficult, perhaps even contradictory, role for CPB. On the one hand, Congress mandated specific pro-

It was not the first time the news media had exasperated **President Nixon**. The news crossing his desk on Sept. 23, 1971, was that the Ford Foundation's National Public Affairs Center for Television (NPACT) had hired newsmen Sander Vanocur, an NBC newsman close to the Kennedy Administration, and Robert MacNeil. "The above report greatly disturbed the President, who considered this the last straw," staff secretary Jon M. Huntsman wrote to Nixon aides that day. "It was requested that all funds for Public Broadcasting be cut immediately."

PB
PB

See online: memos from the Nixon White House released under the Freedom of Information Act.

gram-related responsibilities for the new corporation. CPB's first purpose was to "facilitate the full development of educational broadcasting in which programs of high quality, obtained from diverse sources, will be made available to noncommercial educational television or radio stations, with strict adherence to objectivity and balance in all programs or series of programs of a controversial nature . . ."

At the same time, the corporation also was charged to "assure the maximum freedom of the noncommercial educational television or radio broadcast systems and local stations from interference with or control of program content or other activities."

Among activities the act reserved for CPB were to contract with or make grants to individuals, stations, and other production entities, or otherwise obtain, TV and radio programs for national or regional distribution to noncommercial educational broadcast stations. The corporation also was charged with establishing an interconnection system for public broadcasting.

Questions about the division of responsibility between CPB and PBS also hovered over the infant network. A working agreement outlining these responsibilities became a first, and continuing, order of business when PBS was organized under CPB auspices.

"Banks and the Poor"

A challenge to both organizations came almost immediately. In 1970, public TV aired "Banks and the Poor," a controversial NET

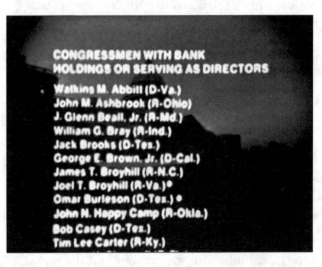

documentary that was favorably reviewed in the *New York Times* and the *Wall Street Journal*, but which brought to the fore all the anomalies and ambiguities then inherent in the structure of public broadcasting.

"Banks and the Poor" alleged that, through practices such as red-lining, major banks were discriminating against the poor, many of whom were minorities. The program closed with a long, scrolling list of senators and congressmen who had (or were alleged to have) ties to the banking industry.

Policymakers at CPB and PBS questioned the program's fairness. So did the White House. Enclosing a clipping about the program from the *Washington Post*, Flanigan wrote Cole, asking how much money CPB had given to NET that year and how much it had budgeted for the production center for 1971. Wrote Flanigan, "Herewith another example of NET activity that is clearly inappropriate for a

Topping off an aggressive critique of banks' failure to serve low-income Americans, Morton Silverstein's **"Banks and the Poor"** featured a crawl of the names of 133 federal officials with banking connections (photo at right). The November 1970 documentary, which brought a sharp response from the Nixon Administration, "snarled and snapped at the hands that fed it," said Columbia University's annual broadcast journalism survey. "No one was spared, from David Rockefeller down to the small-time installment or loan shark." In *Life* magazine, John Leonard said the report "brilliantly dramatized" the indifference and hypocrisy of banks toward the poor, using "tough interviews, concealed cameras, on-location footage of slums . . . pointedly ironic music and a skillful stitching together of the bankers' own TV commercials." The result was too unbalanced for some stations, which chose not to air it, and NET canceled the series *Realities*, of which it was part, at the end of the season. Less noticed at the time was the debut, 11 days later, of *Wall Street Week*, which is still running on PBS three decades later. (Image courtesy of WNET.)

government-supported organization . . . I am directing this inquiry to you in that I think it comes better from you to the board and the management of the corporation than from the White House. Therefore, I'd appreciate you treating this inquiry in that light."

The CPB board—meeting on Nov. 20, 1970, after "Banks and the Poor" aired—spent much of its time discussing the program. In his opening statement, Chairman Pace said the corporation had to deal with the problem of program standards and how best to deal with programs that are objectionable or controversial. Pace observed that the creation of PBS helped by providing stations an institutional representative through which to air their views "in selecting programs, gauging audience reaction, and responding to public protest." But, Pace continued, problems "are bound to arise. The board's obligation is to insure that the corporation is continually on the alert for troublesome situations and be prepared to deal with them promptly and in a forthright and sensitive fashion." Pace and Cole said CPB could not ignore its responsibility to see that federal money was properly spent and said the White House and Congress would inevitably look to CPB, not PBS or National Public Radio, as the accountable agency.

CPB President John W. Macy, Jr., said the program hurt the corporation and described the emerging relationship between CPB, PBS and the producing organizations, which required "national support, creative freedom, and control of the production process." Macy said that PBS—public television's program distribution and scheduling organization—had to have freedom to decide whether programs' content, balance and quality made them acceptable. But Macy agreed with the directors that CPB "as the supporting organization that furnishes funds and leadership . . . is the final accountable agency." Macy cautioned, however, that production houses feared that financial support for programming from the corporation would bring with it attempts by CPB to coerce producers and control editorial policy. "They seek insulation for the producer; the problem lies in furnishing that protection to a desired extent without abdicating the corporation's responsibility to the public," Macy said.

Director Michael Gammino, a Providence, R.I., banker, said he thought "Banks and the Poor" had alienated many CPB supporters and probably hurt the corporation more than it did the banks. Gammino added that public reaction to the program raised the question of whether the corporation needed to participate in determining the philosophy of the programming it funded. He said the board's "No. 1 obligation" was to see that CPB-supported programming met "appropriate legal, moral and ethical standards. . . . Otherwise, the corporation may be lending its hand to a deterioration from within which could destroy it and the country as well."

Some directors worried even whether "Banks and the Poor" was legal. Macy distributed a draft report by PBS programming chief Samuel C.O. Holt and said PBS's board was discussing the issues of taste, fairness, personal attack and advocacy, as well as the possibility of granting equal time for response or correction.

Board member Jack Valenti, then as now head of the Motion Picture Association of America, said Holt's statement would not solve the problem. "The question always remains: What is 'gratuitous'? What are 'good taste,' 'fairness' and 'balance,' and who

A major concern for Nixon aides was the Ford Foundation, which heavily backed public TV in its early years, spending $290 million between 1951 and 1976, aiding the early stations and funding NET. Ford had taken an interest in media after Henry Ford's death. The foundation's 1948 Gaither report on its goals had found that widespread "public apathy" and lack of personal values "bear an important relation to the content of mass communications." In 1966, foundation president, former JFK aide McGeorge Bundy, named ex-CBS newsman **Fred Friendly** (above, in 1988) to oversee its television initiatives. Friendly oversaw NET, backed *Public Broadcasting Laboratory* and supported the influential *Newsroom* local news experiments at four stations. After leaving Ford, Friendly began a series of televised issue seminars that continued on PBS after his death in 1998. (Photo: Andrea Mohin for *Current*.)

determines their meaning? . . . The grisly question is, who has the right of 'final cut?'" Valenti said CPB should.

CPB's responsibility was to the nation at large, not to "a small coterie of the creative," said director Jack Wrather. "Regardless of the difficulties, the corporation must take a definite position in matters of program acceptability."

Dr. James Killian, a CPB board member who had chaired the Carnegie Commission, disagreed with many of his colleagues. Killian said that jumping into censorship would be destructive and that CPB should provide leadership "rather than take an arbitrary, authoritative approach."

At about the same time as the CPB board was preoccupied with "Banks and the Poor," FCC Chairman Dean Burch, speaking at a major public broadcasting meeting, stressed the commission's support for long-range financing, but said that many in Congress and among the public feared "that public broadcasting, if turned loose, will go careening off with its own bent to the issues to be covered and will be a propagandist for one point of view." Burch urged public broadcasters to face up to the issue by being "scrupulously fair— fair in the issues that you decide to cover and fair in the coverage of these issues."

On Nov. 21, 1970, the day after the board meeting, CPB director Cole replied to Flanigan's request, informing the White House aide that CPB's funding for NET was much less than what the Ford Foundation provided, and urging Flanigan to look at the broad range of programs presented by public television, including those of NET.

CPB and PBS agree

Meanwhile, CPB and PBS continued difficult negotiations over their respective roles. By May 1971, the two organizations seemed to have worked things out. Macy wrote PBS President Hartford Gunn a letter outlining their agreement, which defined CPB as the principal policy organization and PBS as public television's principal operating agency for interconnection. "It is clear that the interconnection function implies others: program coordination, national program information and promotion services, nationally acceptable standards and practices, etc. You and your colleagues are to be congratulated on progress made in all of these areas," Macy wrote.

Macy's four-page letter went on to sketch relationships involving distribution, system design, programming and production centers, standards and practices, promotion and program information, station relations, and research. The corporation would have direct responsibility for programming grants and contracts which, however, "will be made in consultation with PBS."

Gunn replied two days later that he was "in complete agreement" with Macy's understanding of the CPB-PBS relationship and looked forward to continued cooperation between the two organizations.

The Public Broadcasting Act of 1967 outlined as one of CPB's principal purposes assuring "maximum freedom of the noncommercial educational television or radio broadcast systems and local stations from interference with or control of program content or other activities." The act also provided that the CPB board elect its chairman and that the board appoint the corporation's president. The corporation, the act said, "will not be an agency or establishment of the United States Government."

But while CPB and the administration continued working on a long-range financing bill, the White House was secretly developing a plan to change these ground rules "to induce CPB to change its orientation and emphasis on public affairs programming," according to a White House staff memorandum later released under the Freedom of Information Act. Involved in hatching the plan were many of Nixon's most senior advisers, including Chief of Staff H.R. (Bob) Haldeman; Domestic Adviser John Ehrlichman; Special Counsel Charles Colson; and Leonard Garment, Nixon's lawyer. "Our friends on the CPB board of directors, notably Jack Wrather, Al Cole and Tom Moore, favor this approach and are working with limited success toward this end," the memo continued. "At a minimum, replacement of Frank Pace as chairman and John Macy as president would be necessary, and more detailed White House intervention would probably be required to keep a rein on the full-time CPB and PBS staffs."

Inflammatory speech in Miami

Recognizing the political consequences of attacking public affairs programming publicly, the Administration's strategy concentrated on replacing the principals of CPB and further decentralizing the public television system.

On Oct. 20, 1971, Whitehead gave a stunning speech to public broadcasters at the NAEB annual meeting in Miami. Contrary to custom, Whitehead's office did not distribute advance copies of the speech; the CPB staff was advised that it would be a rather routine convention address. Instead, Whitehead charged.

"I honestly don't know what group I'm addressing. I don't know if it's really the 47th annual convention of the National Association of Educational Broadcasters or the first annual meeting of PBS affiliates. What's your status? To us there is evidence that you are becoming affiliates of a centralized, national network," Whitehead told the group.

Listing as his first legislative goal for public broadcasting, "to keep it from becoming a government-run system," Whitehead attacked the recently established National Public Affairs Center for Television in Washington and charged that "the Ford Foundation is able to buy over $8 million worth of public-affairs programming on your stations." Whitehead went on to say that public television was imitating the commercial networks. "You check the Harris Poll and the Arbitron survey and point to increases in viewership. Once you're in the rating game, you want to win," he said.

He insisted that the system—largely because of CPB—had strayed from "the bedrock of localism" that underlay the Carnegie Commission's report. Calling the stations "branch offices of a national, public telecommunications system," he charged them to strike "the most appropriate balance in determining the station's role in the public broadcast system—a balance between advancing the quality of electronic instruction and programs for the general public and, ultimately, the balance between the system's center and

Worried by "liberal and far-left producers" providing programs to PBS, as he noted in a White House memo, **Clay Whitehead** played on stations' resentment of their national organizations, warning them that they were becoming a centralized network for programs funded by the Ford Foundation. (Photo: Del Ankers Photographers.)

its parts. You have to care about these balances and you have to work for them. We in government want to help, but the initiative must come from you."

In the final version of a private memorandum Whitehead had drafted the day of the speech, the telecommunications chief described the policy behind his speech:

> No matter how firm our control of CPB management, public television will always attract liberal and far-left producers, writers and commentators. We cannot get the Congress to reduce funds for public television, or to exclude CPB from public affairs programming. But we can reform the structure of public broadcasting to eliminate its worst features.
>
> There is, and always has been, a deep division within public broadcasting over the extent of national control versus local station control. Many local stations resent the dominance of CPB and NET. This provides an opportunity to further our philosophical and political objectives for public broadcasting without appearing to be politically motivated.
>
> We stand to gain substantially from an increase in the relative power of the local stations. They are generally less liberal, and more concerned with education than with controversial national affairs. Further, a decentralized system would have far less influence and would be far less attractive to social activists.
>
> Therefore, we should immediately seek legislation to: (a) remove CPB from the business of networking; (b) make a drastic cut in CPB's budget; and (c) initiate direct federal operating support for local stations on a matching basis.

Whitehead said the key to achieving these goals was to provide the stations with more federal funding than they received from CPB. "Local stations' support for our proposals could be bought for about $30 million," Whitehead wrote. Shortly thereafter, his staff began meeting privately with station managers.

John P. Witherspoon, the corporation's first director of television [and co-author of this history], responded with a memorandum to the stations that charged Whitehead with using the government's financial power to politically pressure the industry. Witherspoon wrote that Whitehead's proposal "says in straightforward political language that until public broadcasting shows signs of becoming what this Administration wants it to be, this Administration will oppose permanent financing. And if we yield to that—well, let's hope the next Administration, and the one after that, agrees with this one, because it will be well known that we can be had."

Two weeks later, NAEB's Public Television Managers Council, preparing for a private meeting with Whitehead, sent him a letter that concurred with his local-station orientation (as had Witherspoon's statement). But the council also rejected the invitation to circumvent CPB and said that public television had adopted improved procedures that already were addressing many of the problems Whitehead mentioned in his speech. The managers emphasized that what they needed most was long-range financing.

But differences existed within public television, and these tensions only exacerbated them. PBS was increasingly apprehensive about CPB. Furthermore, Whitehead's rhetoric appealed to some managers who were concerned about centralism.

Early in 1972 the visible focus of the dispute shifted to the CPB board. At its January meeting the board voted against funding news, news analysis and political commentary. Director Tom Moore also unsuccessfully proposed prohibiting public affairs programming involving controversial political issues.

Three days later, in a draft memorandum to President Nixon, Whitehead wrote that he had made it clear to CPB Chairman Pace and CPB President Macy that CPB would receive an extra $10 million in fiscal 1973—only if the the board agreed to refocus its activities. He also made it clear that further increases depended on the board's willingness to make other changes the Administration wanted. Whitehead wrote that he was making some progress with the board, but that its slow movement and reluctance meant he would have to continue applying public and private pressure. "Also, we will have to change the board in April and replace Pace and Macy as quickly as possible, as all of us earlier agreed," he wrote.

Whitehead wrote that the Administration wouldn't see results immediately. "All of the offensive programs are funded through the end of this fiscal year, and even some of those that are dropped can be expected to be funded through foundations and syndicated outside the public broadcasting network. Changing the board and the management will be necessary to continued progress, but we have made a good beginning."

Against this background, CPB and PBS executives attempted to write an agreement on their organizations' programming responsibilities. In March 1971 PBS established its formal journalistic standards and guidelines; the corporation's board endorsed them at its March meeting. At about the same time, PBS and CPB reached a tentative agreement on program issues.

The agreement had a short life. The natural strains between PBS and CPB, the unrelenting pressure from Whitehead's office, the underlying conflicts in public broadcasting, and the personalities at CPB and PBS combined to create a near-impasse at the national level about public television's course.

Then, on June 30, 1972, President Nixon vetoed CPB's authorization bill, citing the need for increased localism and charging that CPB "is becoming . . . the center of power and the focal point of control for the entire public broadcasting system."

Pace immediately announced his resignation as chairman. On Aug. 10, Macy, ill and under increasing fire, resigned, effective Oct. 15. On Aug. 17, Witherspoon followed suit, also effective Oct. 15.

The Administration got what it wanted. The following day, Whitehead recommended that Nixon approve a $45 million authorization for CPB for fiscal 1973. Soon, nearly all the corporation's principal executives had voluntarily resigned.

In September, the CPB board named Henry Loomis as the corporation's new president. Meanwhile, the board re-examined relations between CPB and PBS.

On Jan. 10, 1973, the CPB board passed a resolution stating that the corporation had during previous years granted to PBS a number of functions that it should have kept, including some programming functions. Among them were the process and ultimate responsibility

Nixon's veto of the CPB reauthorization bill "precipitated a major reorganization of public broadcasting," wrote historian Ralph Engelman. Disappointed that the CPB board did not protest the veto, CPB president **John Macy** (above) followed the lead of chairman **Frank Pace, Jr.**, (below) and resigned in August 1972. The board, controlled by Nixon appointees, discontinued funding of all but one public affairs program, spent more of its money outside the national organizations, and negotiated a larger role in initiating programs. (Photos: City News Bureau.)

Citizen ("lay") leaders from local stations, led by **Ralph Rogers** of KERA in Dallas, assumed a major role when the stations reorganized PBS and divorced it from CPB, which had founded it three-and-a-half years before. The task required the tenacity for which Rogers was known and respected, recalled NAEB leader James Fellows, years later. "He had the powerful presence of a wealthy business-man who was also very smart and dedicated to the public good," said Fellows. Rogers, who had co-founded Children's Television Workshop, later championed public TV's outreach to daycare providers in a KERA project that, with a similar effort at WGTE in Toledo, was a forerun-ner of the PBS Ready to Learn Service. (Photo: Gittings Photography.)

PB
PB

See online: CPB-PBS partnership agreement, May 1973

for decisions on financing program production or acquisition. Another key responsibility the CPB board said it had improperly ceded was "pre-broadcast acceptance and post-broadcast review of programs to determine strict adherence to objectivity and balance in all programs or series of programs of a controversial nature."

The board told Loomis to prepare a plan to establish at CPB the staff and resources necessary for the corporation "to exercise the authority and meet the responsibilities vested in CPB under the Public Broadcasting Act of 1967 and in accordance with the policies expressed in this resolution." The board also told Loomis to negoti-ate a contract outlining relations between CPB and PBS "as may be consistent with sound management, the prudent allocation of resources, and the policies expressed in this resolution."

Gunn responds to CPB

Gunn responded immediately by restructuring PBS to broaden its political base. The organization established dual boards: a lay board of governors, generally consisting of socially, politically and eco-nomically influential people; and a board of managers to represent the interests of the system's professional station managers. Ralph B. Rogers, a Republican who was chairman of Texas Industries and on the board of KERA, the public TV station in Dallas, became chair-man of the new organization. Gunn continued as president. The effect was to erase once and for all any impression that PBS was a subsidiary of the corporation; it would instead be a free-standing organization, largely supported by member stations, operating as the most visible, identifiable part of the public television system.

During the next months, PBS succeeded in rallying the stations and vastly strengthening its national political stature. CPB, far from absorbing PBS as once contemplated, was on the defensive.

On May 31, 1973, the boards of CPB and PBS passed a joint reso-lution, which became known as the "partnership agreement." The purposes stated in its preamble included promoting public televi-sion's independence and diversity and improving its programs; encouraging development—including congressional and executive-branch approval of a long-range financing plan "that would remove public broadcasting from the political hazards of annual authoriza-tions and appropriations"; strengthening local television stations' autonomy and independence; and reaffirming "that public affairs programs are an essential responsibility of public broadcasting." Besides describing program-related procedures, the resolution stipu-lated that fixed percentages of CPB's appropriation would flow through directly to public television stations.

The partnership agreement helped resolve some of the basic dis-putes within the system; Ralph Rogers was the key man in helping the system recover from the first major assault on its basic mandates and assumptions. In the process, many of the original ambiguities of the legislation were—at least in daily operations—laid to rest.

In the process, Whitehead and his colleagues in the White House provided graphic demonstration of the political vulnerability that can strike at the core of American public broadcasting.

The elusive long-term money fix

Are there better ways to help support the services?

Since the earliest days of American radio, reasonably assured, stable, politically insulated financing has been a central issue in public broadcasting—perhaps *the* central issue.

As early as 1934, when the Communications Act was being written and some were proposing reserving radio frequencies for education, planners debated whether educational stations should sell advertising. The founders of the Pacifica network originated the notion of voluntary audience subscriptions in the 1940s. San Francisco station KQED was a step from financial disaster in the 1950s

when it created the now-venerable public television auction. In 1966 the Ford Foundation suggested a satellite system that would offer commercial networks (and National Educational Television) a way to distribute programs to their affiliates while turning over several million dollars "profits" a year to support educational television. And a year later the Carnegie Commission on Educational Television proposed an excise tax on new television set sales. Henry Geller, a former head of the National Telecommunications and Information Administration, proposed a spectrum-use fee, the proceeds of which would help finance public broadcasting. Similar fees have been proposed periodically, with little prospect that they would be levied.

There is underwriting, enhanced underwriting, and there have been experiments with advertising, raising the question: Should public broadcasting be truly noncommercial, or is its purity defended adequately by being "nonprofit?" And, year after year, federal and state appropriations provide critical support for the industry.

Public stations depend upon a complex and diverse mix of revenue sources, including underwriting, subscriptions and appropriations from all levels of government (see box, page 47). Some of them, like audience subscriptions, are the purest philanthropy. Others, like enhanced program underwriting, are nearly commercial. Given the present circumstances and ground rules, all seem essential.

The first Senate debate

Perhaps the earliest major debate on financing public broadcast-

From the start, the Pacifica Foundation planned to support its broadcasting through "listener sponsorship," and held the **first on-air membership drive in 1949**, at KPFA in Berkeley. By 1997, public TV and radio audience memberships were providing 24 percent of total revenues, and the sums would be larger if not for "free-riders." Paying members make up only about one in 12 of public radio's listeners during a week. (Because they listen a lot, they amount to a third of listeners at any given time, the Audience 98 study found in 1998.)

See Chapters 9 and 11: the search for a permanent funding source continues in the 1980s and '90s.

ing occurred on the floor of the U.S. Senate in 1934. During the previous 15 years, educational institutions and other nonprofit groups had been operating a significant number—in the early days, as many as a third—of America's radio stations. But the Great Depression precipitously reduced these numbers. Sen. Robert F. Wagner introduced a complex amendment to the Communications Act of 1934 that would have charged the new Federal Communications Commission to reallocate radio channels, reserving 25 percent for nonprofit stations and permitting these stations to recover their costs by selling ads.

Commercial broadcasters opposed the plan. Bitter fighting over the Wagner-Hatfield amendment consumed the floor discussion on the act. Sen. Clarence Dill led the opposition; the Democrat from Washington state pointed out that the nonprofit stations would compete with commercial stations, that they would not be "what we understand as education and religious stations merely. I cannot believe . . . that there is any hope of their using 25 percent of our radio facilities effectively. They have not the money and there is nowhere they can secure the money except if they go into the commercial field and themselves become commercial stations."

The FCC studied the matter and in 1935 concluded that reservations were not warranted. Congress accepted the recommendation.

When the U.S. Office of Education's J.W. Studebaker wrote in 1937 on "The Government's Responsibility for Educational Broadcasting," he emphasized government use of commercial facilities and tried to persuade commercial broadcasters to devote adequate time and attention to education and public service: "The responsibility of the federal government for educational broadcasting falls within at least three areas: to safeguard the use of radio frequencies to insure the maximum of public service; to use radio frequencies to acquaint the public with the work of the government; and to keep the public posted concerning the services it should expect of radio, and to persuade and assist broadcasters to provide those services."

Studebaker also reported: "When the FCC held a conference in June 1936 to consider the allocation of frequencies among various agencies and for various services, I requested that a minimum of three megacycles be reserved for the exclusive use of local school systems for services, in addition to those which they could normally expect commercial radio stations to perform."

But the Office of Education was principally interested in—and spent its money on—producing programs for national or international broadcast over commercial stations and studying radio's educational applications.

While some early educational AM radio stations operated commercially, organized educational radio didn't emerge until after World War II when a new kind of radio technology, FM—frequency modulation—was assigned its present frequency band. FM broadcasting began to develop—slowly.

Some hoped that FM would bring about radio's rebirth by unlocking its true potential. Charles Siepmann called it "radio's second chance." After an intensive campaign by NAEB and education forces, the FCC reserved frequencies for education in this new, largely unused band, and these frequencies were accompanied by a new

System revenue sources total $2 billion in '97

Tax-based sources 45%

3%
$66 million
Local government
School boards, cities and counties operate 4 percent of stations and contribute other aid.

9%
$178 million
Public colleges
State and local colleges and universities, where educational radio began, still operate about 40 percent of stations, especially in radio. Their aid is largely in-kind support instead of cash.

16%
$299 million
State government
States operate 35 percent of public TV stations and 9 percent of radio stations, and assist independent stations in many states. Per-person aid in 1997 varies enormously from more than $10 per person in South Carolina and Alaska to about 30 cents per person in Texas and Colorado. In total dollars, South Carolina's comprehensive system has the top support at $39 million.

17%
$322 million
Federal government
This is mostly CPB's appropriation: $260 million in fiscal 1997. The rest comes from the Public Telecommunications Facilities Program, the arts and humanities endowments and other grants and contracts.

In fiscal 1997, the public TV and radio systems together brought in revenues of $1.9 billion—75 percent for TV and 25 percent for radio—by CPB's tally.

In addition, CPB said stations earned some $133 million in entrepreneurial revenues not counted in figures on this page, putting total system revenues above $2 billion.

(This compares with $34 billion for commercial TV, $13 billion for commercial radio in 1997 and $33 billion for cable TV in 1998.)

Figures in the chart are for fiscal year 1997, which ran from October 1996 through September 1997.

Private sources 55%

24%
$472 million
Membership
In fiscal 1997, public TV had 4.6 million members and public radio, 2.1 million. Average contributions were $71 per person in TV, $66 in radio. The field's largest revenue source nearly doubled in a decade.

14%
$277 million
Business
Underwriting from both small business and major corporations peaked at $301 million in fiscal 1994 and has slipped since then.

11%
$206 million
Other
This includes $35 million from private colleges, $21 million from station auctions and all other sources. Not counted is entrepreneurial revenue (see text at top of page).

6%
$111 million
Foundations
Their grants have grown five-fold in 15 years and remain an important source for programming.

Tax-based sources

Private sources

license category: noncommercial educational.

The new stations were sustained—typically at a minimal level—by institutional budgets and occasional philanthropic transfusions. During the '40s, Pacifica was first to garner voluntary listener support, but the technique was not widely imitated.

Educational TV's start

In many ways, the Ford Foundation willed educational television into existence. It provided critical start-up money for many early stations. Perhaps more important, the foundation developed an institutional core around which education could rally: the Joint Committee on Educational Television (JCET); the National Citizens Committee for Educational Television (NCCET), which provided a national public relations structure; and National Educational Television (NET), which became a national programming base.

Early community-based educational stations, particularly those in Boston, San Francisco, Pittsburgh and St. Louis, scrambled for a combination of funding sources: contracts to serve public schools, viewer subscriptions (painfully few at first), local and national philanthropy, auctions, and contracts to produce national programs.

In 1955 the U.S. commercial television industry was debating subscription television's prospects as an alternative to conventional advertiser support. The JCET also was interested in using subscription TV revenues to support educational TV. When the FCC formally introduced the idea, however, JCET counsel Seymour Krieger advised against it, on both tactical and philosophical grounds. "To suggest that subscription television operations be authorized for noncommercial stations raises a grave question in my opinion as to whether or not such an operation would be appropriate for a noncommercial educational station," he wrote.

"Of necessity," he continued, "educational television stations must derive their economic support from the entire public within their service areas. To the extent that such stations seek tax funds, which appears to be a most important source of support, it would seem to be a mistake to suggest that any portion of the public be foreclosed from viewing educational television programs by the necessity of securing decoders and paying the required fee."

Sputnik's spur

For their first significant federal support, public broadcasters can thank the Soviet Union. In 1957 the Soviets startled the world when they launched the first earth-orbiting, man-made satellite, Sputnik I. A frantic debate followed in the U.S., both about the military implications of the Soviets' achievement and about America's technological prowess. The debate resulted in, among other things, the National Defense Education Act of 1958, which for public broadcasters provided funding for media-based instruction in science, foreign languages and mathematics.

The first federal funding program directed specifically toward public broadcasting was the Educational Television Facilities Act of 1962, which survives today as the Commerce Department's Public Telecommunications Facilities Program. In its original form, the pro-

Civic leaders with strength and charisma led the struggle to bring educational TV to many cities, one at a time: textiles heir Ralph Lowell in Boston, corporate lawyer and arts activist Leland Hazard in Pittsburgh, steelman and philanthropist Edward Ryerson in Chicago. In Washington, where there were no titans of industry, the job went to school board activist and former college dean **Elizabeth P. Campbell** (above, toasting sign-on with publisher Willard Kiplinger, WETA's first chairman). Before they built a station, WETA's volunteers demonstrated educational TV to the region by producing a daily half-hour science program for fifth- and sixth-graders in 1958, which was aired through a commercial station in town. WETA put its own channel on the air in 1961. (Photo: Bob Young, Georgetown University News Service, courtesy of WETA.)

gram exclusively provided educational TV stations with matching funds totalling $32 million over five years for production and transmission equipment.

As program quality and station coverage gradually improved, educational television stations took a lesson from museums and symphony orchestras, and turned to program underwriting. The Communications Act requires broadcasting stations to identify program funders, so underwriters received brief mentions adjacent to programs. By public broadcasters' own ground rules, these announcements initially consisted only of simple, sparse company identifications: corporate names were allowed, but not brand names or logos.

Through the mid-1960s public broadcasting was financed by a combination of state and local taxes, philanthropy, a modest amount of program underwriting, and institutional budgets. Because this mosaic did not provide enough money to develop a major broadcasting service, public broadcasters paid increasing attention to the problem of long-range financing. That problem, combined with adroit politics, resulted in the Carnegie Commission report in 1967 and the legislation establishing CPB.

But the legislation failed to incorporate an excise tax—which the commission recommended—or any other long-range financing mechanism. President Lyndon Johnson began the pattern of annual appropriations and promised to propose a more satisfactory mechanism the following year. But in 1968 Johnson, under siege because of the Vietnam War, announced he would not seek re-election.

An elusive, perhaps unattainable, goal

"Shibboleth" is defined as "a slogan or saying, especially one distinctive of a particular group." Long-range financing may be public broadcasting's shibboleth. It's a favorite idea, although its terms occasionally shift. It introduces visions of security, if not plenty. When an institution has secure funding sources, it knows that it has its constituency's confidence and that it will be in business for the foreseeable future.

It's not hard to support the idea of long-range financing. What's hard is achieving it. Public broadcasters equate such financing with a solid base of federal money, backed by political independence. Events have proven this an elusive, perhaps unattainable, goal. Public broadcasting has achieved a substantial but quite diverse base of support, but this broad base is inadequate to provide good, diverse and innovative programming. Moreover, it also has shown a potential for permitting political interference.

Nevertheless, public broadcasting has attracted enough money to reach virtually the entire nation, with radio and television stations carrying schedules that few managers would have dared dream about in 1967. It is possible that public broadcasting already has its long-range financing: not ideally defined or assured, not adequate in amount, without proper insulation, but at least for now, as good as we can get.

The first Carnegie Commission estimated that the "Corporation for Public Television" would need $104 million a year to fund public broadcasting's programming, interconnection and related functions. By the late 1960s, the commission estimated, the public television system would require a total of $270 million a year, including $75 million from non-federal sources. The commission also called on the federal government to pay for equipment and station operations through the Department of Health, Education and Welfare. The corporation's funds would come from a tax on new TV sets made available to it through a trust fund. The commission noted that this tax would not be new: the government had levied a 10 percent tax on TV sets between 1950 and 1965.

Commissioner Joseph H. McConnell, president of Reynolds Metals Company, entered a separate concurring opinion, arguing that "those who are licensed to use the airways in the 'public interest'—the commercial television stations—should at least share in the cost of public television." The commercial stations' tax presumably would have been passed along to advertisers.

But Congress adopted neither the excise tax nor the tax on commercial stations; ignoring the Carnegie Commission's objections, it financed public broadcasting through annual appropriations. The commission's steady state-federal target of $200 million—in 1967 dollars—has yet to be achieved.

Shortly after the commission completed its work, the National Citizens Committee for Broadcasting issued a report by Dick Netzer, an economist from New York University. *Long-Range Financing of Public Broadcasting* addressed the best ways to meet the Carnegie target of $270 million a year. Netzer considered eight sources of revenue:

- taxes on gross receipts of radio and TV broadcasters,
- taxes on all FCC long-distance communications licenses,
- taxes on total television advertising outlays,
- taxes on broadcasters' net profits,
- an excess profits tax on broadcasters,
- a charge for leasing access to the radio spectrum,
- a flat per-household radio-TV license fee, and
- a manufacturers excise tax on TV sets.

The tax on commercial broadcasting's gross receipts—at a rate of 4 percent—would have yielded more than $120 million annually, which would be assigned to a trust fund. And the fee for granting commercial broadcasters access to the spectrum was designed to yield at least $50 million a year.

In addition, Netzer believed that the industry should obtain supplementary non-governmental financing by establishing the Ford Foundation's proposed nonprofit satellite system for all broadcasters, which he estimated would yield $20 million a year as well as the substantial value of free interconnection services. Netzer also advocated granting public broadcasters the authority to accept limited advertising and experiment with subscription TV.

While none of his recommendations was considered seriously at the time, several would reappear during the congressionally authorized experiment with advertising in 1982.

Political "insulation" through advance appropriation

The need for long-range financing was underscored in 1970 when CPB's first president, John Macy, told NAEB that "the future of public broadcasting will be very limited unless we succeed in the next couple of years in convincing the nation that we have earned a system of adequate, permanent financing." That "next couple of years," however, consisted largely of turmoil for public broadcasters and culminated in the Nixon veto of mid-1972.

Many stations have dropped labor-intensive on-air auctions of donated merchandise, and public broadcasting's auction proceeds have been declining nationally since 1985. But the frenzied fundraising events have provided income when it was needed, as at San Francisco's KQED, which invented the **on-air auction** in 1953 with a 24-hour event that was credited with saving the young station financially. At left: the circus-like set of a more recent KQED auction. (Photo: National Public Broadcasting Archives.)

But throughout that time, negotiations continued between CPB, the White House, and congressional committees concerning a long-range financing bill. Rep. John Tiernan of Rhode Island introduced a bill in early 1971 that would have established a "public broadcasting trust fund" in the U.S. Treasury and authorized a federal match of $2 for every dollar of non-federal support over $50 million in the public broadcasting system.

In April 1972, CPB created a task force on the "Long-Range Financing of Public Broadcasting." Chaired by former CPB director Joseph D. Hughes, it was broadly based and engaged leaders from stations and national organizations. The goal: to devise a financing plan that the entire public broadcasting constituency could support, fragmented and fractious though it may be. Even before the group's first meeting, the Nixon veto devastated the corporation and made the task force's work all the more pertinent.

The group's plan, released in fall 1973, included several major recommendations. Two were of special significance. One was that Congress should authorize federal funding for public broadcasting "for a period of no less than five years, and a schedule of appropriations for the same period of time should be made part of the authorization." This was designed to insulate public broadcasting from the year-to-year financial and political pressure that annual appropriations imposed. It also called for matching non-federal revenues: "The level of federal support in any fiscal year should match non-federal support for public broadcasting activities for the second preceding fiscal year on a one-to-two ratio, up to reasonable, established ceilings."

Despite a change in the leadership at CPB, the Nixon White House—increasingly under fire because of the Watergate scandal—was divided on whether to support long-range financing. But during Richard Nixon's last days in the White House, in the summer of 1974, the president forwarded to Congress a proposal to provide long-term, insulated financing through a five-year authorization and appropriation, as the task force had recommended.

The 93rd Congress ended before it could take action on the Nixon bill. President Ford submitted a nearly identical proposal in February 1975, and hearings on the Public Broadcasting Financing Act of 1975 continued through the year. But by the time the process was complete, the ingenious link between authorizations and appro-

PB
PB

See online: Carnegie II recommendations.

priations that was the plan's principal insulating mechanism had been uncoupled. On Dec. 31, 1975, the bill was signed into law, with these major provisions:

■ The "public broadcasting fund" was established in the U.S. Treasury.

■ Appropriations were authorized for the period 1975-80, using the ceilings public broadcasters advocated. But the actual appropriations would come separately; yearly appropriations bills provided funding two years in advance.

■ Formula-driven pass-throughs to the stations were included.

■ CPB was mandated to consult with the system.

■ Non-broadcast technologies were included in the Public Broadcasting Act.

The Public Telecommunications Financing Act of 1978 extended the principles of the 1975 legislation, adding emphasis on planning, providing for telecommunications demonstration projects, increasing accountability and reporting requirements, requiring open meetings, and mandating performance in the area of opportunities for women and minorities.

With regard to long-range financing, its major change was to authorize, beginning in fiscal year 1981, a federal match of $1 for each $2 raised from non-federal sources. [Actual appropriations fall far short of meeting that ratio.] The federal funding patterns established in the financing acts of 1975 and 1978 prevailed through the mid-1980s.

Carnegie II

During the stormy '70s, many public broadcasters and their funders continued focusing attention on the issue of long-range financing and the political and structural problems of the Nixon era. The discussion resulted in a second Carnegie group, the Carnegie Commission on the Future of Public Broadcasting. Carnegie II recommended a substantial restructuring of the system and vastly increased federal support. The federal government's appropriate share of support for public broadcasting should be about 50 percent, the report recommended, and the funds should come from general federal revenues, augmented by a spectrum use fee.

The commission estimated that public broadcasting's total revenue should be $1.16 billion (in 1978 dollars) by 1985, and that the federal share of this sum should be $600 million. In addition, the commission recommended a one-time-only allocation of $350 million over five years for new and improved facilities. The report attracted little attention.

Should the field try advertising?

There is an American tradition of commercial enterprises supporting cultural activities. Businesses underwrite symphony orchestras and opera companies, museums, theater groups, and specialized scientific and cultural publications. So it was perhaps inevitable that when public broadcasting began to develop substantial presence, underwriting would be an attractive source of support.

Guidelines established by stations' organizations rigorously restrained the first underwriting announcements: stations would identify the corporate name only, with no logos or reference to product lines. Underwriters were prohibited from supporting programs on subjects related to their businesses. In the '70s, a controversy ensued when a station submitted a program in which the Mobil Oil underwriting credit used a typeface suspiciously similar to the style the company used in its advertisements. The cry went up: "Next we'll be allowing them to use a red 'O'!"

In 1976, CPB's Advisory Council of National Organizations (ACNO), comprised of national groups representing labor, education, civil rights, business and other interests, expressed concern that underwriting might lead to commercialism. Ward B. Chamberlin, Jr., then president of WETA-TV/FM in Washington, D.C., argued that underwriting provides a legitimate and valuable source of support. But he emphasized that corporate underwriting, like any other funding, must be kept in balance with other sources of support.

In 1977, the FCC started investigating underwriting and several other fundraising techniques, striving to "maintain the essentially noncommercial nature of educational broadcasting." The issues raised were not directed toward further underwriting restrictions, but the inquiry served as a general caution to the field.

The specter of commercialism directs attention to the major differences between commercial and public broadcasting in the U.S. Many believe that public stations would damage their prospects for continued noncommercial union agreements by airing out-and-out ads. Some also argue that advertising might hurt voluntary subscriptions by indicating to viewers and listeners that stations are commercially supported, or that ads could cause other support sources to wither.

But the basic difference is more fundamental. Most of the time, a commercial station's salable product is not programs, but people. Commercial stations sell audiences—a combination of demographics and numbers—to advertisers.

Public stations, on the other hand, are intended to offer programs to audiences. To the extent that today's underwriters are sensitive to demographics and audience sizes, this principle may be distorted, but the fundamental difference remains. Lloyd Kaiser, longtime president of WQED in Pittsburgh, put it this way at the time: "Public broadcasting would greatly change while in the swift commercial lane. The proposed limited nature of the advertising in terms of type and placement sounds surprisingly like the beginnings of advertising on commercial broadcasting years ago. It then changed completely, as dictated by the normal forces of the marketplace."

"If advertising were to come to public broadcasting, what then would be our significant difference?" Kaiser asked. "Could anyone really find our reason for being? What then would cause us to be innovative and courageous and a service-first enterprise? Would we continue our search for greatness, or would we merely be known as that ineffective commercial network?"

In spite of these qualms, public broadcasting's financing difficulties invite interest in advertising. The Reagan Administration, for both policy and budgetary reasons, said that it would not support

Most generous of public TV's corporate underwriters over the years was Mobil Oil, in the person of its long-time public relations chief, **Herbert Schmertz**. He recalled when WGBH came to him seeking sponsorship of *Masterpiece Theatre,* to buy and promote 39 hours of BBC dramas for $390,000. "Even in 1970, that was an absurdly low figure, so I was eager to learn more."

increasing annual federal appropriations for public broadcasting. The message was clear: Enterprises such as public broadcasting should rely more on the private sector for support.

TCAF's advertising experiment

The Public Broadcasting Amendments Act of 1981 called for reductions in public broadcasting's direct federal support, and at the same time established the Temporary Commission on Alternative Financing (TCAF), to "identify funding options which will ensure that public telecommunications as a source of alternative and diverse programming will be maintained and enhanced, and that public telecommunications will continue to expand and be available to increasing numbers of citizens throughout the nation." FCC Commissioner James H. Quello chaired the panel.

Under the aegis of TCAF, the first congressionally authorized commission to study financing public broadcasting, 10 public TV stations (radio did not participate) were authorized to conduct demonstrations of limited advertising. They were WNET, New York City; WTTW, Chicago; WHYY, Philadelphia; WQED, Pittsburgh; WPBT, Miami; WYES, New Orleans; WQLN, Erie; and KCSM, San Mateo, Calif. (Stations in Binghamton, N.Y, and Louisville, Ky., did not participate as planned.)

At the end of the experiment, the temporary commission concluded that "limited advertising could be a significant supplemental revenue source for certain public television stations. However, many public broadcast stations would not carry advertising, and the significant financial risks associated with advertising cannot be quantified in advance. Further, these risks could extend to public broadcasting stations—both television and radio—that decide not to air limited advertising."

The group found that overall the risks of advertising were too great. "Advertising benefits would most likely accrue mainly to VHF stations in major markets and other stations well-situated to compete for advertising dollars," TCAF found.

While TCAF recommended against advertising, it recognized that "broadened guidelines for program underwriting (or general support grants) would provide additional revenue for public broadcasting." It said that this enhanced underwriting approach would be more acceptable to the stations and "pose fewer risks to other cost areas."

While the advertising experiments were underway, TCAF examined other non-federal options for alternative financing. These included increased individual contributions, facilities leasing, teleconferencing services, income from subsidiary FM radio services, commercial use of satellite facilities, program sales, subscription television, microwave services, low-power television, cable television enterprises, direct broadcast satellites, teletext, regulatory improvements, and a national lottery. "The alternative financing options studied are unlikely to supplant traditional federal tax-based support within the foreseeable future. Indeed, while some of these options have long-range potential, in the short term there is no reasonable alternative to continued federal funding."

Here are some highlights of TCAF's conclusions:
■ "Public broadcasting clearly has the potential to maintain,

TCAF's verdict was a political judgment in the end, and the product of a compromise among the commission's members. (Above: TCAF chairman **James Quello talks with PBS President Bruce Christensen**.) The seven stations that sold commercials (two others did enhanced underwriting) drew 8 percent of their revenues from the test. Surveys by the ELRA consulting firm found "no evidence that there are any harmful effects attributable" to the test. Proponents of the commercials were exhilarated. "For the first time, we are a real television station," said WYES President Vincent Saele. But the ELRA study pointedly did not address long-term effects, and noted a "slight tendency for contributions to fall in the markets where product commercials were shown." TCAF's final judgment was that the unknowable potential losses of revenue and favorable union pay rates outweighed any advantages of going commercial.

enhance and expand the reach of its services, as suggested in the commission's mandate from Congress."

■ "Significant increases in revenue are essential if public broadcasting is to be maintained, enhanced and expanded."

■ "Venture activities will not become a substantial source of system-wide revenue in the foreseeable future."

■ "Balance and diversity in funding sources are essential to the unique character of public broadcasting services. Federal support stimulates other sources of revenue and is an indispensable part of public broadcasting's financial base."

And TCAF's final recommendations to Congress:

■ "Renew public broadcasting's authorizing legislation for a minimum of three years (1987-1989) and maintain the advance appropriations procedures that afford insulation and aid program planning."

■ "Set a target level of federal funding during this period that provides a strong base that allows public broadcasting to maintain, expand and enhance the reach of its services."

■ "Structure federal funding so as to provide the optimum incentive for local stations to generate non-federal funds."

■ "Continue the existing prohibition on advertising unless it can be established clearly that overall benefits to public broadcasting will exceed the costs, and stations that do not choose to carry limited advertising will not share the risks associated with advertising while not receiving direct benefits."

■ "Further stimulate non-federal revenue sources through the following actions:

■ "Direct the FCC to modify its policies concerning underwriting acknowledgments to permit public broadcasters to identify supporters by using brand names, trade names, slogans, brief institutional-type messages, and public service announcements."

■ "Repeal the unrelated business income tax penalty incorporated in the Public Broadcasting Amendments Act of 1981 and direct the CPB to make refunds to stations that have returned money as a result of this provision."

■ "Reinforce support for regulatory policies that promote the effective distribution of public broadcasting signals."

In March 1984, the FCC broadened its guidelines to permit logos or slogans that identify—but not promote or compare—locations, value-neutral descriptions of a product line or service, trade names, and product or service listings. A public broadcasting station's fundraising activities may not "suspend or alter regular programming on behalf of any entity other than itself," the FCC wrote. PBS, NPR and individual stations have adopted underwriting codes that reflect the FCC standards and apply them to specific situations.

After the advertising experiment, it appeared, the long-range financing of public broadcasting would look very much like the financing arrangements that already existed: diverse, difficult to obtain, and not entirely adequate.

PB
PB
See online: underwriting guidelines and TCAF recommendations

See Chapters 9 and 11: In the 1990s, advocates continue to push for advertising revenue and a permanent funding mechanism.

A civilized voice

CHAPTER 7

Through eight decades, broadcasters and policymakers wrestle with questions of purpose

Ira E. Robinson was the only member of the Federal Radio Commission to oppose its 1928 re-allocation of radio frequencies, which disadvantaged nonprofit stations, wrote historian Robert McChesney. But after leaving the FRC, Robinson became an attorney for commercial broadcasters.

It was 1930 and the Federal Radio Commission's Ira E. Robinson was talking about radio:

> It is the greatest implement of democracy yet given to mankind. It is the voice of the people, indeed, the expression of the soul of the people unto themselves and unto the other nations of the earth. It fits the doctrine of Lincoln that this shall be a government of the people, by the people, and for the people.

But Commissioner Robinson knew commercial broadcasting alone would not meet the nation's needs. He recognized that educational institutions had established a few stations, but observed that their funding was both late and limited. The republic had to do better:

> It is conceded that educational programs over the radio should be devised and directed by professional educators, but this cannot be done under the existing ownership and operation. Will the legislatures provide appropriations of money with which to buy time on the commercially owned and operated stations, and will those stations fairly allocate time for educational uses when others offer to pay for the same period? These and other questions that arise cannot be answered now. But, an evolutionary process will naturally aid in their solution. Radio is intended for a higher use than that now made of it, and the enlightened mind of the public will eventually prevail.

A system of public stations programming as a public service was not a new idea. Public radio—both the mission and the name—had been proposed in 1922 at the Conference for the Voluntary Control of Radio. Instigated by then-Secretary of Commerce Herbert Hoover, the conference raised the question of dividing radio frequencies between educational and non-commercial stations.

Ohio State University's original call letters, WEAO, stood for **"Willing, Energetic, Athletic Ohio."** The stations in Columbus now go by the name of WOSU, and the call letters WEAO have migrated to Akron's public TV station. (Photo: National Public Broadcasting Archives.)

According to the National Committee on Education by Radio, the conference established four priority classes in broadcasting. The first class of station, government owned and operated, was to broadcast within a 600-mile radius "information of the kind which the federal government gathers and is particularly qualified to distribute." The second was the "public station," to broadcast a 250-mile signal, and would be operated by states, municipalities, colleges and universities. Third priority went to private stations, to be operated for "private good-will." Finally came "toll broadcasting stations." These would have operated as the long-distance telephone system, "available to all who desired to sponsor programs." The latter two classes of stations would have served a 50-mile area.

Justin Morrill

In many ways, the father of educational broadcasting was Justin Morrill, a member of Congress from Vermont who in the 1860s fought successfully for the idea of land-grant colleges. These colleges, and the cooperative extension services that came later, were based on the premise that colleges should be broadly useful community resources. Morrill's work laid the path for lifelong learning, universities without walls, education in the practical arts and sciences—and the logic of colleges using radio to reach the people.

In 1933 an astute observer of education and broadcasting noted that educational radio was in a period similar to the early days of agricultural and mechanic arts colleges. "They were endeavoring to find their place." The speaker, A.G. Crane of the University of Wyoming and chairman of the radio committee of the National Association of State Universities, was discussing one of the first public broadcasting surveys. "Like many another fact-finding enterprise," Crane said of *An Appraisal of Radio Broadcasting in the Land-Grant Colleges and State Universities,* "the report calls attention to the importance of what was obvious from the beginning. The heart of the whole question of educational, cultural values in radio depends upon the character and acceptability of the program. If educational stations are to find their places on the air, they must find special services which the schools can render better and more effectively than can be rendered by other agencies. During the free-for-all period of experimentation, institutions have included formal instruction, general information, farm and home information, entertainment and commercial broadcasting."

The study found that 47 college and university stations devoted 48 percent of their broadcasting time to entertainment, 20 percent to farm and home information, 23 percent to general information, and 8 percent to formal instruction. "The experiment of giving formal college courses by radio, and of awarding suitable college credit, seems to have proved unsuccessful," Crane said. "The most acceptable program will include entertainment features that are not available to the general commercial broadcasting companies, such as special school events, sports, drama, lectures and those events in which appear students or faculty whose personal reputations or connections contribute special interest."

An early radio station

Speaking at the 1930 meeting of the Institute for Education by Radio, W.I. Griffith painted a picture of early educational radio. Griffith, director of radio station WOI in Ames, Iowa, told the group that "since our support comes from taxpayers in Iowa, we have not felt at liberty to engage in commercial broadcasting, but we are

Justin Smith Morrill, sponsor of the Morrill Acts of 1862 and 1890, led the movement to extend college education to ordinary Americans by assisting the state universities. The 1862 act, which endowed the schools with 30,000 acres of federal land per member of Congress in each state, was passed when Morrill added military tactics to "agriculture and the mechanic arts" and other subjects to be taught. It was a strong selling point at the start of the Civil War. Years later, NPR President Frank Mankiewicz mused that public radio would get better treatment in Congress if the network were renamed "National Public Radar." (Portrait of Morrill courtesy of Vermont Historical Society.)

PB PB

See online: more about the Morrill Acts.

At Iowa State's WOI in Ames, *Music Shop* still airs daily as it has for decades. In the 1927 schedule, it followed the morning report on expected livestock prices, based on wire dispatches from Sioux City, Des Moines, Chicago and New York. By 1930, half the farms in Iowa were equipped to receive radio, said WOI's **W.I. Griffith** (pictured above) but half weren't. To reach farms without radios, the local phone company in Plainfield, Iowa, repeated agricultural market reports by placing group phone calls to farmers without radios. (Photo: Iowa State University.)

much interested in being of service to all of the citizens of the state."

Griffith said that his station's programs "carry a maximum amount of information with enough entertainment to make the information acceptable." He described the station's program schedule: In 1929, WOI broadcast 7,887 programs, of which 5,570 dealt with market quotations on livestock, grain, poultry and dairy products, and weather reports. In 1930, he reported, half the farms in Iowa were equipped to receive radio programs.

The WOI schedule offered 1,159 educational and 798 entertainment programs. "The lectures broadcast by our own faculty deal for the most part with different phases of agriculture, home economics, engineering, industrial science and veterinary medicine," Griffith reported. "During the college year 1929-30, a series of 30-minute programs was given at 10 o'clock on Tuesdays and Thursdays known as the *Homemakers' Half-Hour*." When the station aired a show called "What Shall We Do with Our Aluminum Cooking Utensils, Throw Them Away or Use Them?," 290 listeners requested copies.

Before broadcasting an art appreciation lecture, the station mailed some of its listeners copies of 12 paintings that would be discussed. "Mrs. Ness discussed such paintings as Raphael's *Madonna of the Chair*, while all through radioland hundreds of housewives paused in their busy morning's work to study a copy of this painting as the talk was being given," Griffith said. "More than 3,000 listeners asked for copies of that broadcast."

Early programming principles

Even in radio's first decade, a number of public programming principles emerged:

■ While many of the early stations were at educational institutions, their programming mission was never seen as heavily instructional. Formal education was seen as a valuable facet of the service that should, perhaps, be enlarged. But public programming has always ranged from stock market reports to drama and self-improvement for adults at home.

■ Alternative programming, drawing upon the unique capabilities of the stations' host institutions to do what commercial broadcasters were not prepared to do, has been present since the creation.

■ Public affairs programs, so controversial in later years, were a valid mission from the beginning.

■ Success lies in providing quality programs that reasonable numbers of people find interesting, entertaining or useful.

Despite these insights, and the accomplishments that brought them about, educational radio was nearly inaudible for years. In radio's infancy, universities rushed to obtain licenses for stations, sometimes for educational or public purposes and often because of the interesting engineering questions behind the new technology.

During the 1920s, 176 educational stations were licensed; with faltering interest from engineering departments and pressure from the Great Depression and commercial radio forces, these dwindled to less than 40 by 1930. Llewellyn White in 1930 described educational radio as "The Light That Failed." Public broadcasting pioneer Richard B. Hull amended that assessment in 1956: "White was essentially correct with one important exception—the light did not fail. It did not go out; it continued, but it flickered instead of burning for many years."

Most universities and colleges, especially private institutions, according to Hull, "found the notion of educating the general mass of people off campus a very foreign one." He noted that Columbia University reputedly "turned down as a free gift what later became NBC's key network station in New York. In almost no instance had these educational radio stations been accepted as major elements in the administrative structures of their universities—the stations were peripheral to the main business of the institution."

Kansas State University's extension service used radio, along with filmstrip lectures and every other new and old technology, to get out the word on agriculture and home economics. Extension official **Lisle Longsdorf** (pictured in 1946) supervised KSAC (now KKSU), whose powerful AM signal reached much of the Midwest. To extend the reach of its information, the extension service distributed scripts (and later tapes) to stations around the country. Before the school started its own station in 1924, former KKSU manager Ralph Titus recalls, it tried making programs on a station owned by J.R. Brinkley, a famed purveyor of "goat gland" treatments for restoring sexual pep. Kansans appreciated the radio service, and the new station launched a daily farm report that continues 75 years later. (Photo: National Public Broadcasting Archives.)

Television—and NET—enter the picture

When Hull was looking back at educational radio, educational television was less than four years old. The first station, KUHT—licensed to the University of Houston and the Houston Independent School District—went on the air in May 1953. The second station, WKAR, at Michigan State University in East Lansing, took to the air eight months later. Six additional stations were born in 1954, and nine more a year later. Twenty-four noncommercial educational television stations were on the air (and seven more under construction) by December 1956.

These stations operated, on average, nearly 32 hours per week. They aired in-school programs (in 1955, more than 30,000 children in 1,400 central Iowa classrooms regularly watched *Iowa School Time*), formal adult education (in 1954, more than 2,000 adults enrolled in WQED's High School of the Air); in formal adult instruction (shows ranged from *Today's Farm* to *Transatlantic Televiews*), instruction for home and business (*Parents and Dr. Spock* to *Industry on Parade*), cultural programs in the arts, and public affairs and children's programs (including Fred Rogers' early work).

During 1955-56, the Educational Television and Radio Center, predecessor of National Educational Television (NET), distributed 775 hours of programming by more than 75 producers, including educational institutions and stations. In late 1956 it was supplying six hours per week and had secured a $6 million Ford Foundation grant to help double its output.

A decade later the organization had moved from Ann Arbor, Mich., to New York City. Under John F. White's leadership, NET vigorously strove "to provide a national program service that tangibly contributes to the knowledge and wisdom of the American people

In the years just after NET's 1970 merger with New York's local Channel 13, creating WNET, programmer Jack Willis and colleagues launched *The 51st State*, a local news program that was "purposely provocative, unpredictable, irreverent and probing" in the words of James Day, who was then president of WNET. At right: host/editor **Patrick Watson** and guests, during a segment on youth gangs. (Photo: National Public Broadcasting Archives.)

on subjects crucial to their freedom and welfare and to the continuing cultural growth and renewal that are vital in any healthy society."

By late 1964—with the first federal public broadcasting funding law three years from the president's signature—planning that would lead to the first Carnegie Commission was underway. In November 1964, NET, which was providing educational TV stations with their core programming, published *NET Program Philosophy and Purpose: A Guideline for Staff Planning*. In practical terms, the document laid out the network's philosophy toward public affairs, cultural and children's programs.

NET public affairs programs aimed "to induce people to think critically about the important national and international issues confronting our society." The document gave public affairs producers "test questions" to ask themselves:

"Is this subject significant for the American people and important to their welfare?"

"Do the American people have an unfilled need for information on this subject?"

"If the need does not exist now, will it exist in the future?"

"Is full information on this subject available elsewhere on television?"

"Does this subject fit into a current or projected NET series?"

"Does this subject fit into the overall program pattern?"

"Can this subject be presented effectively on television?"

"Can this subject be presented effectively for the money available?"

"Is this subject worth the money that must be spent to produce an effective program?"

"Is this the right time to produce a program or series on this subject?"

"Is this subject too topical for effective presentation through the NET distribution system?" (NET distributed programs to stations by mail.)

"Would this program or series contribute positively to the NET service?"

"Our Lyceum, our Chatauqua, our Minsky's and our Camelot"

By this time, a program philosophy had evolved for public broadcasting. It was summarized in a 1971 book by Robert Blakely: "The objectives of commercial broadcasting are to get people to listen and to view and to buy. The objectives of broadcasting for public purposes pertain to what happens in the lives of people as a result of the process of programming—the planning, the production, the presentation, the reception, the consequences. Public broadcasting clienteles are made up, mostly, of the same people who make up the audiences for commercial programs, but they are people acting in different roles, with different kinds of concerns, interests and reasons, just as the same person may concurrently read a mystery story for relaxation and a sociological report for understanding; just as he may attend a baseball game with 10,000 other fans one evening and a voluntary

organization with 20 or 100 other members another evening. Broadcasting for public purposes may serve a large clientele at one time and a small clientele at another; it must serve a wide array of different clienteles in any one day or week. The members of these clienteles change and shift from program to program, according to interests and objectives. But they are always publics, and never a mass."

The programming vision of the 1967 Carnegie Commission was a major factor in passing the Public Broadcasting Act of 1967. At the head of *A Program for Action* is this statement by E.B. White:

"Noncommercial television should address itself to the ideal of excellence, not the idea of acceptability—which is what keeps commercial television from climbing the staircase. I think television should be the visual counterpart of the literary essay, should arouse our dreams, satisfy our hunger for beauty, take us on journeys, enable us to participate in events, present great drama and music, explore the sea and the sky and the hills. It should be our Lyceum, our Chatauqua, our Minsky's and our Camelot. It should restate and clarify the social dilemma and the political pickle. Once in a while it does, and you get a quick glimpse of its potential."

Public television would be, the commission believed, "a civilized voice in a civilized community."

"Public television is capable of becoming the clearest expression of American diversity, and of excellence within diversity," said the commission. "Wisely supported, as we conclude it must be, it will respect the old and the new alike, neither lunging at the present nor worshipping the past. It will seek vitality in well-established forms and in modern experiment. Its attitude will be neither fearful nor vulgar."

The Public Broadcasting Act of 1967, the federal law that resulted from the Carnegie Commission's work, deals gingerly with pro-

Since 1972, WNET producer Jac Venza has given PBS viewers a front-row seat for theater, music and dance on *Great Performances*, offering national exposure to such artists as Beverly Sills, Wynton Marsalis, Yo-Yo Ma and Alvin Ailey. (At left: **Virginia Johnson of the Dance Theatre of Harlem** in a dance version of "A Streetcar Named Desire.") Over the years, *Great Performances* has become more populist and diverse, often trying crossover acts, such as Linda Ronstandt singing Mexican folk songs and Itzhak Perlman playing klezmer music. Despite the work of Venza and his producers, the arts get somewhat less airtime than in the past (peaking at 22 percent in 1982, now down six points). But Venza continues to look after artists—bringing a wooden floor to dance tapings so that dancers don't have to perform on concrete studio floors. Perform-ers on PBS may not be paid the highest fees, but as Pulitzer-winning playwright Wendy Wasserstein said, the good treatment made her "a sucker for a three-figure deal."

Few series have done so much to "restate and clarify the social dilemma and the political pickle"—what E.B. White hoped public TV would do—as *Frontline*. It has repeatedly challenged the campaign finance status quo and virtually prosecuted numerous cases against abuse of power. Its executive producer, David Fanning, got public TV into a hot spot with the "Death of a Princess" docudrama in 1980, but WGBH and CPB bet on his conviction and storytelling skills, making him executive producer of the new series that debuted in January 1983. In one exceptional series within the series, producer Ofra Bikel made three films—eight hours airing between 1991 and 1997—on the questionable Edenton, N.C., child-abuse case against daycare providers. Four days before the third documentary aired, local prosecutors dropped remaining charges. (In the photo, a **defendant learns that charges have been dismissed**.)

gramming. In its declaration of policy, the Congress "finds and declares that it furthers the general welfare to encourage noncommercial educational radio and television broadcast programming which will be responsive to the interests of people both in particular localities and throughout the United States, and which will constitute an expression of diversity and excellence."

A principal concern of Congress was to set forth the ground rules for public broadcasting's treatment of public issues. CPB, the agency Congress established in 1967 as both heat shield and distributor of federal funding, was forbidden to support "any political party or candidate for public office" and individual stations were not permitted to "engage in editorializing or . . . support or oppose any candidate for public office." In 1984, the Supreme Court held that the station-editorializing prohibition was unconstitutional.

Congress went beyond the FCC's Fairness Doctrine and equal-time provisions to require of public broadcasting "strict adherence to objectivity and balance in all programs or series of programs of a controversial nature."

Much of the congressional debate behind the act centered on the importance of educational programming, with "educational" subdivided into formal instruction and informal "material to be presented in the home for credit or improvement of specific skills." There was a considerable, albeit minority, feeling that the educational potential of broadcasting had been given too little attention by the legislation's authors.

"To coat the philosophic pill with innocent merriment"

The House report that accompanied the bill struck a middle course concerning programs CPB would finance: "Educational television or radio programs are defined . . . as 'programs which are primarily designed for educational or cultural purposes and not primarily for amusement or entertainment purposes.' Notwithstanding the difficulties of defining 'entertainment,' the committee deems such a provision advisable in order to preclude the corporation from granting funds for programs which are designed primarily to amuse and for no other purpose. Education is often entertaining as well as enlightening; indeed it is often more palatable if it is. For example, Shakespeare, Toscanini, Gilbert and Sullivan, and Will Rogers have all been great teachers as well as absorbing entertainers, and their works would, of course, not be excluded by this definition. In short, Section 397(9) is not intended to inhibit programs which coat the philosophic pill with innocent merriment."

In the bill's final version, Section 397(9) reads simply: "The term 'educational television or radio programs' means programs which are primarily designed for educational or cultural purposes." The House committee's addendum, "and not primarily for amusement or entertainment purposes," did not survive.

The second Carnegie Commission devoted most of its attention to structural issues and made no profound statements about programming. The commission generally used a wide definition of appropriate programming. Its proposed "Program Services Endowment" would have had "the sole objective of supporting creative excellence and will underwrite a broad range of television and radio productions and program services, including public affairs, drama, comedy, educational and learning research, and new applications of telecommunications technology."

The second commission also recommended increased emphasis on education, encouraging more research in the use of media for instruction and urging the endowment to "finance and stimulate the development of quality programs that both test and demonstrate the potential of telecommunications for learning."

The issues of public television programming were set forth in PBS's statement of "Programming Goals and Objectives," adopted in 1982, reaffirmed in 1984 and reviewed in 1985:

■ "programs that foster American creativity and new talent,"

■ "innovative programs of quality and imagination for children,"

■ "major programs and series portraying the concerns and achievements of women and minorities,"

■ "the use of public television programs for life-long learning, in school and at home,"

■ "public affairs programs that dig into the major issues and problems of our time,"

■ "programs and series that provide service to specialized audiences, including the handicapped and the aged," and

■ "coverage of high-quality cultural and performing arts festivals and events, throughout the nation, including, where practical, the capability of multichannel (stereo) sound."

Through decades of public broadcasting, there have been established by consensus, practice or law a number of fundamental principles of programming:

■ Public broadcasting programs are intended to address specific interests of specific audiences. They are not intended to generate mass audiences for sale.

■ Public broadcasting has special responsibilities to certain audiences, particularly children and other groups not likely to be well served by commercial broadcasting, given its economic imperatives.

Many public broadcasters form a human link between the system's early days and its present. **Bill Siemering**, the light-haired young man in the photo at left, worked in educational radio at WHA in Madison, Wis., and then, with Jack Mitchell and other colleagues, set the course for *All Things Considered* and the present sound of NPR. Siemering went on to start *Fresh Air, Soundprint* and other programs and in the 1990s consulted with broadcasters in Africa and Eastern Europe. (Photo: NPBA.)

■ Public broadcasting has its roots in education, although formal instruction has always been a relatively small part of the schedule.

■ Public broadcasting programs are intended as alternatives to commercial programs.

■ Public broadcasting's traditional program categories are public affairs, cultural programs, programs for children, programs for other special audiences, programs for informal education and self-help, and instructional programs.

Audiences in the plural

They're students (enrolled or not), they're citizens, and they're minorities that add up to a majority

The relationship between public broadcasting and education is integral. Most of the early noncommercial radio stations were associated with universities, and radio's potential for instruction was recognized immediately. In 1931, with broadcasting barely a decade old, the editor of the *Journal of the National Education Association* said:

> It is now an established fact that radio may be used effectively as a supplementary method of teaching children the common branches even as low as the third grade; that it can be used to enrich and vitalize many school subjects; that it can be made the means of bringing children in the classroom into closer contact with the actual processes of citizenship and government; that it has large possibilities in training for music appreciation; and that it is the most powerful tool so far devised for reaching large numbers of adults.

Since at least the mid-1970s, the percentage of broadcast hours devoted to instruction has declined, even among the stations licensed to states and local school boards, which have the closest relationships with the schools. In radio, the stations licensed to states or local authorities devoted more than 10 percent of their 1978 schedules to instruction. By 1984 the stations licensed to local school boards and other units of government reported that instruction accounted for 1.5 percent of their broadcast hours. Other radio licensee categories reported 0.2 percent or less.

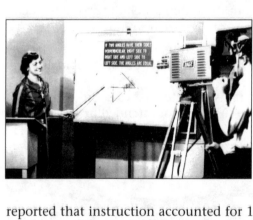

Public TV began with classroom instructional programs in many cities and states, as in South Carolina, where **Cornelia Trumbull taught geometry** in 1958. In South Carolina and several other states, multichannel satellite and fiber-optic systems continue to bring formal course materials to schools and colleges and at-home learners. But in most places, the "last mile" to the student's desk is increasingly a direct satellite link, a videotape from the school media center or other "narrowcasting" delivery systems, instead of the broadcast channel. (Photo: South Carolina ETV.)

In television, 17.1 percent of public stations' broadcast hours were devoted to instruction in 1974. A decade later, stations reported that instruction accounted for 13 percent. [And in 1994, it occupied 8.9 percent of airtime.]

But one must be cautious about raw percentages. In public television, for example, instruction's percentage dropped four points by 1984, but the stations' total number of broadcast hours increased by nearly a third. Furthermore, it is important to look at individual cases. While some stations broadcast little formal instruction, others offer substantial schedules. Moreover, broadcast hours don't tell the whole story. Stations use alternative technologies, such as cable TV systems or a microwave technology that the FCC calls the Instructional Television Fixed Service (ITFS), to provide more material and increased schedule flexibility, sometimes at lower cost.

CPB began exploring its educational role soon after it was organized. At first its educational mission was ambiguous. The interests of education had been retarded somewhat by the first Carnegie Com-mission's relative lack of attention and the fact that the Public Broadcasting Act provided the legislative equivalent of a fourth-down punt: it called for a study, as Carnegie had. Furthermore, the resulting study became diffuse and, at least from public broadcasting's standpoint, its report was ineffective.

Even before the congressionally mandated report was issued, CPB began to consider its future course in education. By summer 1969 CPB staffers gave President John Macy suggestions for possible initiatives. During the fall an informal committee composed of a few education-oriented public broadcasters considered the problem. That was followed by a six-month International Council for Educational Development study, which recommended a focus on television and radio courses toward a high school equivalency certificate. The study also recommended that CPB work with other institutions concerned with non-formal instructional services. For the formal education system, it was said that CPB should fund high-quality, broad-appeal programs on specific important subjects. The report's priority list was ageless: it was headed by drugs and sex.

The corporation's now-defunct Advisory Committee of National Organizations, originally established as a broadly representative advice and support group, studied CPB's educational role. It provided a status report, probed some principles of education and broadcasting, and pointed out the changing context of American education and public broadcasting.

Given the enormous scope of American education and the relative limitations of the corporation's financing, how could CPB best make a difference? CPB had undertaken some useful initiatives, and some distinguished programs had been produced, but they didn't constitute a strategy for making a difference.

After starting to develop a coherent educational program under Douglas F. Bodwell's direction in the mid-1970s, the corporation in 1981 completed negotiations with Ambassador Walter F. Annenberg and the Annenberg School of Communications to establish the Annenberg/CPB Project. Backed by annual grants of $10 million [through 1990], the project is a major effort for using telecommunications in higher education, particularly for the off-campus, non-traditional learner. [By 1997, the project had aided the production of 40 college-credit telecourses totalling 600 hours of video. Under separate grants from Annenberg, the project later began developing materials to improve teaching in elementary/secondary schools.]

PBS distributes college-level telecourses through its Adult Learning Service. [And for elementary/secondary schools, the National Instructional Satellite Service, operated by the National Educational Telecommunications Association and the American Telecommunications Group, provides satellite feeds of classroom video programs.]

Rising steadily and perhaps already No. 1 among the many Annenberg/CPB Project video courses is its introductory Spanish series, **Destinos.** Above: series stars Liliana Abud and Arturo Puig ("Raquel" and "Arturo"), who lead a cast of 62 characters through a storyline that crosses three continents. In the U.S. alone, some 250 colleges and universities have used the WGBH-produced series as a telecourse for distance learners and 1,400 use the series in traditional classrooms—implying that at least 500,000 students have used the series, by CPB's estimate. It's also used in 1,900 secondary schools. (Photo: CPB.)

Programs for kids

Public television has considered children's programming a special mission since its earliest days. Programmers from the 1950s will

In 1953, **Fred Rogers and Josie Carey** (at right) put together *The Children's Hour*, a local forerunner of *Mister Rogers' Neighborhood*, for which he was producer and puppeteer and she, the on-camera host. Rogers developed his own series for preschool-age kids during a short stint at the Canadian Broadcasting Corp., and returned to WQED for a long run, which continues more than 30 years later. "Somehow, early on," he said, "I got the idea inside of me that childhood was valuable, that children were worthy of being seen and heard, and who they were would have a lot to do with how our world would become." (Photo: National Public Broadcasting Archives.)

recall Buckskin Bob and the *Friendly Giant*. The *Children's Corner*, produced by WQED, Pittsburgh, might also come to mind. The program's host, Josie Carey, became a favorite with children and their parents. The producer, a young newcomer named Fred Rogers, also handled a puppet character, Daniel Striped Tiger. When Daniel invited viewers to stop by the studio on his birthday, hundreds circled the block on a rainy day.

A decade later, Rogers appeared in a new program on the Eastern Educational Network stations. When Boston station WGBH held an open house for the creator of *Mister Rogers' Neighborhood*, they made provisions for a crowd of 500. The event attracted 10,000 children and parents, and outdrew that day's Red Sox game.

Sesame Street, produced by the Children's Television Workshop (CTW), debuted in 1969. It was an instant success, and during 1984 claimed a regular audience of nine million children under the age of six. Since then, CTW has produced other series in language, science and math, plus numerous specials and a magazine. It also receives royalties on sales of program-related toys and other products, which are plowed back into program production.

Perhaps CTW's most important contribution to children's program production is the integration of research and studio production. Before a *Sesame Street* segment is broadcast, the producers know that it will achieve its educational objectives.

Herman W. Land, engaged to analyze CTW's structure and products, wrote: "As conceived by the CTW, research should be used as a program building tool from the earliest stages. This view is characteristic of the empirical orientation of the workshop. It seeks to be guided pragmatically by what objective experience points to as that which will be most effective in reaching and educating its audience. This results in a process of production, testing, feedback and revised production which is, in effect, a self-regenerative process of improvement always in motion. It results, too, in an open-ended attitude toward production as a continuing process, rather than as a system with fixed limits. Research directed toward program development is termed 'formative' research. At CTW it consists of two main parts: that designed to test the ability of a program to hold the viewer's attention; and that designed to see how much of the educational objective is being achieved."

In 1985 the Central Educational Network and WTTW, a public TV station in Chicago, hosted the first American Children's Television Festival. There were 100 entries from public and commercial producers; 25 of these were nominated for the festival's Ollie Awards. Half of the 10 awards went to public television producers. They were: *Mister Rogers' Neighborhood, The New Image Teen Theatre,*

Reading Rainbow, Sesame Street and *WonderWorks*.

CPB figures show that "general children's and youth" and *Sesame Street* programming accounted for about 23 percent of public TV stations' schedules in 1984. [A decade later, with the advent of the Ready to Learn Service, the share had risen to 29 percent.] In radio, children's shows accounted for less than 1 percent of public radio stations' schedules by 1978. Producers have tried to revive the production of radio programs for children with series like Kathy O'Connell's *Kid's Corner* at WXPN-FM in Philadelphia.

At one point recently, **Sesame Street** (cast at left) counted 71 Emmys, two Peabodys and dozens of other awards. Founder Joan Ganz Cooney received a Presidential Medal of Freedom in 1998. And a sample of Americans voted the series one of 15 "icons" of the 1970s to appear on postage stamps in fall 1999 (it came in No. 2, after the "smiley face"). Cooney recalled that the idea for a school-readiness series came out of a 1966 dinner party she threw, attended by Lloyd Morrisett (then a vice president of the Carnegie Corp.), who later funded the start-up, and her boss at public TV's Channel 13, Lewis Freedman. Three years later, in November 1969, *Sesame Street* went on the air. Cooney headed the production house, Children's Television Workshop until 1990 and since has remained chair of its executive committee.

Minority audiences of various kinds

The Public Broadcasting Act of 1967 includes a mandate to provide alternative programming that is responsive to the nation's entire citizenry. Public broadcasting responds to this mandate by including programs for minorities, and targeted groups, such as the elderly, children and the handicapped. Black, Latino, Native American, Asian and Pacific Islander program groups are also active in public broadcasting, with annual assistance from CPB.

Two NPR programs illustrated a national response to minority needs. *Horizons* was a weekly half-hour documentary intended for special audiences and *Enfoque Nacional* was the only national Spanish-language public radio program in the country.

It should be acknowledged that station managements, scrambling to attract funding and recognizing the need to increase audience numbers, have been caught in a dilemma about such programming. On the one hand, no one questions the mandate, but on the other hand, how does one honor it, take the consequences of attracting very small audiences of specialized programming, and survive?

Supporting its mandate for minority programming, public broadcasting also has an equal employment opportunity mandate, and CPB plays a mandated training role. The issue of minorities in public broadcasting has been difficult, and progress has never been fully satisfactory. In 1978, a task force called upon Congress, CPB and the other national organizations to increase participation in public broadcasting and to increase the number of minority-oriented programs.

Public television's major venture in programming specifically for the elderly was the series *Over Easy*, produced by KQED, San Francisco. A 1980 CPB report said that "special or target audience programming in 1978 showed an increase of 130 hours per year to 424 hours per broadcaster over 1976, and the percentage of all air time it represented jumped from 6.5 percent to 8.7 percent. Much of this increase was accounted for by the single program for older viewers, *Over Easy*, which constituted nearly one-third of the 1978 target programming."

Public television was a leader in developing captioning for the hearing-impaired. Open captioning—visible to all viewers—began in 1972 with WGBH's federally supported captioning of *The French Chef*. PBS engineers soon developed closed-captioning technology, which displays captions only on TV sets with special decoders. Closed captioning began experimentally in 1976 and became a regular service in 1980. In 1990, Congress required that all future TV sets be capable of receiving closed captions.

To serve audience members whose *sight* is impaired, many public radio stations use a "subcarrier" of their FM signals, inaudible to conventional radio receivers, to provide extensive information service for print-handicapped people. For example, KPBS-FM, San Diego, transmits 24 hours a day of readings from newspapers, books and magazines, plus other features of particular interest to people who can't see well.

Public TV also serves sight-impaired viewers with an optional audio narration, developed by WGBH, called Descriptive Video Service (DVS). In this supplementary soundtrack, received by stereo TV sets over the SAP (Separate Audio Program) channel, a special narrator describes visuals that sighted viewers are seeing.

Aggregating funds for production

Nowhere is public television's decentralized structure more clearly illustrated than in its longtime processes for choosing programs.

For years, public TV stations assembled a large part of their schedules by participating in the Station Program Cooperative (SPC), an annual program market operated by PBS. In October 1972, fresh from the trauma of the Nixon veto and the change of command at CPB, PBS President Hartford Gunn envisioned the SPC in an article in NAEB's *Educational Broadcasting Review*. Gunn proposed that most of CPB's public TV funds go directly to the stations. Then a sort of programming marketplace would allow stations to choose which programs they would support. The idea had surfaced earlier in a variation called the "Market Plan for PTV Programming."

PB
PB
See online: Gunn's paper proposing the SPC, 1972.

"Under such an arrangement," Gunn wrote, "programming would be, and would be perceived to be, the result of station and community needs rather than political expediencies. CPB would be seen to be facilitating those station decisions, rather than be suspected of controlling programming for its own purposes."

The idea was controversial. CPB was not sure it could meet its programming mandate by such a mechanism. Nevertheless, the idea clearly had appeal in that beleaguered time, and the SPC was born. It became public TV's major financing mechanism. In 1985, stations spent $39 million in the SPC, providing a major portion of funding for programs such as *Sesame Street, Great Performances, American Playhouse* and the *NewsHour*. Typically, SPC funds were mixed with CPB grants, corporate underwriting, and foundation or government support to make up a program's cost. An individual station's share of the cost was based on the number of stations making a commitment and a formula based on the station's total non-federal financial support. [In the 1990s, as discussed in Chapter 10, public TV replaced the SPC mechanism with a "chief program executive" at PBS.]

Public radio also moved toward decentralization when it adopted a "new business plan" for NPR in 1985. Under the plan, most of CPB's radio funds now go directly to stations, which buy programs from NPR or elsewhere. In fiscal 1986, CPB began funding national radio programs through national program grants that public radio stations could use to produce their own more-than-local programs or acquire them from suppliers such as NPR and Public Radio International. The CPB Radio Program Fund has provided seed money for such radio series as *Marketplace* and *World Cafe*.

A semi-autonomous program fund

In 1979, the second Carnegie Commission proposed replacing CPB with a "Public Telecommunications Trust," which would contain an insulated "Program Services Endowment." Neither Congress nor the president picked up on the idea, but CPB President Robben Fleming was intrigued with the idea of an insulated, semi-autonomous program unit. In August 1979 he proposed that CPB's board reorganize the corporation and establish a Program Fund headed by a director empowered to make final decisions about programs CPB supports.

The proposal "is experimental in nature and will be reviewed for possible modification and change at the end of a two-year period," Fleming said. "The fund will be independent in matters of individual program decisions but will rely upon the board for guidance and upon the management services division for administration and other support." The board would appoint the fund's director from candidates selected by CPB's president. Nominations would originate with a search committee from outside the board. The fund's structure would emphasize political independence.

The board accepted the idea. Here's how the Television Program Fund operated: The fund's director reported quarterly to the board and once a year proposed program priorities, which the board could accept or modify. In establishing categories and judging program proposals the director was assisted by a complex advisory structure mandated by CPB's enabling legislation. [CPB later discontinued the semi-autonomous structure of the fund; the fund now reports to the president of CPB.]

Exercise of the First Amendment

The first Carnegie Commission made the political insulation of public broadcasting a major point of its recommendations. The ensuing federal law and its successors admonish CPB to assure the freedom of the system from undue external influence. Public broadcasting's stations and national organizations have adopted codes to assure that programs meet the standards required, including "objectivity and balance in all programs or series of programs of a controversial nature."

It has been demonstrated, however, that the system can be penetrated at several points, and potentially serious attempts at inappropriate influence can occur. Sometimes it's from an agency of govern-

In public TV's most fertile period of series creation since its earliest days, veteran producer **Lewis Freedman**, first director of CPB's Television Program Fund, assembled consortia of stations to create several of public TV's longtime staple series— *American Playhouse, Frontline* and *WonderWorks*. Freedman's successor, Ron Hull, arranged for CPB to help start *The American Experience*. Above: Freedman makes a point to his bosses on the CPB board. (Photo: *Current*.)

If "credibility is the currency of our programming," as public TV leaders resolved in 1984, the *NewsHour* is one of its most valuable assets. The nightly program helps establish PBS's reputation for fairness with its careful partisan balance. Longtime co-hosts **Jim Lehrer and Robert MacNeil** (above, circa 1981) worked together four months on NPACT's Watergate hearings coverage in 1973, and started the nightly half-hour in 1975. In 1983 the producing stations WNET and WETA expanded it to an hour in 1983— the first national hour-long news program. MacNeil retired in October 1995, leaving the anchor chair to Lehrer. MacNeil, after a heartfelt tribute to his partner and friend, told a gathering of public broadcasters: "I thank you for letting me work in a place where I didn't have to check my ideals at the door."

**PB
PB**

The Wingspread statement on editorial integrity

ment, and sometimes it's from a funder or underwriter. The threat has been a continuing point of concern for public broadcasting managers and trustees.

In November 1984, a group of trustees and managers, plus invited speakers and discussion leaders, met at the Wingspread conference center of the Johnson Foundation in Racine, Wis. Their purpose was to discuss public broadcasting and editorial integrity and to start creating principles that could serve public broadcasting. They proceeded from five major principles:

■ "Public broadcasting responsibilities are grounded in constitutional and statutory law."

■ "Because public broadcasting is a public service, it should be responsive to diverse public views and opinions."

■ "Public broadcasting can be justified only by offering a consistent range of good program choices."

■ "Public broadcasting must assure credible public service programming by creating programming which meets the needs and stimulates the interest of the audience; ensuring that programming will be free of undue external influence from all sources; basing programs on their value in the marketplace of ideas, not on financial considerations or pressure."

■ "Public broadcasting must conduct its financial affairs in order to assure its supporters and its audiences that their time and resources are used efficiently and effectively."

The group's "Statement of Principles of Editorial Integrity in Public Broadcasting" was subsequently endorsed by the boards of PBS and the National Association of Public Television Stations and commended to all public TV licensees. Here is the statement's full text:

■ **"We are the trustees of a public service:** Public broadcasting was created to provide a wide range of programming services of the highest professionalism and quality which can educate, enlighten, and entertain the American public, its audience and source of support. It is a noncommercial enterprise, reflecting the worthy purpose of the federal and state governments to provide education and cultural enrichment to their citizens.

"As trustees of this public service, part of our job is to educate all citizens and public policymakers to our function, and to assure that we can certify to all citizens that station management responsibly exercises the editorial freedom necessary to achieve public broadcasting's mission effectively."

■ **"Our service is programming:** The purpose of public broadcasting is to offer its audiences public and educational programming which provides alternatives in quality, type and scheduling. All activities of a public broadcasting licensee exist solely to enhance and support excellent programs. No matter how well other activities are performed, public broadcasting will be judged by its programming service and the value of that service to its audiences.

"As trustees, we must create the climate, the policies and the sense of direction which assure that the mission of providing high quality programming remains paramount."

■ **"Credibility is the currency of our programming:** As surely as programming is our purpose, and the product by which our audiences judge our value, that judgment will depend upon their confidence that our programming is free from undue or improper influence. Our role as trustees includes educating both citizens and public policymakers to the importance of this fact and to assuring that our stations meet this challenge in a responsible and efficient way.

"As trustees, we must adopt policies and procedures which enable professional management to operate in a way which will give the public full confidence in the editorial integrity of our programming."

■ **"Many of our responsibilities are grounded in constitutional or statutory law:** Public broadcasting stations are subject to a variety of statutory and regulatory requirements and restrictions. These include the federal statute under which licensees must operate, as well as other applicable federal and state laws. Public broadcasting is also cloaked with the mantle of the First Amendment protection of a free press and freedom of speech.

"As trustees we must be sure that these responsibilities are met. To do so requires us to understand the legal and constitutional framework within which our stations operate, and to inform and educate those whose positions or influence may affect the operation of our licensee."

■ **"We have a fiduciary responsibility for public funds:** Public broadcasting depends upon funds provided by individual and corporate contributions; and by local, state, and federal taxes. Trustees must therefore develop and implement policies which can assure the public and their chosen public officials alike that this money is well spent.

"As trustees, we must assure conformance to sound fiscal and management practices. We must also assure that the legal requirements placed on us by funding sources are met. At the same time, we must resist the inappropriate use of otherwise legitimate oversight procedures to distort the programming process which funding supports."

Historical family sagas engrossed PBS viewers in the 1970s, starting with the British imports *The Forsyte Saga* and *Upstairs, Downstairs*. WNET gave the genre a Yankee try with the 13-part *Adams Chronicles* in January 1976, but the high production costs discouraged thereafter all but a few American-made mini-series for PBS. Above: **Nyree Dawn Porter** of *The Forsyte Saga*. At left: *Adams Chronicles* stars **George Grizzard and Kathryn Walker** as John and Abigail Adams, with the younger Adamses. (Photo: Carl Samrock.)

The creative spark

Programs are our only purpose. Statements of principle, mechanisms for decision-making, and arrangements for funding are only steps toward serving that fundamental mission.

Public broadcasting has every right to be proud of its program-

In January 1973, WNET got viewers buzzing over the unexpectedly sensational fly-on-the-wall documentary about **William and Pat Loud's household** (at right), *An American Family.* In seven months of shooting in Santa Barbara, producer Craig Gilbert and filmmakers Alan and Susan Raymond rolled 300 hours of film, watching as the marriage came apart and one of the five children declared he was gay. The series led the way for such intensive, intimate PBS documentaries as *Hoop Dreams* in 1994, *The Farmer's Wife* in 1998 and *An American Love Story,* 1999.

ming record. Public television has become America's medium for presenting constructive programs for children. While *Sesame Street* and *Mister Rogers' Neighborhood* come immediately to mind, they are in distinguished company with *Zoom!* and other programs.

Public broadcasting has, to a greater extent than generally recognized, contributed to the forms of broadcast programming. *An American Family* and "Trial: City and County of Denver vs. Lauren Watson," presented by NET many years ago, broke new ground in documentary production and captured the attention of the country at a time when public television was in its youth. *The Great American Dream Machine* is sometimes remembered for its controversies but its contributions to program production are seen on everything from topical revues to *60 Minutes.* The *MacNeil/Lehrer NewsHour* and *All Things Considered* are major developments in the presentation of news, and they in turn owe a debt to *The Advocates,* the work of the National Public Affairs Center for Television in the '70s, and programs like *Kaleidoscope* from the pioneering Educational Radio Network. The WGBH crew that produces the programs of the Boston Symphony and the Boston Pops have set the national—perhaps world—standard for televising major concerts. It was *Nova* and its association with the BBC that explored America's growing taste for programs about science and nature. Programs like the *National Geographic Specials* and William F. Buckley's *Firing Line* began in commercial television and found a natural home with public broadcasting. A combination of economics and program quality led to importing the series which constitute the venerable *Masterpiece Theatre,* its trailblazing predecessor The *Forsyte Saga,* and Jacob Bronowski's stunning *The Ascent of Man.* And, on a less profound note, it was public television that broke with the conventional wisdom of the day and demonstrated that people will indeed watch tennis on television.

The constant problem, however, is to assure that new program ideas will be developed and that producing organizations can afford to turn the best of these ideas into programs. Successful new programs seem to require equal amounts of money, marketing and magic. Anyone who has tried it knows how difficult it is to attract and maintain the creative spark, sell the idea and then the program, promote it so it will be watched and heard, and then find a way to pay for the whole complex effort. The work of public TV's major producing stations has proved difficult to sustain, and teams capable of top-quality work cannot be casually disbanded and reassembled. An elegant California department store once used the slogan, "Good taste costs no more." Public broadcasting sage Frank Norwood once paraphrased it: "Bad taste costs no less."

☞

See Chapter 10: Programming in the 1990s.

Mission v. Market

By Robert K. Avery and Alan G. Stavitsky

A chili cookoff might draw more viewers, but a four-hour series that looks at a significant but little-known war in America's past, like KERA's *The U.S.-Mexican War, 1846-1848*, qualifies as a "mission" program for public TV. At left: a Steadicam-equipped cameraman operates in the smoke of a reenacted battle. (Photo: George Stone for KERA.)

Persistent structural frailties

National institutions: system leaders confront gaps in revenues and governance, 1986-99

When public broadcasters discuss what they are going to put on the air next week or next season, they commonly use the words "mission" and "market" to explain their reasoning. If a program falls into the mission category, they are choosing it to fulfill the many public-service promises that the field has made over the years, even if the ratings are low. Or if it is a market program, they are trying to boost the audience somewhat and thereby bring in some more memberships and underwriting grants to meet the station's payroll. On a good day, a program succeeds in both ways.

In theory, public broadcasters were not supposed to worry about "market," but they do, more and more, as their underwriters increasingly expect higher ratings, as legislatures consider cutting "no-strings-attached" appropriations, and as they discover that audiences send larger checks if they see certain kinds of emotionally gratifying pledge specials. "Mission" and "market," therefore, are not academic classifications but real-world choices that broadcasters make each month when they draw up their schedules.

Evidence that the balancing act is succeeding at least by some measures can be seen in the groundswell of fans and donors who defended public broadcasting when its federal aid was under attack in the mid-1990s, but numerous gaps remain between the sky-high mandates for the system and its limited financial resources. By that standard, public broadcasting remains undernourished and handicapped by its own inabilities to boldly advance its cause or even react decisively.

Throughout its history in this country, public broadcasting has been institutionally disenfranchised, scholar Willard D. Rowland has observed. From the earliest days of radio, the U.S. government has favored broadcasting as a business, with only relatively weak factions truly committed to use it for education and cultural enlightenment. In Rowland's words, "The historic contradictions in U.S. politics and social thought about the 'public,' technology and private enterprise always have been reflected in the structure and purposes of [American] broadcasting."

In the period 1986-99, covered by these latter chapters of this book, opponents of public funding for the field have made their case more explicitly and publicly than ever, capitalizing on three strains in contemporary thought and culture:

■ **Discontent with the public sector.** In the 1980s, growing dissatisfaction with the unresponsiveness and inefficiencies of various public institutions led many ordinary people to new doubts about the public sector and greater confidence in the workings of commercial market forces. In this political setting, private broadcasters questioned the public-trust obligations imposed on them, and conservative populists attacked public broadcasting as elitist, self-serving and unaccountable. Anti-deficit crusaders, playing on taxpayers' feelings that their standard of living was slipping away, strove to eliminate funding of CPB to help balance the federal budget.

■ **Expectations of a programming cornucopia.** The expansion of cable TV and direct broadcast satellite systems, along with the home video boom, showed that it was commercially feasible to serve some smaller specialized audiences previously served only through public television. In many minds, this called into question the need for an alternative, publicly supported system. Many academics and journalists, as well as politicians, came to accept an optimistic scenario: that technology would bring viewers the plenty of 500 channels.

■ **Intolerance on the rise.** In the highly polarized political climate of the 1980s and early 1990s, conservative ideologues could refuse to tolerate any views to the left of their own. They openly campaigned against the use of tax dollars to produce (or even transmit) programs with a "liberal bias."

The question of leadership

In October 1993, a group of public broadcasting "Old Timers," as they called themselves, gathered at a Washington, D.C., hotel to swap reminiscences before attending the opening of the National Public Broadcasting Archives at the University of Maryland, which Donald McNeil had lovingly nurtured into existence. Many of those educational radio and television pioneers had little good to say about what was happening to public broadcasting in its adolescence. One speaker after another lamented the tangible loss of the sense of mission that had burned so brightly in the early years. For some, the undoing of public broadcasting seemed to be its endeavor to compete head-to-head in the commercial marketplace. Like Rowland and other critics of the field, many of the old-timers that afternoon placed much of the blame for the system's recurring problems on the present leaders of the system's three major national organizations, PBS, NPR and CPB.

In fairness to those leaders, however, the fervent convictions of the 1950s and 1960s are unable to withstand today's persistent economic pressures and institutional conflicts. The people who have guided the system since the mid-1980s have been talented and well-intentioned, though none has been able to lead the field on an imaginative new course, while fighting fires that erupt frequently.

PBS: From Gunn to Duggan

It is probably safe to say that no one who has taken the helm of the Public Broadcasting Service since its inception has been a match for its gifted first president, Hartford Gunn. He was a man of remarkable intellectual strength who could not only formulate a clear vision for public television but also articulate it in a way that was accessible and empowering for those who accepted it as their own. But despite Gunn's invaluable contributions, PBS reached the point in 1975 when a change in its leadership was needed, and Lawrence Grossman seemed the best fit for the time.

With his aggressive leadership style, Grossman led PBS into the early phase of its transformation to an organization that was market-sensitive on a variety of levels. Yet Grossman knew when it was

In a media world accustomed to sudden mergers and acquisitions, a leading advocate of "privatizing" public broadcasting, **Sen. Larry Pressler** (R-S.D.), briefly put CPB "in play" during January 1995. He mentioned on a talk show that Bell Atlantic was interested in assuming the federal government's role in CPB, prompting other companies to rush to the phone. It turned out that he, as the Senate's telecom regulation overseer, had raised the startling idea with Bell Atlantic executives, who expressed *other* interests in public TV—especially in picking up any TV channels that might become available.

PBS presidents since Gunn (from the top): **Lawrence Grossman, Bruce Christensen** and **Ervin Duggan.**

time to exit the top position, and the role was filled in 1984 by Bruce Christensen, a 41-year-old Utah native who had cut his teeth on local station issues in Provo and Salt Lake City. Christensen had moved to Washington, D.C., less than two years earlier to head the National Association of Public Television Stations, and many within the system worried that he had not yet gained the experience necessary to handle the responsibilities of this important post. On May 15, 1984, Christensen hit the ground running, moving quickly to close ranks in the system and build confidence among station managers and lay leaders alike that he was the right man for the job.

The Christensen years at PBS, 1984-93, were marked by repeated challenges to the system from both within and without. Christensen's firm but soft-spoken style complemented well the period's fiery attacks on program content, efforts to redefine noncommercial use of the spectrum, congressional demands for system accountability, and the ascendance of marketplace ideology. Christensen also dealt with disruptions caused by a major fire in 1984 that forced the relocation of PBS headquarters. When he retired to return to Brigham Young University as a dean, concluding a record nine-year tenure as PBS president, observers praised him as an effective diplomat who had succeeded in helping the system withstand both internal and external attacks. Others privately conceded that he was getting out in the nick of time, before public broadcasting encountered a series of political battles that would be difficult to win.

In the summer of 1993 came the release of the Twentieth Century Fund's report on public television, *Quality Time*. Some hoped the foundation's 21-person panel would be regarded as a third Carnegie Commission, which could move public television issues once again onto the front page. And *Quality Time* did draw some media attention, though it was far more newsworthy within the field than to the public. Its most notable recommendation was a call for federal monies now earmarked for local stations to be reserved for the production and distribution of national programming.

Active on the task force were members Lawrence Grossman and Markle Foundation President Lloyd N. Morrisett, and task force staffer Chloe Aaron, who had been Grossman's programming chief at PBS. They and others on the task force had been outspoken about the importance of strong national programming. The threats to public TV—and the standard of efficiency for comparison—were the national cable networks like the Discovery Channel that are not burdened by the expense of staffing nearly 180 licensees that operate 350 stations around the country.

Perhaps no portion of the report has been read more closely than the brief supplemental comment by Ervin S. Duggan, a task force member who at the time was a member of the Federal Communications Commission. His remarks, which filled less than three pages, explained that he differed from the report's general recommendations in two respects. First, he did not agree with the redirection of federal funds away from local stations. Second, he believed that fairness in program balance must be achieved within every individual program—that achieving balance across the entire schedule would not be adequate. Not too surprisingly, PBS station executives were attuned to the first item of dissent, particularly this paragraph:

. . . I have real misgivings about reconstituting public television's funding in a way that would diminish the resources of local stations. Public broadcasting has long been identified with the public interest, and one bedrock principle of broadcasting in the public interest is localism. In my view, the service that public stations bring to their communities should include serious attention to local needs. Diluting the amount of money that public broadcasting's funding sources provide to local stations could directly undermine the hope for improved local service. Such an undermining, in my judgment, would be most unfortunate.

Less than six months later, on December 1, 1993, the PBS search committee seeking Christensen's successor announced that Ervin Duggan would become the fourth president of PBS. The committee reportedly had interviewed as many as eight candidates, but rejected popular front-runners from inside the system in favor of an outsider—someone who could bring a fresh perspective and who could be an effective spokesperson for public television in Washington's circles of political power.

Duggan would demonstrate a year later that he could hold his own in debates over federal funding for the system, but he was less effective against challenges from within the system. Soon his statements about the bedrock of localism were being thrown in his face as he attempted to enforce what he believed was the will of the majority of stations, pushing for common carriage of key programs to facilitate tune-in promotion and to boost viewing and underwriting. The system's internal field of battle resembled Grossman's early years at PBS. To build a programming war chest to stay ahead of the competing cable networks, Duggan centralized "back-end" rights in PBS's hands, and with the help of a robust U.S. economy was able to add $50 million to PBS's program budget in five years. At the same time, as a former FCC member, he felt strongly that public TV should hold the line on commercialism and limit 30-second underwriting credits. After five years punctuated by clashes with factions of the system, Duggan resigned in 1999.

After Bennet, NPR tries a businessman

For all that Frank Mankiewicz did at National Public Radio to strengthen its news operations and attempt long-range entrepreneurial business ventures, he will be remembered as the president who allowed NPR to run a $6.4 million deficit in 1983. During congressional hearings, Mankiewicz, who had already been replaced by Douglas Bennet, continued to insist that the financial collapse was not his fault, that subordinates had not informed him of the perils.

NPR presidents in the 1980s and '90s (from the top): **Frank Mankiewicz, Douglas Bennet, Delano Lewis** and **Kevin Klose.**

The tight-lipped, wry Bennet did not mingle readily with NPR's journalistic troops, as Mankiewicz did, but he did oversee the network's recovery. He is given credit for working closely with the NPR Board of Directors, which, on July 17, 1984, agreed unanimously with the plan that the stations accept what was by then a $6.9 million debt. Bennet helped mount a national fundraising campaign and created confidence at NPR. With firm management practices and a welcome stability based on a new business plan, NPR in 1985

was able to create *Weekend Edition* as an extension of the successful weekday newsmagazine, *Morning Edition.* After a two-year effort, the public radio system made the final payment on NPR's debt in September 1986. NPR had added staff to strengthen the cultural side of its schedule and in 1987 began national distribution of such important programs as *Performance Today, Fresh Air* and *Car Talk.*

But an expanding NPR also needed increasing membership fees, and relations with the stations soured. Late in Bennet's term, in January 1993, the stations and their network called a five-year truce in the annual dues wars: they linked the program fees paid by stations directly to the growth of stations' own revenues rather than to NPR's spending needs. The dues "lock-down" bought peace within the system but put more burden on NPR's own fundraising efforts.

With Democrats back in the White House, Bennet returned to the State Department as an assistant secretary in March 1993—the same rank he had held during the Carter Administration. With Bennet gone, CBS News veteran Joseph Dembo held the fort as acting president. It took NPR until August of that year to sift through more than 200 resumes and interview nine finalists. The end result was the appointment of Delano E. Lewis as NPR's fifth president.

Well known in influential Washington circles, Lewis had established himself as a skilled "people person" as president of Bell Atlantic's phone company in the city. A businessman hired to boost NPR's revenues, Lewis set out to overcome what he called "the legacy of '83"—a fear of risk-taking dating back to the disastrous end to NPR's previous entrepreneurial streak under Mankiewicz. NPR's 25-year audio archive and its respected brand name held enormous value, Lewis figured, but after seeking and considering many possible media deals, network leaders encountered few that they wanted to make. As he approached the end of his fifth year at NPR, Lewis acknowledged: "There doesn't appear to be any 'low-hanging fruit' we can easily pick that will bring millions of dollars into NPR."

One deal Lewis did endorse was a merger with the rival network Public Radio International, though it did not come to pass. While NPR fought PRI in the trenches for program carriage, Lewis maintained friendly ties with Stephen Salyer, president of the Minneapolis-based network, and for a while the networks collaborated on a joint satellite service for Europe called America One. Contending that public radio's real competition was outside the field, they both presented merger proposals to their boards in the fall of 1997.

Though NPR was the larger force in public radio because of its strong news department, Lewis quite likely was impressed that Salyer and his board had raised millions by 1996 to start *The World,* a daily newsmagazine co-produced with the BBC and WGBH-FM in Boston. (NPR moved quickly to compete with the program, rushing to start *All Things Considered* an hour earlier than before.) Lewis envied PRI for having a board that raised money effectively while he answered to a board of elected station managers; he repeatedly suggested that NPR split its program roles from its membership organization.

If the PRI merger had occurred, it could have brought that structural change; indeed, PRI's board did insist on maintaining its "private nonprofit governance structure." NPR's board likewise preferred for the stations to keep hold of NPR. Their greatest fear remained that their prized news service would "bypass" the local stations or turn against them as a competitor, via satellite or the Internet.

When Lewis retired in August 1998, NPR did not seek another businessman as president, but instead hired Kevin Klose, a 25-year *Washington Post* correspondent and editor with recent experience as head of Radio Free Europe and then the U.S. International Broadcasting Bureau, parent of Voice of America. Klose took charge in December 1998.

CPB: interplay with partisanship

Partisan politics is built into the governance of CPB, with board members appointed by the White House, often from the ranks of loyal campaign donors and public relations staffers. Though the law allows no more than a majority of one board member from a party, that safeguard does not prevent partisan politics from intermittently showing itself at CPB. When Republicans rule, the board is more likely to worry about liberal bias in programming, and when the Democrats are in charge, there's more talk about minority programming and independent producers.

A sudden conflict in 1985 began the recent sequence of presidential succession at CPB: the sudden, public clash between the Republican board chairman, Sonia Landau, and President Edward Pfister, over a programming trade excursion to Moscow (see caption on opposite page). Pfister quit with a fiery speech, and his successor, a commercial broadcaster named Martin Rubenstein, lasted only 10 months before the board fired him.

CPB's sixth president, named in July 1987, was Donald Ledwig, who had served as vice president for finance, and then acting president. No one expected Ledwig to be a charismatic spokesperson or visionary, but board members got what they hoped for—a solid fiscal manager who helped put congressional appropriations on a firmer footing. It was during Ledwig's tour of duty that the public radio and television satellite distribution systems received their much needed overhauls, with special appropriations totalling $198.3 million paid out in 1991-93. But Ledwig suffered a crushing personal blow during testimony on behalf of an appropriation. Sen. Ted Stevens (R-Alaska) lashed out at him, charging that CPB's grant policies—with the larger grants going to populous places with successful fundraising—were shortchanging minority-controlled, rural and small-town stations, such as those used by the senator's constituents in Alaska. When Stevens heard that CPB had assembled a rebuttal entitled "Myth and Fact: A CPB Response to Senator Stevens," he was incensed that CPB employees had responded flippantly. The senator's public rebuke left Ledwig visibly wounded. Ledwig submitted his resignation six months later, effective January 1, 1992.

Recent CPB presidents: **Donald Ledwig, Richard Carlson** and **Robert Coonrod.**

In March, CPB for the second time turned to the U.S. Information Agency for its president. The first was USIA official Henry Loomis, hired 10 years earlier. The second was Richard W. Carlson, a former director of USIA's Voice of America who had been serving as ambassador to the Seychelles islands. Carlson, unlike his predecessor Ledwig and his successor Robert Coonrod, was an ambitious, combative political personality. He had achieved a reputation as a highly articulate spokesman and used his gift to defend editorial freedom at VOA. A onetime TV anchorman and San Diego mayoral candidate, he also was a certified Republican, chosen for office as a wing of his party mobilized for the second great assault on federal aid to public broadcasting.

The right builds, and loses, an argument against federal aid

Public television has always had its share of critics, but Carlson and his counterparts—Bruce Christensen at PBS and David Brugger at America's Public Television Stations (formerly NAPTS)—were caught off guard by the hostile rhetoric increasingly seen in opinion columns and heard on Capitol Hill. For years, Reed Irvine and his organization, Accuracy in Media, had accused PBS documentaries of leftward leanings, but by 1989 right-wing think tanks were focusing on public broadcasting as one of the most objectionable survivors of LBJ's Great Society. In 1991, the Heritage Foundation, a key new-right think tank in Washington, hired a young Ph.D. from UCLA, Laurence Jarvik, to study public broadcasting. At the same time in Los Angeles, a onetime left-wing journalist, David Horowitz, made the system one of the first targets of his new Center for the Study of Popular Culture. Jarvik's go-for-the-jugular broadsides, regularly published in Horowitz's quarterly, *Comint*, won him the attention he was seeking. Soon Senate Majority Leader Bob Dole—and later House Speaker Newt Gingrich and Senate Commerce Committee Chairman Larry Pressler—would wage their attacks on public broadcasting with ammunition crafted by Jarvik.

When Carlson took office at CPB, the corporation was already struggling with revived conservative demands that it use "content analysis" to rebalance the political weight of the public TV programming paid for with tax dollars. It was not a new issue for CPB. Five years earlier, in March 1987, the board had rejected board member Richard Brookhiser's proposal for a study of "balance" by social scientists S. Robert Lichter and Linda S. Lichter, then at George Washington University. The Lichters did their study anyway, in 1988, and they released it in March 1992, when a CPB funding bill was pending in Congress. The content analysis, published by their Washington-based Center for Media and Public Affairs, found that 225 public TV documentaries aired in a year "tilted consistently in a liberal direction."

The documentaries, according to the Lichters, revealed a liberal agenda, which they said favored peace over war, preservation of the environment at the expense of human expansion, and absolute separation of church and state. South Africa's apartheid was "condemned by two out of three sources," the report complained, and the people filmed defending apartheid "tended to be so extreme as to lack credence within the American political structure." The public TV programs also tended to claim that minorities and women still suffered from discrimination in America, and portrayed national enemies in a favorable light.

"This so-called study is clearly a political tract, not scientific fact," responded Robert Ottenhoff, PBS executive vice president. "It is motivated by the same political bias that it purports to study." Although public broadcasters said the study focused on certain doc-

What public broadcasting needs is a $1.00 check-off box on the federal income tax form, said **longtime Arkansas ETV volunteer Jane Krutz** (above, left), a Little Rock businesswoman. Lobbyists didn't rank the idea high on their list, but Krutz got a big hand during a grim legislative update at the PBS Annual Meeting in June 1995. "I'll guarantee you that 98 percent of Arkansans would check it off," she said. "I could stump it across the nation." And from her assertive presence, and speaking skills developed on the Salvation Army circuit, it seemed she easily could. Krutz was named public TV volunteer of the year by the National Friends of Public Broadcasting. She concluded: "You give us a chance to put a check on that tax and, honey, we'll put it on there."

When Congress asked public broadcasting for a plan for phasing-out federal aid, it got two somewhat different plans in May 1995—one from CPB and the other from the other national organizations. At left: **NPR's Delano Lewis speaks for the station organizations**, flanked by (left to right) PRI's Stephen Salyer, APTS's David Brugger and PBS's Ervin Duggan. Neither plan gave Congress much hope of a politically easy, cost-free phase-out. CPB ventured deeper into the touchy area of station efficiencies and avoided recommending funding sources for a trust fund. The other groups dared to name a half-dozen funding sources with implications for the federal budget, though House subcommittee chairman Jack Fields had warned them not to bring back tax proposals. Lewis dodged the issue: if Congress took proceeds from spectrum auctions to endow the trust fund, he argued, that would be private money, not tax money. (Photo: Photopress.)

umentaries that were unrepresentative of the total PBS schedule, congressional leaders who shared the Lichters' viewpoint found it most helpful in the campaign against the system.

Encouraged by writings of the Lichters and Jarvik, Congress put the issue of program balance back in CPB's lap. Since its beginning, CPB had been responsible for "strict adherence to objectivity and balance," but in a June 1992 amendment to CPB's authorizing law, Congress ordered the corporation to solicit public views on objectivity and balance in programming (and certain other desired qualities); to review national programs and make grants to meet those criteria; and to report on the matter annually to the President and Congress. As in the struggle with the Nixon Administration, politicians were asking CPB to police unbalanced programming—while the stations counted on CPB to act as their heat shield.

Though the corporation did not formally set out to redress imbalance, Carlson himself gave a public drubbing to PBS's 1992 election night coverage—onlookers in the WGBH studio were clearly heard cheering Bill Clinton's election. CPB also came up with funds for several conservative-leaning projects, including an issues series, *Reverse Angle* (later *National Desk*), which premiered in 1993, and *Adventures from the Book of Virtues,* a 1995 children's series based on a book by former Education Secretary William F. Bennett. CPB responded to the congressional mandate with an "Open to the Public" campaign to collect public views on program balance, holding hearings around the country and releasing a poll in 1994. Though 33 percent of the poll's sample said public TV programming was "too slanted to liberal positions," 28 percent said it was "too slanted to conservative positions." That was balance of a sort.

Results from that survey and others indicated little grassroots support for "zeroing out" federal aid to public broadcasting. Three separate polls in February 1995, for instance, indicated the public backed the funding by majorities ranging from 62 to 84 percent. Then a Roper poll said public TV and radio yield the best value for the tax dollar of all government services except for police and the military.

Newt Gingrich did not carefully weigh public appreciation for public broadcasting, however, when he was riding high on the Republican congressional elections victory that made him speaker

Profile of a relationship with Congress

Millions of dollars

Opponents of aid to public broadcasting created plateaus in CPB spending in early 1980s and again in 1990s.

But the general upward swing of this chart doesn't mean more spending power. After adjusting for inflation, FY2000's $300M is worth 5% less than FY90 figure of $229.4M.

Authorizing bills, which set ceilings for spending and are handled by different Hill committees, are often 15-35% more generous than these actual appropriations.

Reagan-era cutbacks, halted CPB's rise for years, starting with $35M cut in in FY 83 (to **$137M**). ▼

$400							
$350							
$300							
$250							
$200							
$150							
$100							
$50							
$0	1969	1971	1973	1975	1977	1979	1981	1983

▲

CPB's first appropriation in FY68 was just **$5M**, but from there the sum often rose by $10M or $20M a year.

As a portion of public broadcasting's total revenues, the appropriation to CPB has hovered around 14-15% for a decade. For FY97, the portion was 13.5%. For more about the other sources, see page 47.

The prophetic bumper sticker from Draper, S.D.

of the House. Soon after the November 1994 vote, he and Senate Commerce Committee Chairman Larry Pressler (R-S.D.) led the charge against federal aid to the system. But calls and letters to congressional offices agreed with the polls, favoring a reprieve for Big Bird, as did newspaper editorialists and hundreds of well-connected station board members of both parties.

In the fore of the national debate, month after month, were three articulate system spokesmen with distinct strengths of position. Ervin Duggan took the microphone as a parable-quoting South Carolinian, who had worked as a young man in the Johnson White House. Delano Lewis appeared as a fully credentialed veteran of the private sector. And Richard Carlson spoke as a Republican who had cut the CPB staff by 25 percent.

As Republican leaders came to realize that zeroing-out federal aid to public broadcasting was not a winner with voters, their threat receded. Before the 1996 election, the proprietor of a cafe in Draper, S.D., had printed up bumper stickers urging, "Let's Keep PBS and 'Privatize' Pressler," and voters heeded the call. It may have been Pressler's advocacy of telephone deregulation that cost him the election, but it did not help his candidacy that he was out front in the campaign to "privatize" CPB. In November 1996 Pressler would be the only incumbent Republican senator to lose a seat.

Though the attack on CPB funding petered out, it energized reforms of inefficiency in the system. Under Carlson, CPB began research and development to rectify the system's problems of overlapping infrastructure and inadequate revenues. It risked the wrath of stations in 1995 by freeing up $11 million from its highly compartmentalized budget to begin twin Future Funds for radio and TV research-and-development projects. Future Funds (phased down to $7 million by fiscal 1999) help stations plan various revenue-generating ventures as well as efficiency-minded consolidations.

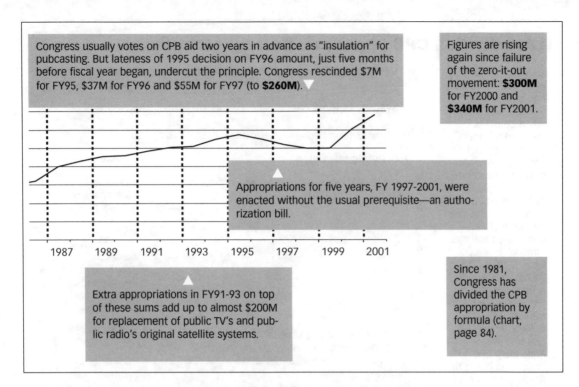

Congress usually votes on CPB aid two years in advance as "insulation" for pubcasting. But lateness of 1995 decision on FY96 amount, just five months before fiscal year began, undercut the principle. Congress rescinded $7M for FY95, $37M for FY96 and $55M for FY97 (to **$260M**). ▼

Figures are rising again since failure of the zero-it-out movement: **$300M** for FY2000 and **$340M** for FY2001.

▲ Appropriations for five years, FY 1997-2001, were enacted without the usual prerequisite—an authorization bill.

1987   1989   1991   1993   1995   1997   1999   2001

▲ Extra appropriations in FY91-93 on top of these sums add up to almost $200M for replacement of public TV's and public radio's original satellite systems.

Since 1981, Congress has divided the CPB appropriation by formula (chart, page 84).

Carlson's G.O.P. partisanship may have helped save federal aid from the Gingrich assault, but it eventually ended his term. With a Republican majority led by board Chair Sheila Tate, a former Reagan spokeswoman, Carlson clashed repeatedly with Democrats on the CPB board in 1995, at one point proposing to hire a friend of Gingrich's as a consultant. In January 1997, four months after Clinton appointees took the board majority, Carlson announced he would step down as CPB president that spring.

In a memo to station managers, Carlson wrote:

. . . After nearly five years on the job, I believe we have met or exceeded the goals and expectations the CPB board presented to me when I was hired in the summer of 1992. . . . We have reacted responsibly and constructively to the rapidly worsening budget climate here in Washington. We have begun to address the painful but unavoidable issues of overlap and consolidation, and have taken important steps toward more realistic grant criteria. . . . At the same time—as you all well know—broadcasting is entering a revolutionary era of new digital technology. It is clear to all of us that this transition will force extraordinary demands on the system—not only financial challenges but a need for long-term planning and commitment. This is a logical juncture for CPB to seek new leadership . . .

Carlson's executive vice president, Robert T. Coonrod, served as acting president until the board promoted him to succeed Carlson on October 1, 1997. Carlson had brought the 25-year foreign service officer from VOA, where he was deputy director. But Coonrod was a product of the civil service meritocracy, with the style of a professor popular with his students. He was as collegial as Carlson was confrontational, as informal as Carlson was imperious. With Coonrod's

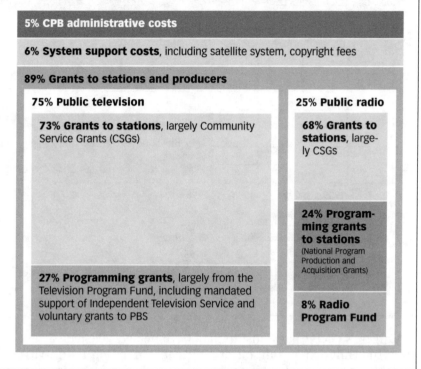

Law divides CPB appropriation by formula (chart not to scale)

Dividing CPB funds between TV and radio had been a repeated struggle until 1981, when Congress imposed a formula proposed by Rep. Tim Wirth (D-Colo.), allocating CPB spending. The 75-25 split was based on experience. Robben Fleming, then president of CPB, complained that the formula "emasculates" CPB, and his successors periodically have objected to the loss of discretion over spending. Outside the formula, CPB also spends Annenberg/CPB Project funds and the Ready to Learn appropriation.

5% CPB administrative costs

6% System support costs, including satellite system, copyright fees

89% Grants to stations and producers

75% Public television

73% Grants to stations, largely Community Service Grants (CSGs)

27% Programming grants, largely from the Television Program Fund, including mandated support of Independent Television Service and voluntary grants to PBS

25% Public radio

68% Grants to stations, largely CSGs

24% Programming grants to stations (National Program Production and Acquisition Grants)

8% Radio Program Fund

arrival came a period of reconciliation between CPB and the system.

Underwriting: a well-timed push for marketplace thinking

Well before Speaker Gingrich's assault on public funding of the system, some of public television's own leaders were concluding that the system would have to look to the private sector to support itself, to compete with cable networks for audience, and to grow. The 12-year Reagan/Bush era had already deeply injured Americans' faith in the public sector. The ideals of public service inherited from the radio pioneers at midwestern land-grant colleges had lost stature, along with the phrase "public television," popularized by Carnegie I. In 1992, an Illinois station manager, Lee O'Brien, wrote a commentary in the trade newspaper, *Current,* suggesting that, with the failures of public housing and the public schools, the system might benefit by dropping the faded word "public" from its name.

This view gathered strength in the 1990s with the retirement of many station leaders who had founded and built stations in the 1950s, 1960s and 1970s. In Los Angeles, Dallas, Detroit, South Carolina and elsewhere, veterans were replaced by younger executives from commercial media who had the eagerness to advance public broadcasting but often lacked the old-time religion of deep skepticism toward all things commercial. The debate naturally centered on ways to expand underwriting revenues, or even get permission to sell outright advertising.

For a new generation of station managers, the FCC's clear distinction between underwriting announcements and commercial advertising seemed blurred at best. Ironically, the very concept of underwriting credits grew out of an FCC rule driven by a populist suspicion of business: the rule directs public stations to identify on-air the source of grants that supported the production and distribution of specific programs. The rule gave birth to underwriting campaigns that polished corporations' images by associating them with educational or culturally enriching programs on public TV.

In the late 1970s, the meek little underwriting credit—always forbidden by FCC rules from utilizing Madison Avenue's entire bag of persuasive tricks—looked more and more like the main chance for public broadcasters. It seemed clear then that the stable and growing federal support called for by the Carnegie Commission would never materialize. In 1982-83, the FCC's Temporary Commission on Alternative Financing (TCAF) had monitored experiments with limited advertising at a handful of public TV stations and had recommended against full-fledged advertising.

The danger of going any further—selling "limited" or even outright advertising—was not that stations would fail to generate new money; the danger was that it would injure traditional revenue streams—government aid and viewer/listener dollars. Some argued that public broadcasting could never serve as an innovator and social conscience if market forces began to dictate programming decisions. Instead, TCAF opted to support "enhanced underwriting"—compromise guidelines that would give underwriters a more effective billboard to tout their generosity, without letting them go all the way to commercials.

In March 1984, the FCC issued new regulations that permitted corporate logos, brand names and product listings, and otherwise loosened rules restricting underwriting credits. PBS and NPR interpreted the rules, writing specific guidelines for underwriting credits on the networks. Under the new rules, enhanced underwriting announcements would gradually become almost indistinguishable from some soft-sell corporate image commercials.

The positions of individual stations on these matters often coincided with their economic circumstances. State TV networks backed by generous legislatures tended to accept or even demand restrictive underwriting rules. Likewise, few public radio leaders pushed for looser rules; the bigger stations were doing well without risking a flare-up of controversy among their educated listeners. Big-city public TV stations like Chicago's WTTW, however, knew from constant conversation with underwriters that they were losing revenue because of the rules.

Stations with strong underwriting potential—some already selling run-of-the-schedule spot announcements unrelated to particular programs—pushed to further loosen the guidelines or even run outright advertising. But there was no consensus at an Underwriting Summit called by PBS in 1985. The heated debate would return again and again in coming years.

In March 1988, after more than 10 months of study, PBS returned to revising its guidelines, which attempt to interpret the FCC rules for member stations. The new guidelines limited how long an underwriter could exhibit its products on the air, but loosened restrictions on showing products in motion and depicting corporate slogans and mascots. While in public television PBS tried to walk a tightrope between the warring camps of its member stations, in public radio the FCC sporadically cracked down on a handful of stations that violated its rules.

By September 1994 the debate that had been raging for years was situated in a more compelling context. As a national medium, public television was not only competing against proliferating cable networks, its series producers were also competing for corporate underwriting with the system's local stations. In a period of sagging revenues from underwriting, some big-city stations were selling 30-second underwriting credits locally, potentially undercutting the 15-second spots that WGBH and other producers could offer on national programs. In January 1995—soon after Gingrich had launched his campaign to zero-out federal aid—the PBS Board experimentally adopted a schedule of "nonstandard usage fees" to discourage 30-second spots. The penalties outraged many station executives: PBS was trying to impose national policy on local practices. Some 40 stations refused to sign PBS program contracts.

By May, advocates for the penalty called it off. The dispute remained unresolved within the field, while a faction of major-market station executives privately lobbied Congress for looser rules. Maverick managers asked key congressmen to give them the local option of being "nonprofit" rather than "noncommercial" stations—a change of definition that appealed to Rep. Jack Fields (R-Tex.), chairman of the House subcommittee that oversees CPB. In September 1995, the split surfaced briefly on Capitol Hill when Jeff Clarke, manager of public TV station KUHT in Houston and vice chairman of APTS, testified in favor of advertising in a House hearing chaired by Fields, his hometown congressman. At the same time, NPR President Del Lewis delivered the opposite message—the official position of both APTS and NPR. (Clarke was later defeated for reelection to the APTS board.)

Fields, who tried in vain to pass a CPB reauthorization bill after the zero-it-out fight, told a delegation of public broadcasters the next year that he would be willing to open the door to advertising. As one radio station manager recalled, Fields said: "Well, it's not that we're *telling* you to advertise. It's that we don't think we should be in a position of telling you that you *can't*."

Reacting to the behind-the-scenes lobbying by some of their market-minded colleagues, executives from some 30 public TV licensees, including most of the state networks, issued a memo in April 1997 reaffirming their commitment to noncommercial operation. They pledged not to carry 30-second spots and to abide by PBS standards, commenting: "What we do affects one another, often in profound ways. In the case of more commercial practices, we fear that the differences among stations are quickly becoming a liability to us all."

The system's divided views about commercialism not only confused politicians, who wanted a consensus delivered to their desks, but it also deepened the distrust within the field. Station leaders with strong views often talked openly only within their own factions, "in the hallways" outside of system meetings.

A trust fund: can an ideal become the practical choice?

While the practical route to stronger revenues was through incremental changes in underwriting rules, the ideal had always been a permanent funding source such as a trust fund—a permanent endowment that, when invested, would yield stable annual operating revenues, insulated from political or corporate pressures.

Most proposals that surfaced over the years were based on the notion that because the airwaves belong to the public, the privilege of using these scarce resources for profit-making should carry with it some financial responsibility to assist an alternative noncommercial system. Methods proposed over the years have included taxes on TV sets, fees for use of spectrum, auction of unused spectrum, or profits from the operation of a satellite system. But when would an ideal permanent funding source become politically practical?

In October 1987, a long-awaited bill proposing permanent funding suddenly appeared on the horizon. The Senate Commerce Committee, chaired by Ernest Hollings (D-S.C.), voted to create a public broadcasting trust fund that would yield more than $340 million annually beginning in 1990 (an amount 70 percent higher than the level at the time, not to be equaled by an actual CPB appropriation until 2001). Conceived as part of the committee's deficit reduction package, the proposal sought to generate the trust fund revenue from a 2-to-5 percent fee on the sale of FCC-licensed stations. (The sliding fee would be based on such criteria as fair market value of the property, whether the involved stations had violated the Fairness Doctrine, and the length of time the property had been in the seller's hands.) The Hollings proposal prompted what some described as the largest grassroots campaign ever waged by the National Association of Broadcasters. In December, the Senate rejected the trust fund vision by a vote of 66-28.

Sen. Ernest Hollings (above) was not the first or last to propose a fee or tax to support a trust fund for public broadcasting. Carnegie I (1967) recommended a tax on TV sets; Carnegie II (1978), a spectrum fee on commercial broadcasters; Hollings (1987), a tax on sales of commercial stations; Rep. Jack Fields (1996), proceeds from sales of excess public stations and vacant reserved channels; and Reps. W.J. Tauzin and Edward Markey (1998), fees paid by commercial broadcasters for exemption from public-service obligations. In 1995, public TV and radio listed most of these options as possible sources, along with proceeds from auction of analog TV channels after the DTV conversion.

Opponents criticized Hollings for inserting the proposal in the committee's budget reconciliation bill just hours before the bill came up for a committee vote, circumventing the usual review process, including hearings. But to the public broadcasting establishment, politicians' complaints about Hollings' tactics seemed just an easy excuse for voting against a long-term funding plan bitterly opposed by commercial broadcasters, undoubtedly Washington's most powerful lobby.

In April 1988, Hollings tried again to breathe life into the proposal by opening hearings on the matter, showcasing veteran public broadcasting advocate Fred W. Friendly, who along with Ford Foundation President McGeorge Bundy had called in vain for another insulated funding mechanism 20 years earlier. Friendly waxed eloquent about the virtues of public broadcasting and the need for a trust fund to protect the integrity of its programming. He stood his ground against such powerful opponents of the transfer fee as Sen. Robert Packwood (R-Ore.), but in the end, Friendly and colleagues proved no match for commercial broadcasting lobbyists.

The public broadcasting trust fund would remain on the back burner until 1995, after Republicans won a congressional majority and Speaker Gingrich trumpeted plans to zero-out CPB. It was Republicans who put forth plans for a public broadcasting trust fund—notably Sen. Pressler and Rep. Jack Fields (R-Tex.). In February 1996, Fields' subcommittee held hearings on his Public Broadcasting Self-Sufficiency Act, which put a ceiling of $1 billion on federal contributions to the trust fund. The funds would have been raised, among other ways, by auctioning off overlapping public TV channels or using them for commercial purposes. Some observers speculated that the trust fund might now be politically feasible because it could be seen as a way of getting public broadcasting out of the annual federal budget.

Pressler, who had been the most vocal critic of CPB funding for months, sought to dispose of the issue by informally proposing a trust fund. Both Fields and Pressler sought to preserve annual appropriations to CPB at the $250 million level through the year 2000, maintaining aid to stations until the trust fund could begin operating. Fields, however, proposed an endowment of $1 billion, an amount that would have paid out only about $50 million a year—far less than public broadcasters had received or claimed necessary to keep the system afloat. The level was too high for legislators seeking to end deficit spending and too low for supporters of public broadcasting. The bill never left Fields' subcommittee.

Bigger pieces of the action

If there were stubborn obstacles to expanding revenues from on-air advertising as well as federal aid, there were also open invitations for public broadcasters to join in the crazed world of media deal-making. Most members of Congress smiled on public broadcasters "earning their way" through private-sector ventures, and some insisted upon it.

As it happened, PBS's least-expected program phenomenon of the 1990s, *Barney & Friends*, was twice engulfed in controversy over entrepreneurial behavior. PBS had bought the cheerful but crudely produced program from a Dallas-area producer, the Lyons Group, to help fill out its sagging schedule for preschoolers in 1991, and was planning to drop it until kids flocked to the show by the millions.

In the first uproar, initiated within public broadcasting's traditional constituency and picked up by politicians, public television was accused of being *too aggressive* in making money with Barney. In March 1993, the *Wall Street Journal* reported that parents of young Barney fans were angry about the way public TV stations were displaying Barney dolls and videotapes as incentives for pledge-drive donations. At least two outraged parents filed complaints with the FCC. To some parents, the on-air offers of Barney merchandise during children's viewing hours crossed the line into the realm of craven commercial manipulation and violated the Children's Television Act. In response, a PBS task force later that summer reiterated existing PBS policies regarding fundraising adjacent to children's programming and recommended that appeals be directed at parents, not children, and that they be clearly separated from kids' programming. The flap resulted in a system-wide reexamination of pledging practices; PBS decided not to repeat the program for the August 1993 drives.

The second accusation, largely from the right, was that public television was *not aggressive enough* in making money from Barney. Laurence Jarvik and other conservative critics said public television was providing free advertising for commercial programs and merchandise, letting private companies make big profits without any return to the taxpaying public that was paying broadcast costs and at least part of the program's production costs as well. Criticism focused on product sales associated with *Barney and Friends* and *Sesame Street*, but also struck at the sale of videocassettes and books associated with primetime programs made by Ken Burns and Bill Moyers.

With growing press attention, estimates of the ineptly forgone revenues rose to unrealistic heights. Pressler repeatedly claimed that Barney had made $1 billion in a single year—money that, he argued, could be redirected to support public broadcasting. Hoping to squelch the exaggerations, CPB President Carlson went before the House appropriations subcommittee in January 1995. Carlson pointed out that manufacturers, retailers and others take the lion's share of the retail dollar, while the production company, the Lyons Group, probably netted income closer to just $20 million. Public broadcasters were then entitled to only a fraction of that. While still a healthy sum, all of the producer's share of the Barney product proceeds would not replace CPB appropriations, even if public broadcasting had the right to take that money, which it did not. CPB and PBS officials did, however, upshift their ancillary rights policies, and PBS began demanding larger shares of ancillary and "back-end" revenues from programs it funded and/or distributed.

Perhaps the greatest gains from product sales were made by Minnesota Public Radio, where President Bill Kling built its sideline of *Prairie Home Companion* merchandise into a major catalog retailer. The network sold most of the operation for $120 million in 1998, giving itself the biggest endowment in public radio, capable of supporting one-sixth of its annual budget.

As the Barney experience demonstrated, it was not easy for PBS to "earn its way" as Pressler and other politicians demanded. Videocassettes of PBS programs sold better than expected, but by fiscal year 1998 the net income from cassettes came to just $2.8 million for PBS and $3.6 million for the programs' producers. Of course, gross retail sales were much higher, as in the case of Barney dolls, but the net income from cassettes—after subtracting what the retailers, middlemen, duplicators and publicists get—amounted to a minor income stream for PBS.

Given these limited returns, it was all the more disturbing when in February 1999 a federal district court jury imposed damages and fines of nearly $47 million on PBS for the way it dropped its original retail distributor, Michael Nesmith's Pacific Arts Video, in 1993. (PBS in the meantime had taken up with Turner Home Entertainment, now Warner Home Video.) Stunned by the verdict, PBS hired new lawyers and settled privately with Nesmith in July 1999.

The success of Barney products in Christmas 1994 gave politicians hope—false hope, most likely—that public TV could live off of ancillary sales. At left: the Texas mother who created Barney for her own kids, **Sheryl Leach, with Dennis DeShazier and Kathy Parker, fellow executive producers of *Barney and Friends*, and** their stars, B.J. and Barney. (Photo: The Lyons Group.)

How to make decisive decisions?

For all the criticism of public broadcasting over the years, no one has ever accused it of racing into a decision, without adequate deliberations. Indeed, outsiders who discover the system's jerrybuilt institutional structures and painstaking attempts at democratic involvement almost always ask how anything gets decided at all.

Recognizing that slow and often inconclusive processes are seriously handicapping public TV in its lobbying as well as strategic moves, both PBS and APTS initiated governance studies in 1995.

With a consistent push from Chairman Gerald Baliles, a former Virginia governor, the PBS board responded to manager unrest by amending its bylaws in 1997. The proportion of station managers on the board rose from two-fifths to a half, and to make sure all stations were involved in building consensus on system issues, PBS established an annual Members Meeting where all station chief executives can vote on advisory petitions to the PBS Board.

A parallel movement in APTS was launched by Joseph Traigle, a Louisiana businessman. The "laypeople" on stations' boards, Traigle said, look at public TV as an important national institution, not just as 177 local institutions that happen to be interconnected. A working group—steeped in "productive conversation" techniques by process-oriented consultants—proposed a separate group for managers to meet and consider system issues, without PBS executives drawing up the agenda or even listening in. The National Forum for Public Television Executives was begun in November 1997 with a shoestring budget and almost no staff, but with high hopes. In its draft charter, the forum recognized that public TV needed a new inclusive, fact-based decision-making process to make its way in the digital mediascape:

> The winners in this new world will make decisions based on the best possible information, they will be agile enough to capitalize on developing opportunities, and they will form alliances with each other and with entities outside public television. Good information, agility, and meaningful collaborations are not the first attributes which come to mind about public television.

Founded in 1997 at a convention of stations at Austin, Tex., the National Forum for Public Television Executives devoted all of its first regular meeting, and much of its later meetings, to discussing how the stations will use their digital TV channels. Above: **James Pagliarini of KTCA in the Twin Cities and Judy Stone of Alabama ETV** at the organizing convention. Guided by an elected council of 13 station chiefs, the entire Forum membership meets once or twice a year for discussions and resolutions. By early 1998, the Forum included about 100 of the 180 public TV licensee organizations, including most of the larger ones.

With the nearly simultaneous creation of the PBS Members Meeting and the independent Forum, public television's leaders now have two settings where they can discuss issues and build consensus. And in their talks, they have recognized the need for research to give them a factual basis for making decisions. The PBS board, for example, spent $450,000 during 1998-99 on studies to inform its decisions about enhanced underwriting. But the research has been acquired on an ad hoc basis. Stations in the Forum initially chose not to impose fees on themselves for an ongoing research office. Similarly, the system has yet to act on the proposal by former NAEB President James Fellows to fund a Hartford Gunn Institute to coordinate systematic research and planning for public television.

Advocates for better decision-making pointed to public TV's failure to start one or more cable channels when cable networking was young in the early '80s. But they did not have to go back that far for a dramatic example of how the system's commitment to station autonomy and democratic decision-making left it hopelessly gridlocked.

Early in the 1990s, PBS's decision-making process robbed its viewers of an intriguing public-affairs experiment. The incident began in 1989 when Lloyd N. Morrisett, president of the John and Mary Markle Foundation approached PBS with a program idea. Morrisett—who helped put *Sesame Street* on the air, years earlier— was no stranger to public broadcasting. His seminal essay, "Rx for Public Television," had a long life on the required reading lists of graduate public broadcasting seminars across the country. Morrisett wrote that he was ready to help public television play a major role in creating an informed electorate and preserving American democracy.

The foundation's study of media practices and public perceptions during the 1988 presidential campaign led Morrisett to conclude that the public needed genuine, direct exposure to the major candidates—quite unlike the slickly produced ads and 15-second TV news items that were, sadly, their main information sources. Morrisett proposed that public television make itself "The Voters' Channel" in time for the '92 presidential campaign. PBS would provide free airtime to let the presidential candidates directly address the electorate. Morrisett had already hired veteran independent producer Alvin H. Perlmutter to prepare a comprehensive feasibility study that revealed the potential for this innovation and estimated the cost of making it go—more than $12 million. Toward that sum, Morrisett pledged $5 million from Markle, PBS would put up $3 million, and Morrisett would lead the campaign to raise the rest.

PBS was not ready to pick up the challenge immediately. In the spring of 1989, the system had just given extensive programming authority to its first "chief program executive," Jennifer Lawson, as we will discuss in the next chapter. She entered talks with Morrisett, Perlmutter and station representatives, but few stations seemed interested in giving unencumbered airtime to candidates or taking up other Perlmutter ideas. Discussions went nowhere and ended in June 1991. The foundation withdrew its $5 million offer and eventually backed political coverage on CNN. PBS ended up spending $3 million on its campaign coverage—twice its spending in 1988, but a fraction of what Morrisett had proposed.

The Voters' Channel idea suffered from the not-invented-here syndrome in public TV. It came from a growing consensus of political observers that television should assist the political process rather than inflate pre-election advertising costs and drive candidates' desperate search for campaign dollars. Free airtime for candidates, in particular, had nothing to do with normal measures of TV production values (it might even be boring sometimes), and it clearly surrendered the gatekeeper's prerogative to edit and mediate what viewers are shown.

Were Bruce Christensen and his senior staff too timid to take the lead on this attractive proposition, as some critics asserted, or did the incident prove that public television's independence could not be bought for an ill-considered plan, as some insiders said?

The idea "was simply too big an idea for PBS," Christensen reportedly told Morrisett after the episode. From an institutional standpoint, PBS was not prepared to deal with such an opportunity. System and station leaders did not share a firm understanding of common purpose and did not invest enough trust in their leaders to make decisions for them. Without an alternative to PBS—like the National Forum created six years later—Morrisett had nowhere else in public television to take this rare opportunity for public service. If the system had worked out a pact with the funder, perhaps public television's role in the nation's political process could have been worthy of more than a brief historical footnote.

Though the Voters' Channel proposal collapsed in 1991, individual public TV and radio stations have expanded their campaign coverage— some inspired by the trend toward "civic journalism." **Maine Public Broadcasting aired candidate debates** in October 1998 (above), as did 40 other public TV stations. Wisconsin PTV, Chicago's WTTW and Rochester WXXI gave free airtime for candidate statements. CPB, PBS and NPR advocated and assisted the local coverage. (Photo: Maine Public Broadcasting.)

See online: Perlmutter's Voters' Channel recommendations.

See Chapter 11: Politicians talk "trust fund" but have trouble finding cash to endow one.

Not your father's public broadcasting:

The programming environment, 1986-99

The often-singular programs that are the signature of public television and radio continue to enlighten, enrich and entertain audiences and impress critics.

One measure of their value is the 71 prestigious George Foster Peabody Awards the programs have won in six recent years, 1992-98. Public TV's production powerhouse in Boston, WGBH, took home seven for *American Experience* histories, three for *Frontline* documentaries and six others, not counting its British imports. NPR News programs received five. Independent producers won many of the Peabodys; three aired on *P.O.V.*; David Isay produced two for radio.

Among the Peabody winners were musical panoramas of jazz,

Educational radio came out of the universities originally, but it was also part of a medium that thrives with engaging personalities as hosts and producers. Four of public radio's 1990s stars appeared in a 1998 seminar at the Museum of Television and Radio in New York City. Left to right: *Car Talk* producer **Doug Berman**, **Ira Glass** of *This American Life*, **Terry Gross** of *Fresh Air* and independent producer **David Isay**. (Photo courtesy of the museum.)

rock and gospel; "event" programs such as "Hoop Dreams" and *Tales of the City;* incisive journalistic reports on Bosnia, health care reform and the Waco cult disaster; career awards to Fred Rogers, folk singer/host Oscar Brand and newsman Daniel Schorr; and the latest must-hear series on public radio, Ira Glass's *This American Life.*

Less widely known are programs that aired locally, such as *Chicago Tonight*, WTTW's must-see-TV for people who follow public affairs in the city, hosted for 16 years by John Callaway; the steady streams of state history and cultural documentaries from the state networks in Nebraska, Kentucky and elsewhere; the jazz programming at KPLU in Seattle/Tacoma, and the alternative music at Philadephia's WXPN, both repeatedly recognized by the *Gavin Report* as best in the country; and the highly clued-in radio talk shows hosted by Warren Olney on KCRW in Los Angeles and Faith Middleton on Connecticut Public Radio.

These and the regular servings of preschool, how-to, news, science, college-credit and other programs were valued enough, by another measure, that audiences donated $472 million to public TV and radio in fiscal year 1997—about a quarter of the system's revenues.

At the same time, however, critics within and outside public broadcasting have noted trends toward centralized operations, reduced local programming, a timorousness toward hard-hitting public affairs coverage, and a penchant for quasi-commercial fare, especially during pledge periods.

These forces have plagued the industry for years, but in recent years have been exacerbated by competition from new cable networks that covet public broadcasting's turf, as well as a strident political climate in which public broadcasters feel increased heat for presenting controversial programming.

Localism: challenges to an American ideal

One of the recent major trends in the system has been centralization. For decades, U.S. communication policy has been grounded in a doctrine of localism—the notion that communities need local broadcast stations as outlets for expression of citizens' needs and concerns. In practice, however, commercial broadcasters delegated the bulk of their programming decisions to networks and syndicators.

Public broadcasters traditionally resisted this trend, for reasons both ideological and economic. They philosophically opposed the notion of networking in the commercial style, and in the early years, they could not afford interconnection, anyway. Further, there were strong cultural divides: between public broadcasters from the cosmopolitan cities and those from the rest of the country, and between the more commercially attuned community licensees in big cities and the generally more purist stations licensed to states or universities. Today, futurists say localism can be a distinct virtue when most programming originates nationally, but strong centripetal forces pull on all public broadcasters.

In public television, localism largely has become associated with local autonomy, relative to PBS in particular. The field's long-running debates over centralized program decision-making reflect the eternal conflict between local station prerogative and the need to finance and coordinate a national service. PBS's Station Program Cooperative, an annual market mechanism developed in the wake of the Nixon veto to allow stations (instead of CPB) to exercise control over programming, was replaced in 1989 by a chief program executive, with broad authority to make program decisions. The first top programmer, Jennifer Lawson, was an unflappable executive from the CPB Television Program Fund, who said she would revamp the national schedule and render a "distinctive" service.

Lawson's powers fell short of the autocracy implied by the "program czarina" nickname that befell her, however. Her decisions had to be agreeable to diverse local managers with final authority over their schedules. And with long-running series commanding most of her budget, Lawson had relatively little discretionary money. The result, writes veteran public TV executive James Day in his book *The Vanishing Vision: The Inside Story of Public Television*, was continued "consensus programming, not risk taking." Lawson resigned the job after new PBS President Ervin Duggan announced plans to appoint an executive above her; he eventually promoted PBS programmer Kathy Quattrone to succeed her. (Quattrone would stay in the top job almost four years, leaving in 1999 to develop a new cable service for the operators of the Discovery Channel.)

The long-simmering dispute over common carriage of the PBS primetime schedule underscored the schism between PBS and some of its member stations. The conflict reached a boil in 1995 when a PBS task force proposed that stations commit to carrying about 350

During her younger days, **Jennifer Lawson** (above) spent three years working in the civil rights movement in the South, but the PBS program chief will be remembered by some critics for the reason she gave in 1994 for rejecting *Rights & Wrongs*, an independently produced weekly newsmagazine about human rights. Ordinarily the most cautious of speakers, Lawson said human rights was "an insufficient organizing principle for a PBS series." She explained her view: that existing PBS public affairs series do an excellent job on the subject.

hours a year of selected, highly promoted primetime programming at designated times, or face "nonstandard usage fees" assessed by PBS. Proponents of common carriage argued it was necessary to attract national underwriting and permit national promotion of programs. Indeed, coverage of some major series occasionally had slipped to 70 or 80 percent of the population, short of the 90 percent goal, judging from PBS data. But managers of about 40 stations balked at the common-carriage rule, along with the penalty on 30-second underwriting credits (see Chapter 9), claiming the policies violated their independence. Duggan said the protest exemplified "a kind of feudalism . . . that prevents us from acting like a system." But PBS had underestimated the stations' resistance, and eventually dropped the penalties. Most stations already were complying and continued to do so voluntarily.

Public broadcasting's deeply held ethic of localism has been further challenged by a thrust for consolidation. Efficiency advocates, increasingly funded by CPB in the 1990s, believe that many local stations have such sparse audience and economic resources that they will seldom produce local programs of consequence and, in television, never be much more than "pass-through" distributors of the national PBS feed. Outside of large markets, reformers recommend statewide or regional networks of transmitters with central staffs and greater economies of scale.

But there is no answer without vexing complications: for example, the outlying transmitters in each state network often overlap at the state line. Ironically, these border-area overlaps—an unintended consequence of efficient statewide networks—are sometimes lumped with other offending overlap stations as targets in the consolidators' campaigns for efficiency.

The problem with overlaps, now well recognized by budget-cutters on Capitol Hill, is that they sometimes air the same programs. As CPB President Richard Carlson noted in a widely cited *New York Times* op-ed piece, *Barney & Friends* was available 29 times a week on channels in the New York City area. "The patchwork quilt of public stations across the nation must be reorganized so viewers can have more choice and better services," Carlson wrote in 1994. He pointed approvingly to the Maine Public Broadcasting Corp., the 1992 union of the state's two, previously independent, public TV operations. The combination pooled staff and facilities to run two differentiated channels, each reaching much of the state, instead of running two similar channels separately. (One channel was eliminated soon after, however, for budget reasons.)

Though Carlson's critique infuriated the smaller overlapping stations—the newcomers that are usually blamed for overlap inefficiencies—his commentary played well with the dominant stations, as well as with the CPB board and Congress. In 1996, the board adopted new grant eligibility criteria that are gradually reducing grants to overlapping public TV stations. At the same time, CPB exempted radio from the new rule, recognizing that neighboring radio stations usually choose different formats.

Even before the new grant rules, stations were feeling economic pressure for consolidation. In 1991, for instance, a fledgling public radio station in Grand Junction, Colo., merged with Denver's Colorado Public Radio (KCFR), simulcasting the Denver signal.

Consultant Tom Thomas called the case a "bellwether" for public radio. Stations in small cities often find they lack the population base to support even a modestly paid staff. In South Carolina, the state radio network closed a freestanding station in Charleston in favor of simulcasting programming from network headquarters in Columbia. In these and other cases, money was saved but locally originated programming was lost or cut back.

Other stations kept their autonomy while gaining economies of scale by consolidating specific functions. In the late '90s, CPB prompted a new wave of efficiency experiments by subsidizing them with Future Fund grants. In one of the first large-scale collaborations, several Florida public TV stations shared direct-mail fundraising operations, while others in the state shared program scheduling experts and pooled their underwriting sales efforts.

Locally produced programs: endangered species?

If localism implies making programs locally, the principle is rarely followed in public television and is on the wane in public radio. According to CPB data, only 4.9 percent of public television programming was produced locally in 1996, down from 11.4 percent in 1974. In public radio, where local production is far less expensive (it may involve simply spinning CDs), the amount of local programming has declined nonetheless, from 57 percent of airtime in 1988 to 50 percent in 1996. Clearly, economies of scale favor regional and national production, and public broadcasting's satellite systems provide ready access to a booming marketplace of public TV and radio fare.

Producers, managers and consultants have argued in recent years over the role—and future—of local production. In public radio, idiosyncratic local programs have often given way to "focused formats," or consistent streams of programming, designed to please the station's core audience and members. And much of that consistent programming, with the highest production values, can now be plucked from the satellite. As many music/news stations switched to news/talk formats, NPR and PRI competed avidly to offer news and talk programming across the midday hours. For those stations that kept music formats, Minnesota Public Radio's Classical 24 service, the Beethoven Satellite Network and a newer Classical Public Radio Network feed co-produced by Colorado Public Radio and Los Angeles' KUSC, offer classical music "off the bird," 24 hours a day. While some producers and listeners lamented the loss of local voices, many programmers asked what's so local about an announcer playing music that was recorded elsewhere, anyway.

New conceptions of localism in public TV

The production of local programs, already limited, was criticized as uneconomic in a high-profile 1991 report by the Boston Consulting Group. The report, commissioned by CPB, underscored public television's increased concern with its national service. National programming "is the chief value delivered and the chief motivator of donations" to public TV, the consultants concluded, "but requires substantially increased investment if it is to survive

Though public TV stations' local production has continued to decline, at least 20 produce nightly public affairs or news programs like the New Jersey Network's *NJN News* (that's **anchor Kent Manahan** above), and several have begun weekly arts or business newsmagazine shows.

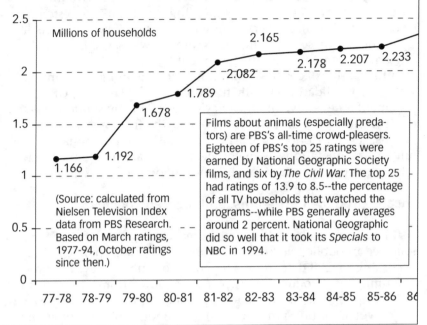

Public television audience, 1977-97

Nielsen primetime average households tuned in to public TV stations.

PBS's evening audience (graph) grew rapidly in the 1950s-70s, peaking above 2.3 million households in 1986-87. But as cable and other channels proliferated, Its primetime audience plateaued around 2 million households. (The big networks have lost bigger parts of their audiences.) Note that ratings services measure TV audiences by the household and radio audiences by the individual.

Millions of households

2.165
2.082
2.178   2.207   2.233
1.789
1.678
1.192
1.166

(Source: calculated from Nielsen Television Index data from PBS Research. Based on March ratings, 1977-94, October ratings since then.)

Films about animals (especially predators) are PBS's all-time crowd-pleasers. Eighteen of PBS's top 25 ratings were earned by National Geographic Society films, and six by *The Civil War*. The top 25 had ratings of 13.9 to 8.5--the percentage of all TV households that watched the programs--while PBS generally averages around 2 percent. National Geographic did so well that it took its *Specials* to NBC in 1994.

77-78 78-79 79-80 80-81 81-82 82-83 83-84 84-85 85-86 86

the intensifying competition of focused cable networks."

Numerous cable services have ventured onto public television's turf, particularly Nickelodeon for children's programming, Discovery for science and history, and A&E for mysteries and biographical documentaries. For public TV to remain competitive in the multichannel age, the Boston Consulting Group report suggested gingerly, stations "could divert spending as necessary" from local production to supporting quality national programming.

Some stations remain committed to locally originated programming, though only about 20 of 200 produce nightly public affairs or news. KTCA in Minneapolis/St. Paul produces an acclaimed local newscast, *NewsNight Minnesota*, four nights a week. Jack Willis, the former KTCA president who started it (and who earlier produced a feisty newscast, *The 51st State*, at New York's WNET in the 1970s), says local production is "what we really have to offer—otherwise, we're just pass-throughs"—airing a national service like most cable networks.

On public TV, the prototypical local program has been an inexpensively produced weekly roundtable of city and state journalists. Any additional production requires a difficult hunt for outside underwriters. But stations increasingly are saving up production dollars to make handsomely produced documentaries, modeled after national programs. Some make their way into the national arena through PBS distribution, such as the Wisconsin Collaborative Project at Wisconsin Public Television. In the 1990s, many stations began producing local history programs with light, nostalgic specials inspired by "Things That Aren't Here Anymore," from WQED in Pittsburgh, and, like WQED, have since ventured into fuller histories of states, cities, immigrant communities and neighborhoods.

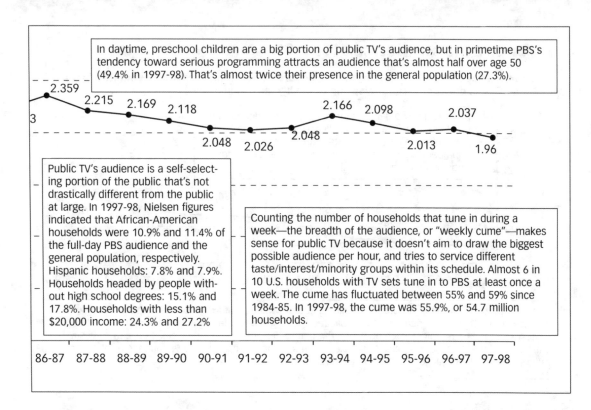

In daytime, preschool children are a big portion of public TV's audience, but in primetime PBS's tendency toward serious programming attracts an audience that's almost half over age 50 (49.4% in 1997-98). That's almost twice their presence in the general population (27.3%).

2.359   2.215   2.169   2.118   2.166   2.098   2.037

2.048   2.026   2.048   2.013   1.96

Public TV's audience is a self-selecting portion of the public that's not drastically different from the public at large. In 1997-98, Nielsen figures indicated that African-American households were 10.9% and 11.4% of the full-day PBS audience and the general population, respectively. Hispanic households: 7.8% and 7.9%. Households headed by people without high school degrees: 15.1% and 17.8%. Households with less than $20,000 income: 24.3% and 27.2%

Counting the number of households that tune in during a week—the breadth of the audience, or "weekly cume"—makes sense for public TV because it doesn't aim to draw the biggest possible audience per hour, and tries to service different taste/interest/minority groups within its schedule. Almost 6 in 10 U.S. households with TV sets tune in to PBS at least once a week. The cume has fluctuated between 55% and 59% since 1984-85. In 1997-98, the cume was 55.9%, or 54.7 million households.

86-87   87-88   88-89   89-90   90-91   91-92   92-93   93-94   94-95   95-96   96-97   97-98

Audience research: "guys in suits with charts"

Public broadcasting's past 15 years have been marked by renewed attention to audience interests and behaviors. Several factors contributed:

■ flat or declining levels of tax-based support,

■ "missionary work" by audience researchers, spreading what they've learned about how to build audiences, and

■ the popularity of certain high-profile public radio and TV programs, which helped managers realize they could boost member donations and underwriting revenue by engaging a larger audience.

For decades, public broadcasting managers and programmers resisted using ratings data in their decision-making, regarding Nielsens and Arbitrons as marks of encroaching commercialism. In the 1980s, however, CPB and increasing numbers of stations embraced audience research as a tool for assessing programming and fundraising. The influence of a cottage industry of consultants was acknowledged formally when independent researchers Tom Church and David Giovannoni were honored with CPB's Edward R. Murrow Award for service to public radio in 1994.

Debates continued to roil around the use of ratings data in a field that was still guided in large part by its public-service mission. The conflict has been more pronounced in public radio than in public television; the higher-profile TV system was always more comfortable with using research to justify public succor.

"I think there's been an influx of commercial people (in public radio)," Garrison Keillor told *Broadcasting & Cable* magazine. "Guys in suits with charts and pages of numbers. I think this is a pretty dreadful development." Pacifica correspondent Larry Bensky was

Audience researchers including **Tom Church (above)** and **David Giovannoni (below)** helped transform public radio's notion of ratings from anathema to a widely used tool for decision-making.

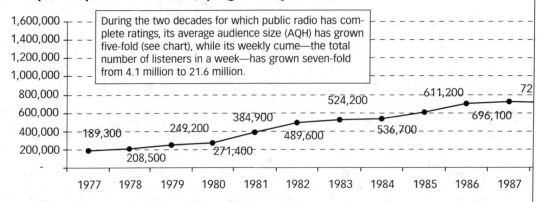

Public radio audience, 1977-98

Arbitron full-day (6 a.m. to midnight) average quarter-hour audience (AQH) estimates for all CPB-qualified public radio stations, spring of each year. (Source: NPR.)

During the two decades for which public radio has complete ratings, its average audience size (AQH) has grown five-fold (see chart), while its weekly cume—the total number of listeners in a week—has grown seven-fold from 4.1 million to 21.6 million.

Values on chart: 189,300 (1977); 208,500 (1978); 249,200 (1979); 271,400 (1980); 384,900 (1981); 489,600 (1982); 524,200 (1982/83); 536,700 (1984); 611,200 (1985); 696,100 (1986); 72 (1987)

A smaller portion of Americans listen to public radio than watches public TV, but they spend more time with it. One in 10 radio listeners tunes in public radio during a week, for an average of more than 8 hours. Almost six in ten households watch public TV, through for less than 3 hours a week. Public radio has a smaller audience because it appeals to people with more education, Audience 98 found; 63% of public radio's audience has college degrees but just 26% of public TV's.

even more strident in reacting to the awards given to researchers Church and Giovannoni: "Not since Henry Kissinger won the Nobel Peace Prize has there been a more inappropriate award."

Proponents of research said they use the numbers in the service of mission. "The bottom line for all radio stations is that a mission . . . cannot be achieved if there are no listeners," wrote Church. "Those who fear the audience's impact understand neither the listener nor the mission of public radio," said Giovannoni. "Public radio cannot afford to serve audiences of any size with insignificant programming, just as it cannot afford to serve insignificant [small] audiences with any sort of programming."

A contemporary theater of conflict is public radio's local news programming. Station-based and independent journalists at a 1994 conference expressed concern that local news would be replaced at many stations by syndicated or network news programs or by music, which is less expensive to produce. Much of the talk at the 1994, 1995 and 1996 conventions of Public Radio News Directors, Inc. (PRNDI) involved the need to "defend" local news. Their concerns were fueled by cut-backs of news staffs in Tampa and other markets, and by some programmers' views that local journalism should be tucked into cutaways in national programs, instead of being presented in daily local newsmagazines.

Even the Pacifica stations, which pride themselves for resisting the tyranny of the marketplace, fine-tuned their programming to seek to reach more listeners during the 1990s. For its flagship station, KPFA in Berkeley, Pacifica hired a consultant who concluded that the station's progressive offerings represented "castor-oil" radio—"good for you but not necessarily easy to take." KPFA followed through by revamping its schedule. It canceled some of the volunteer-produced, eclectic shows in favor of a more uniform for-

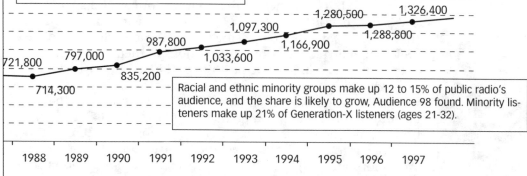

721,800 714,300 797,000 835,200 987,800 1,033,600 1,097,300 1,166,900 1,280,500 1,288,800 1,326,400

| 1988 | 1989 | 1990 | 1991 | 1992 | 1993 | 1994 | 1995 | 1996 | 1997 |

mat of public affairs and music that included more programs from Pacifica's national production facility in Washington. Other Paci-fica-owned stations underwent similar restructuring. Displaced volunteers and some listeners reacted angrily; graffiti sprawled on KPFA's building called then-Executive Director Pat Scott, architect of the new schedule, a "Yuppie Stalinist." But Scott maintained, "We're getting away from equating being progressive with being unprofessional." The conflict escalated in 1999 when Pacifica fired several KPFA staffers and briefly put the station's entire staff on leave, damaging the organization's reputation among its leftist fans and prompting a series of sit-ins and marches.

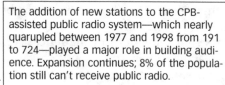

Instead of celebrating its 50th anniversary in prosperous stability in 1999, Pacifica Radio marked the occasion with internal warfare. Executive Director **Pat Scott** (left) and successor Lynn Chadwick caught flak from furious volunteer staffers by pushing for stronger programs and displacing volunteer hosts. Scott committed heresy, to some ears, by arguing against the organization's traditional commitment to give airtime to a program "as long as there is one intelligent listener and one intelligent speaker." Using airtime that way undercuts Pacifica's commitment to "progressive social change," Scott wrote. "As long as we speak only to ourselves, we cannot fulfill this commitment." (Photo: Moya Photography/ Design.)

CPB, which paid for much of the ratings research in public radio, reinforced audience awareness in 1996 by adding its first audience-size standard to the criteria for radio stations seeking annual grants. As of fall 1997, stations had to meet standards based on Average Quarter Hour (AQH) listenership, *or* local financial support. The policy roused the old mission-versus-market debate, and raised questions of accessibility and purpose. "When people say mission and audience are unrelated, I say, 'No audience, no mission,'" argued Public Radio International executive Bruce Theriault, a member of the CPB-appointed task force that helped draft the new standards. But in a 1995 Public Radio Conference session, Ralph Jennings, g.m. of WFUV in the Bronx, N.Y., spoke for many managers: "We all know if we put on wall-to-wall formats we might increase our ratings. . . . But I don't think that's what public broadcasting is supposed to devote itself to."

The new standards put about 35 stations in danger of losing their grants. Most chose to fight for their eligibility, albeit reluctantly, by focusing their program schedules, often eliminating eclectic offerings. WFUV dropped some shows that served ethnic audiences, such as Italian-Americans, and KPFK, Pacifica's Los Angeles outlet, cancelled programs on medicinal hemp and atheism, among others. Pasadena's KPCC switched from a daytime format of Big Band music and jazz to news/talk, but drew the line and kept its Latino music show with a stay-in-school theme. When the axe fell in fall of 1997, only six public radio stations lost portions of their CPB grants.

Overall, the changes were positive, said KPCC manager Rod Foster, but "it's what animated the change that bothers me, and the way CPB had morphed from being a political insulator for public broadcasting to becoming a political conductor." But CPB's Bob Coonrod defended the standards as "reasonable": "Mature institutions ought to periodically assess their impact on the community. We're not suggesting they have to become rock-'n-roll stations to get reasonable support."

Service to under-served minorities

Educational radio today is "educated radio," with listeners that are 42 percent more likely to have some college education than the population at large, and to have correspondingly upscale incomes. And the tendency is reinforced by many stations' determination to "super-serve" their existing audiences by dropping programs with less appeal.

This means that most public radio stations do not aim squarely at the least-educated, lowest-income segments of the minority populations—whose needs justify most government policies assisting minorities. But public radio does have a substantial non-white listenership. One-seventh of its listeners identify themselves as non-white, David Giovannoni's Audience 98 study reported, and the proportion is almost certain to grow as more Latinos and African-Americans attend college. Significantly, the study found, non-white listeners make up 21 percent of public radio's young adult (21-35) audience.

Some of these listeners tune to minority-controlled public radio stations that target one ethnic group. Two dozen stations sent delegates to an African-American Public Radio Summit in 1998, including big-city stations as well as small ones operated by traditionally black colleges. To bolster these cohorts of minority stations, CPB funds two satellite networks providing targeted programming—Satélite, for Latino Americans, and American Indian Radio on Satellite (AIROS) for Native Americans. Satélite was launched in 1993 by Radio Bilingüe, a public radio licensee in Fresno, Calif., and AIROS in 1994 by what is now Native American Public Telecommunications, based in Lincoln, Neb.

But most of public radio's minority listeners are attracted by the same programming that whites want, as Giovannoni and Frank Tavares of Audience 98 reported: "what public radio does best: programming that transcends racial and ethnic differences, programming that embraces the values and attitudes of an educated citizenry."

Though they're usually categorized as "educational" rather than "minority" programs, public TV series like FASE Productions' *The Eddie Files* and CTW's *Ghostwriter* follow *Sesame Street*'s practice of putting minority faces in prominent roles, both children and authority figures. Above: Harlem teacher **Kay Toliver**, who, like another master educator, Jaime Escalante of East Los Angeles, starred in a series that says clearly: all kinds of people can love and benefit from knowing math and science. After public TV's *American Playhouse* dramatized Escalante's life in *Stand and Deliver*, FASE put the real Escalante in *Futures* for PBS; Toliver appeared as herself in *The Eddie Files*.

This strategy to "transcend" rather than to "target," as the researchers put it, dominates in public TV as well. Jennifer Lawson and other program decision-makers generally "mainstreamed" minority subjects and performers for the broader audience—a policy that could be witnessed most clearly in a shift away from traditional elite music and drama on *Great Performances* and *American Playhouse* during the 1980s.

A thin stream of programs by and about African-Americans, Latinos, Native Americans, Asian-Americans and Pacific Islanders comes to public TV from the five "minority consortia" backed by CPB with annual funding of about $1 million apiece.

With these and other programs, public TV draws an audience nearly as diverse as the general population, even during primetime when *Sesame Street* is not a factor (see box, page 97).

Though public television has aired many extraordinary programs for and about minorities, the volume is disappointing to advocates who point to the ongoing congressional mandate for CPB to facilitate service to minority groups.

A "permeable membrane" between public and commercial

In the 1990s' multimedia, multichannel environment, the bright line between public and commercial media has become blurred. Public TV producers have found the only way they can raise funds for some programs is to enter into partnerships with commercial companies, which typically have better access to capital than nonprofits. In 1998, Children's Television Workshop joined with Viacom, owner of the Nickelodeon network, to announce a new cable channel for children, Noggin. To the dismay of public TV stations, they would soon find reruns of *Sesame Street* competing with their own broadcasts of new episodes—much the same situation that befell NBC when the producers of *Seinfeld* put it into syndication.

One journalist noted "the increasingly permeable membrane between public and commercial TV" in an account of the 1996 annual National Association of Television Program Executives conference—the commercial television industry's major program marketplace—at which public TV programmers were hawking their wares. WGBH's *This Old House*, Maryland PTV's *MotorWeek*, KCTS's *Bill Nye the Science Guy* and countless cooking shows were among the programs seen on both public TV and commercial stations or cable networks. While some critics argue that such sales erode the distinctiveness of public television, programmers say they need the income to produce new shows.

Oregon Public Broadcasting's *Neat Stuff* is an exemplar of the new quasi-commercial age. A kitschy, MTV-influenced melange of quick cuts and driving surf guitar, with a former *Brady Bunch* cast member serving as roving reporter, *Neat Stuff* features a wry, albeit affectionate, look at sci-fi, Barbie dolls and other pop culture artifacts. OPB sold the program to cable's Learning Channel, which airs each episode one week before OPB does. It's not your father's public television, but OPB Vice President John Lindsay says money from *Neat Stuff* will allow the network to make more programs for and about Oregon.

Seattle public TV station KCTS made a pilot of **Bill Nye the Science Guy**, but when PBS declined to put money into the slapstick children's science-education series, the station got backing from the Walt Disney Co., which successfully syndicated it to commercial stations in 1993. For its second season, KCTS struck a deal to offer the show to public TV on weekdays and commercial TV on weekends, with the National Science Foundation and PBS together paying less than half the cost. An FCC rule requiring commercial stations to air educational children's shows encouraged them to pick up the show, as well as *Magic School Bus*. In 1999, Nye and his show joined the Viacom-CTW children's network, Noggin. (Photo copyright 1994, Walt Disney Co.)

PBS also began concentrating on the art of the deal. Aware that stations, during the Gingrich siege, would resist increases of PBS dues, Duggan in 1995 tried a variation of what NPR had done almost three years earlier: pledged to hold down program fees for the next four years. In PBS's case, it tied increases to the inflation rate. Over the same four years, PBS would boost its revenue-generating efforts, buying and reselling additional rights for selected programs. By fiscal year 2000, Duggan pledged, PBS would increase its National Program Service budget by 50 percent to $165 million. Despite the collapse of a major co-production deal with the faltering Reader's Digest Association, PBS met Duggan's goal. PBS pursued the strategy on a smaller scale with a Disney/ ABC subsidiary, Devillier Donegan Enterprises, founded by two onetime PBS programmers. Working with the firm, PBS launched a new program "thread" of world history documentaries that could readily be sold to broadcasters overseas.

Through these years of growing competition for public TV, its radio counterparts have suffered fewer challenges. Cable-delivered audio services that offer commercial-free music failed to catch on with consumers. Public radio news programs remained superior to commercial radio journalism, which has generally declined in quality. And relatively few commercial stations took up broadcasting of classical music and jazz. This may change, however, as multichannel digital audio broadcasting (DAB) networks begin to send out their signals by satellite early in the next decade. (Two satellite firms were licensed in 1997.) More immediately, after the 1996 Telecommunications Act eliminated limits on how many radio stations a company may own, some analysts speculated that multistation owners would increasingly direct some of their stations at the demographically attractive public radio audience. (Reflecting this interest, Arbitron began publishing income and education demographics with its radio ratings in fall 1998.)

Indeed, Phoenix public radio station KJZZ was forced out of the "smooth jazz" format when a commercial station switched to it. The competitor also owned a successful rock station in a duopoly, and thus could afford to reach the relatively small but potentially lucrative jazz audience. "They were doing this with one live person and the rest was automated," says KJZZ Program Director Scott Williams. "They didn't care if they were top 10, they just wanted to add to the audience they already had."

KJZZ responded as several other public stations have, by replacing midday music (airing between *Morning Edition* and *ATC*) with news and public affairs programming. Like many other public radio stations, they adopted public radio's franchise for in-depth news and civil talk. The satellite provided a bevy of options: NPR's *Talk of the Nation* and the expanded, earlier-starting *ATC*, PRI's *The World* and *Marketplace*, and talk shows from stations in Philadelphia, Washington and Boston.

The strategy of creating a more uniform news/talk "program stream" flowed from consultants' recommendations that stations should seek to "super-serve" a consistent body of listeners with programming that appeals to them. Critics argue that catering to this somewhat upscale audience merely imitates the commercial market. "What the government should fund is any station that's willing to explore possible alternatives to commercial media and is willing to show the culture and diversity of the area they're in," says Dennis Cronin-Doyle, g.m. of St. Louis community station KDHX. But Dennis Kita, former g.m. of WJHU in Baltimore, which switched from midday music to news, says, "I am not at all apologetic for airing nationally syndicated programs that have won the most prestigious awards in broadcasting."

Tending the young end of the audience

While public radio increasingly edits its programming to appeal to its core audience of NPR News fans, public TV has been working in the 1990s to bolster its hold on one of its key constituencies: children and their parents. After a 40 percent decline in its child audience in the early 1990s, PBS engineered a comeback that it counts as one of its most successful programming initiatives. For school-age kids, PBS found large audiences with *Wishbone* in 1994 and public TV's first animated series, *Arthur*, in 1996. And for toddlers, it imported *Teletubbies* from Britain in 1998. Preschoolers were the target of the network's first big kidvid investments, buying *Barney & Friends* and bringing back ageless 1950s ventriloquist Shari Lewis in 1991 to supplement *Sesame Street* and *Mister Rogers' Neighborhood*.

Shari Lewis was 23 episodes into production of her second PBS series when she was taken by cancer in 1998 at age 65. The 1950s star ventriloquist on NBC returned to regular series work with the PBS program *Lamb Chop's Play-Along* in 1992, won five consecutive Emmys with it, and then moved on to *Charlie Horse's Music Pizza*, which she developed to encourage children's interest in music.

PBS further expanded its preschool programming with the help of a pedigreed educational movement then gaining strength among politicians. When President Bush brought together the state governors for an educational summit in 1989, they agreed their No. 1 objective was to make sure that all children entering school in 2000 are "ready to learn." Ernest L. Boyer, a prominent educational reformer and key figure in the summit, followed up with a book in 1991, *Ready to Learn: A Mandate for the Nation*. Based on a survey of kindergarten teachers, Boyer said, more than a third of children were not ready for school—their health was poor, and they had little proficiency with language. Though then-Rep. Ron Wyden (D-Ore.) proposed extensive federal efforts in child and maternal health as part of the package, the part that survived was television programming and related outreach. In 1993, responding to congressional interest, CPB issued a report proposing that one public TV station in every community set aside 10 to 12 hours a day for educational programs for preschoolers. Though nobody answered CPB's call for spending $42 million to $81 million a year, Congress has appropriated $7 million to $11 million a year.

The PBS Ready to Learn Service, launched in 11 cities in 1994, now offers at least six-and-a-half hours a day of preschool programming through stations covering 90 percent of the population. Participating stations employ outreach workers to train local day-care workers in using TV for its educational value, and not just as a babysitter.

The changing ideal of public TV programming

For many adult viewers, independent filmmaker Ken Burns' documentary films redefined PBS in the 1990s. An 11-hour montage of old photos and talking-historian-heads set to mournful fiddle tunes,

Masters of the multi-part documentary, **Ken Burns** and the late **Henry Hampton** (above) took on enormous subjects, wrestled history into scenes and episodes, and gave experience to dozens of young producers who will be their heirs. Extensive airtime gave them the option of telling ambivalent stories—what Hampton called "messy" history. "People want neat, fully told stories with proper conclusions, and everybody goes out the door relatively happy," said Hampton. "That's not always possible with this kind of film. And so, in some ways, it's helping the audience redefine its viewing responses—to help an audience understand that going through messy history may take a little more energy, a little more effort, and a little more risk." (Burns photo: Lisa Berg for General Motors.)

The Civil War confounded conventional television wisdom in the fall of 1990. The series broke public TV records for viewership, reaching an average of 14 million homes for each of the five successive nights it was broadcast—an unprecedented 13 percent audience share. "A kind of video miracle," gushed *Newsweek*. *Variety* called the series "a masterful, compelling achievement." Further, a companion book sold well, and *Civil War* videocassettes became staples of neighborhood video stores and premiums for public TV fundraisers.

When Burns scored another success in 1994 with *Baseball*, an 18-hour history of the national pastime, his lesson was not lost on the public television community. His success inspired other historical documentaries on both local and national levels, and even provided impetus for an all-history cable network. More important, the very model of a modern major public TV program had begun to shift. The combination of an important topic, powerful narrative and expert filmmaking approached the ideal of a program that serves both mission and market. In practical terms, this emerging ideal promised three things: to attract a broad audience, to garner corporate underwriting support (General Motors signed on as a major funder for *The Civil War* and later Burns films), and to generate ancillary income through the sale of related products and videocassettes.

Burns' success gave public TV a new taste for hits. "They [PBS] weren't excited about *The Civil War* because it was just good programming," said a producer quoted in William Hoynes' book, *Public Television for Sale*. "It was a huge ratings success." Though other public TV producers interviewed by Hoynes said they did not feel explicit pressure from PBS to deliver big audience numbers, some did see a new climate. The editor of *Harper's*, Lewis Lapham, took note in a scathing article in his magazine, "Adieu, Big Bird: On the terminal irrelevance of public television." Lapham recalled his lunch with PBS programmer Jennifer Lawson when he was seeking $200,000 to continue his *Bookmark* program. Lawson said she had little use for "cheap little half-hour service shows," according to Lapham. "Bring me big projects," Lawson reportedly said. "Bring me Streisand or the Civil War. I'd rather give you $2 million than a paltry $200,000."

With the success of *The Civil War* PBS learned the value of intense promotion, which General Motors had bought. Major publicity efforts, coupled with strategic scheduling (such as "stripping" a series across consecutive nights and "stacking" two or more episodes on one night) helped attract and hold more viewers. The desire to build audiences through promotion gave PBS renewed interest in common carriage, as described earlier in this chapter. Corporate underwriters knew from experience with commercial TV that promotion works most effectively when it specifies the date when a program can be seen nationwide, instead of vaguely inviting viewers to "check local listings." PBS's senior vice president of advertising, promotion and corporate information, Carole Feld, came to public television from HBO, bringing a commercial sensibility and a desire to bolster PBS as an attractive "brand" in viewers' minds.

The corporate support lavished upon the Burns films recalled broadcast historian Erik Barnouw's assessment of public television fare as "safely splendid." Such high-quality, noncontroversial programs as the Burns epics are attractive to corporations. In 1999, G.M., which had already contributed to Burns' budgets for 12 years, committed to aid every documentary he would make for 10 more years. Herbert Schmertz, top public relations executive for Mobil Oil, a longtime public TV underwriter, wrote that "when we give certain publics a reason to identify with the projects and causes that we have chosen to support, they will translate that identification into a preference for doing business with us." In 1995, PBS officially recognized Mobil's perennial aid, adding the oil company's name to a famous series title, now *Mobil Masterpiece Theatre*.

Producers addressing touchy subjects had a harder road. Henry Hampton, for example, chased dollars for six years before he could complete his award-winning 1987 chronicle of the civil rights movement, *Eyes on the Prize*. Part way through production, the Boston producer mortgaged his house so he could meet payroll and continue. The continuing shift of production support from public to private dollars exacerbates the timorousness of public broadcasting's programming, especially in the area of public affairs.

The emphasis on corporate-friendly, non-controversial fare isn't new to public TV, nor is the system's interest in broader appeal and ancillary income. But what is of contemporary concern is that policymakers and critics no longer automatically accept and defend the legitimacy of the public broadcasting system. If they and the public lose sight of the values differentiating public broadcasting from the commercial world, the field will not be able to count on their continued support.

Public television and controversy

The new ideal for public television programming represents a sharp contrast from a procession of PBS documentaries that engaged public TV in a series of fiery left-right controversies in the late 1980s and early 1990s. The furor over programs such as "Days of Rage: The Young Palestinians," "Stop the Church," "Tongues Untied" and "Dark Circle" reflected the conflicting obligations and crisis of mission facing public television managers. Here were conflicts between the objectives of "quality" and "alternative" programming, the clash between providing programs of cultural significance with high production values and providing media access to marginalized and minority voices. The contention over these programs called attention to the fragile economic foundations and amorphous mandates of public broadcasting.

While federal aid to public broadcasting has left the industry vulnerable to criticism over controversial programming since the days of "Banks and the Poor," these latest conflicts developed in the heated climate of the Culture Wars of the 1980s and 1990s, whose

With "Days of Rage," like other volatile documentaries of the 1980s, PBS put together a package of balancing material for broadcast the same night in September 1988. The documentary by **Jo Franklin-Trout** (at left with an interview subject) explored the angry Palestinian reaction to the Israeli occupation, and PBS added a shorter pro-Israeli film and a panel discussion, extending the airtime from 90 to 150 minutes. Critics said the film was one-sided and objected that the producer had taken funds from the Arab-American Cultural Foundation. But PBS programmer Barry Chase told scholar B.J. Bullert that the film was worth airing: "We put it on because it provided a point of view not well provided before. That doesn't mean it was the correct point of view. It was a piece of the puzzle. Unfortunately, in television, only one thing comes out of the box at once."

Marlon Riggs was "pushing America's anxiety button" with his film "Tongues Untied," wrote *Los Angeles Times* critic Howard Rosenberg. He called it an "exciting, free-form film . . . about black men loving black men." But the poetic film violated America's "triple taboo"—against sexuality, blackness and homosexuality, the filmmaker said. Some managers aired the film at risk of bitter controversy, as in Georgia, where manager Richard Ottinger aired the show at 11 p.m. Ottinger's board backed him up, pledging not to shrink from controversial programs. Other station managers said a year later at the PBS convention that the first-person advocacy and raw language were too advanced, and wished that PBS hadn't put them in the position of having to choose publicly whether to carry the program. "There is some heat," PBS President Bruce Christensen replied to the objecting managers, "but that heat goes with part of the job." (Photo: ITVS.)

combatants had little tolerance for contrary opinions. The very notion of government intervention in fostering "public culture" came under assault, and the National Endowment for the Arts and the National Endowment for the Humanities had barely survived calls from congressional conservatives for their elimination. As former NEA Chairman John Frohnmayer described his job: "I was caught between the uncompromising forces who, on the one hand, saw the arts endowment as promoting obscenity and nonmajoritarian values and, on the other, condemned it for capitulating to censorship and artistic repression. I sought the middle ground and was creamed."

Public television officials often felt similarly trapped. The case of "Tongues Untied," Marlon Riggs's intensely personal video-essay on gay, African-American life, was a watershed. Distributed by PBS in July 1991 as part of the *P.O.V.* documentary series, the program came under fire from conservative think tanks, legislators and critics. Sen. Jesse Helms (R-N.C.) claimed the film "blatantly promoted homosexuality as an acceptable lifestyle." Columnist James Kilpatrick, while defending Riggs's right to produce the film, wrote that "the producer has no right whatever to produce his film at public expense." In the end, 174 of the 284 transmitters that usually broadcast *P.O.V.* carried "Tongues Untied." At WOSU in Columbus, Ohio, General Manager Dale Ouzts described the bind for many PBS managers: "Some say, 'If you show it, you're a pornographer.' Others say, 'If you don't run it, you're a censor.'"

The controversy, wrote producer/scholar B.J. Bullert, sparked "a crisis within public television over its reason for existence and its role in a heterogeneous and multicultural society." In this climate, according to *New York Times* critic Walter Goodman, too many public TV stations have resorted to "risk-free offerings"—old movies, Britcoms, how-tos, nature docs, Lawrence Welk reruns, and ballroom-dancing championships—to complement the traditional PBS cultural and public affairs programming.

Declarations of independents

"Instead of simply complaining and decrying the degeneration of public television from its original public-service orientation, we actually had a solution and an answer," said documentary distributor/producer Lawrence Daressa in 1989. That answer was to find money for freelance producers to make public TV programs "independently of the priorities of the stations."

The evidence to support his proposition was already on miles of film and videotape. When the programming envelope is pushed in public television, it's often by an independent producer. Many of public TV's noteworthy—and controversial—programs are produced by independents, ranging from young muckrakers to big-name veterans. Producers like Bill Moyers, Ken Burns and even Children's Television Workshop qualify as independents under some definitions; by CPB's count, 35 percent of public TV hours aired in fiscal 1996 were produced by indies, compared to 47 percent by stations.

Since 1978, the laws that authorize funding of CPB encouraged the corporation to steer production money to indies, but Daressa and other advocates found that CPB's Television Program Fund was spending less and less on independent productions. As it turned out, Daressa was one of three Larrys who took the lead in redirecting some of CPB's money to an "independent program service." In 1988, Laurence Hall, a retired physicist and tireless gadfly for reform of KQED, came with Daressa

from San Francisco and joined with Lawrence Sapadin, head of an indie trade association, to push for new legislation. Rhetoric flew. Independent documentarian Frederick Wiseman painted public TV as an incompetent, bureaucratic "mess." In response, a station-based producer, *MacNeil/Lehrer* executive Al Vecchione, accused indies of "simply seeking employment through the back door," and demanding "a private sandbox" to play in. "Why should they have the right," Vecchione asked, "to circumvent the central authority?" Traditionally, that's the stations.

The indies' argument caught the ear of leaders in the House but not the Senate, which had a different idea—giving the stations control of most of CPB's TV production money. It's pertinent that both houses sought to reduce CPB's authority—both were Democrat-controlled and both had been watching CPB in recent years as Reagan appointees on its board considered various schemes for adjusting public TV's ideological balance.

With the session waning, in November 1988, Congress finally enacted a three-year CPB authorization bill, directing the corporation to establish an independent program service "to expand the diversity and innovativeness of programming available to public broadcasting." The founders of the Independent Television Service (ITVS) saw the entity as, in the words of scholar Pat Aufderheide, "a political organization, not in the liberal/conservative sense, but in terms of making a strong case for a radically new kind of media." A board including the three Larrys, and chaired by Sapadin, incorporated ITVS the next fall. After long negotiations with CPB, ITVS began operations in 1991 in St. Paul, Minn. Annual funding fell short of indies' hopes. Taking a cue from House report language that suggested $6 million a year, CPB has granted ITVS approximately $7 million or $8 million a year, though the corporation has sometimes chafed at the mandate. In 1996, Senate supporters of ITVS had to scurry to delete a five-word House amendment that would have removed CPB's mandate to support ITVS.

Static on public radio

Public radio has drawn fire from both the right and the left flanks in the '90s. Conservatives have long charged its networks and stations with bias: the right-wing media watchdog Center for the Study of Popular Culture refers to NPR's "liberal news team" that goes easier on Bill Clinton than it did on Presidents Reagan and Bush. On NPR, Clinton accuser Paula Jones was treated like "a troublesome bimbo," wrote the center's Tim Graham, while Anita Hill, who said

In a lobbying campaign that peaked in 1988, the founders of the Independent Television Service argued that independent producers bring creativity and diverse viewpoints to public TV. Pictured at left: **Lawrence Daressa, Lawrence Sapadin** and **Louise Lo** of the National Asian American Telecommunications Association. Defending public TV, CPB program chief Ron Hull gave one reason why indies are unhappy with the system. Because it can give production grants to only 20 out of 200 applicants, Hull said, CPB maintains "a very large group of dissatisfied producers."

PB
PB

See online: founding documents of ITVS.

conservative Supreme Court justice Clarence Thomas had harassed her, "remains the heroine of the liberal myth that NPR reporter Nina Totenberg did so much to create." Pacifica's KPFK in Los Angeles enraged some members of Congress in 1992 when speakers on the station's Afrikan Mental Liberation Weekend, a marathon discussion of African-American culture, made anti-Semitic comments. And NPR had to apologize for essayist Andrei Codrescu's 1995 commentary deriding as "crap" the fundamentalist Christian belief in a forthcoming event of mass salvation called "the Rapture."

But liberal critics have also attacked public radio with gusto. The watchdog group FAIR published a report entitled "NPR: Tilting Center"; others on the left similarly claimed that NPR had drifted into the media mainstream and no longer serves as an alternative news source. (*Newsweek* in 1992 labeled NPR part of the nation's "cultural elite.") A Pacifica local-station host referred to NPR as "gravy-sucking dogs" for the network's reliance upon corporate support. And Pacifica itself took heat from volunteers and listeners for its shift toward centralized programming and on-air "professionalism," as noted earlier in this chapter.

First Amendment, second class?

The issue of public broadcasters' free-expression rights, always complicated by their relationships with government entities, has been rendered even more complex by a number of recent legal challenges. Most notable was a case involving the Arkansas Educational Television Network and a minor-party candidate for Congress named Ralph Forbes. When AETN refused Forbes a spot on a televised 1992 debate, the former American Nazi Party member brought suit, claiming that AETN, as an agency of state government, was obligated to provide access to all legally qualified candidates. Though AETN argued that it made an independent editorial judgment that Forbes was not a viable candidate—and indeed was neither actively campaigning nor raising funds—a federal district court sided with Forbes in 1996.

AETN appealed, and the U.S. Supreme Court agreed to hear the case. In May 1998 Justices ruled 6-3 in favor of the state network. Justice Anthony M. Kennedy, writing for the majority, noted that the state network's exclusion of Forbes was "a reasonable, viewpoint-neutral exercise of journalistic discretion." Public broadcasters who had been watching the case with concern heaved a communal sigh. "This is a great decision for viewers," said AETN Executive Director Susan Howarth.

The Forbes case offered public broadcasters a modicum of protection by declaring that public radio and TV did not constitute a public forum, which would have opened it to all comers, and severely undercut the state network's editorial discretion. However, the narrowly construed ruling did not go so far as granting pubcasters the same First Amendment footing as their private, commercial counterparts. Thus public broadcasters may continue to find their editorial decision-making challenged and may remain susceptible to lawsuits that take time and money to fight and could discourage producers from dealing with touchy public affairs topics.

In one such case, the Missouri chapter of a Ku Klux Klan group

The state-owned Arkansas Educational Television Network survived Supreme Court scrutiny in its long court struggle with Ralph P. Forbes by having objective, not politically motivated reasons for excluding minor candidate Forbes from a broadcast debate. If the state network had to give broad rights of access to outside speakers, the high court ruled, it would be "antithetical, as a general rule, to the discretion that stations and their editorial staff must exercise to fulfill their journalistic purpose and statutory obligations." Above: **AETN chief Susan Howarth and attorney Richard D. Marks** recap the Supreme Court arguments for reporters.

PB
PB

See online: the Supreme Court decision in the Forbes case.

sued St. Louis public radio station KWMU after the station, licensed to the University of Missouri, refused to sell the Klan underwriting. (The proposed message would likely have caused some rush-hour fender-benders: "Support for All Things Considered is provided in part by the Knights of the Ku Klux Klan, a white Christian organization, standing up for the rights and values of white Christian America since 1865.") A district court judge in St. Louis threw out the suit in 1998; the Klan promised an appeal.

In another episode, a convicted murderer sued NPR in 1996. The network had earlier agreed to broadcast the death row commentaries of Mumia Abu-Jamal, himself a former public radio journalist sentenced to death for the killing of a Philadelphia police officer. When NPR cancelled the deal under pressure from police groups and Sen. Robert Dole (R-Kansas), Abu-Jamal brought suit for abridging his First Amendment rights. A judge dismissed the claim on grounds that NPR is a private organization.

Click and Clack, the Magliozzi Brothers of the national program *Car Talk,* even figured in a minor First Amendment flap in 1996. Wisconsin Public Radio's managers were summoned by a state legislative committee to explain their decision to replace a locally produced auto-advice show with NPR's *Car Talk.* After an uncomfortable hearing, WPR stuck with Click and Clack, but network director Jack Mitchell, who had been tarred by opponents of the program change, soon quit his 21-year position and became a journalism professor.

The programming challenge

In its continuing mission-versus-market debates, public broadcasting repeatedly faces questions about its goals, its distinctions from commercial media and the very nature of its "alternative" role. Do public radio and TV exist to *complement* commercial broadcasting, to "serve the unserved" first of all? Or should public broadcasters provide "better broadcasting" for its educated audiences—programs of higher quality than commercial radio and TV—with limited obligations to innovation and minority interests? And what of attending to our nation's educational needs, and fostering democratic processes—obligations that are accepted enthusiastically by some, but not all, public stations?

Public broadcasters often regard these questions from well-meaning activists, academics and blue-ribbon commissions as divorced from the economic and operational realities of the industry. The outsiders have lacked the right combination of organizational understanding and political savvy to create a consensus for change, either inside or outside of the profession. And leaders of the field, in the tradition of editors and publishers, give themselves credit for resisting outside influence.

Nonetheless, these are not simply "blue-sky," academic questions. Clearly, a tough-minded assessment of the mission of public broadcasting, and its future, must situate the field within the multichannel world, without losing sight of what the "public" in its name implies. The final chapter considers some of the pertinent issues.

Should death row inmate **Mumia Abu-Jamal** be given airtime to speak for the 1.2 million Americans in prison? NPR news executives said it was "inappropriate" to air his commentaries without contrasting opinions, and pulled the tapes in 1994, the day before they were to start airing. Though NPR said it reversed its course for journalistic reasons, Abu-Jamal's lawyers later claimed in an unsuccessful suit that government pressure on public radio had forced the decision, making it a violation of the First Amendment. This time it appeared to be leftists instead of right-wingers who were trying to manipulate public radio through its public funding. But lawyer Debra Katz denied that was happening: "We are not contending in this suit that people have the right to dictate what goes out on public broadcasting. What we contend is that the government doesn't have a right." The appeal was one of many legal actions that have kept Abu-Jamal alive on death row for more than 17 years. He was convicted in 1982 in the 1981 shooting death of policeman Daniel Faulkner.

Great prospects, deep divisions

The view from 1999: a mixed outlook

Prospects for public broadcasting in the next century depend largely upon how the system's leaders navigate between the Scylla of market temptation and the Charybdis of high purpose.

There's no way to roll back the forces that rocked the enterprise worldwide in the '90s. Though federal aid to CPB has been restored for the moment, legislators will periodically question the legitimacy of public succor and may someday reject it. Tax-based support will remain unpredictable and may decline precipitously. Commercial competitors will covet segments of public broadcasting's "turf" and occasionally annex them. And technological advances will dictate costly re-engineering. Accordingly, how can—should—public broadcasters adapt and thrive in the coming mediascape?

The trust fund outlook

After more than seven decades, public broadcasting still lacks a funding source that is both generous enough to enable it to fulfill the many expectations and promises of public service, and unintrusive enough to give it independence from commercial and political interests. Public broadcasting's best recent hope has been to avoid the political hoops and hurdles of the annual appropriations process and win approval of a trust fund, to be capitalized with some of the billions of dollars the FCC is collecting by auctioning off electromagnetic spectrum to commercial broadcasters, digital pocketphone companies and other ventures.

Newton Minow, the well-known former chairman of the FCC, and now a superbly connected Chicago lawyer, has tried to inspire support for the cause with the story of Justin Smith Morrill, a 19th century Republican member of Congress. The Morrill Act of 1862 took a huge public windfall—proceeds from public lands—and dedicated the funds to support higher education, eventually endowing 70 state universities and extending higher education to young people of limited means. Spectrum auction proceeds, Minow suggested repeatedly in the 1990s, should go to similarly high public purposes, supporting educational children's programming or public broadcasting.

But the proceeds of the auction windfalls already had been claimed by the deficit-cutters in Congress, driven by a reputedly unstoppable anti-tax sentiment in many states.

The field did have an opening after the failure of the Gingrich "zero-it-out" campaign. Republican leaders, including Fields and Pressler, were emboldened to endorse the concept of a "trust fund." But public broadcasters' national organizations could not agree on many details, including the crucial amount and sources of the money to capitalize the fund—details that could wreck their long detente with commercial broadcasters.

Fields' trust fund bill died with his retirement in 1997 and returned in somewhat different form the next year. Fields' successor in the chair of the House telecommunications subcommittee, Rep. Billy Tauzin (R-La.), repeatedly hinted he might offer commercial broadcasters further deregulation in exchange for their support of a spectrum fee to support public broadcasting.

Taking a purist line with potential appeal for both the left and the right, he suggested the trade-off: the commercial industry should be freed of obligations that public broadcasters should handle, who in turn should be cleansed of the need (and authority) to pursue commercial revenue. In June 1998, during the PBS annual conference, Tauzin announced his legislation, co-sponsored by the subcommittee's ranking minority member, Edward Markey (D-Mass.). The bill not only proposed to reauthorize CPB at a high level, but also to assign a blue-ribbon panel to propose a trust fund or other revenue sources.

Rep. Jack Fields' successor as chair of the House subcommittee that oversees CPB, **Rep. Billy Tauzin** (R-La.) was caught in an awkward position in 1999. When news of WGBH's mailing list exchanges with the DNC reached Washington, he had just set aside his plans for reforming public broadcasting in hopes of expediting a major boost in CPB funding. To his right, Rep. Mike Oxley (R-Ohio) was competing with him for the chair of the powerful Commerce Committee—a factor that may well have raised the volume of both congressmen's denunciations during their grilling of public broadcasting leaders. (Photo: *Current.*)

Before Tauzin or Markey would dare confront the NAB or the House deficit-cutters, however, they would need solid endorsement from the public broadcasters themselves. No one else mattered so much at this juncture, to help the subcommittee move the bill its first inch. Indeed, during the House telecom subcommittee hearing in October 1998, everyone else on the Hill was watching the Clinton-Lewinsky hearings. The public broadcasters, as usual, called the bill a good first step, but they didn't like one trade-off: that underwriting spots would be rolled back to an unadorned, 10-second credit giving only the underwriter's name. APTS President David Brugger said the underwriting rollback could wipe out gains from the proposed annual CPB payment of $475 million a year.

Markey warned bluntly: "This is the condition we've got to sign on to, if we want this unusually high level of support." Tauzin and Markey left the bill on the table. The divided Congress stuck with the status quo of annual appropriations to CPB in 1998.

Then, in the summer of 1999, all bets were off. Tauzin and his subcommittee were infuriated to learn that WGBH had exchanged fundraising lists with the Democratic National Committee—and later that dozens of public stations had also swapped lists with groups on both sides of the aisle, even at stations with rules against the practice. Professional fundraisers grumbled the list deals were routine ways to get addresses of member prospects. Coonrod and Duggan said the deals were legal but "stupid" because of the appearance of partisan connections, and Coonrod outlawed them for CPB grantees.

See online: texts of Fields and Tauzin bills.

Advice from the "Gore Commission"

Until the uproar over mailing lists there was a wider than usual opening for progress on the federal front. There was bipartisan support for federal aid to the system and renewed hope for a trust fund. There was a rising coalition of outside reformers on the left, some with foundation backing, including a potentially powerful coalition, People for Better TV, and a fledgling Citizens for Independent Public Broadcasting, launched in 1999. And there was also the timely coincidence of digital TV and, attending that, the Gore Commission.

Back in 1996, in the rush to reach agreement on the technical side of DTV broadcasting, the FCC had delayed entirely any deci-

sions about what the broadcast industry might have to do for the public in exchange for its new channels for digital transmission. The channels would be worth billions if auctioned off the way the FCC was disposing of other spectrum. The commission did give notice that it would consider the matter later on, but by the mid-1990s had already lost its leverage because the commercial broadcasters had already been promised their channels.

In October 1997, President Clinton nevertheless appointed an advisory committee to revisit the matter—22 members, including only seven commercial broadcasters and a larger contingent of public-interest advocates, including seven with close ties to public broadcasting. Officially it was the Advisory Committee on the Public-Interest Obligations of Digital Television Broadcasters, though outsiders called it the Gore Commission. Clinton and Gore made it clear that they wanted the panel to endorse free airtime for political candidates during campaigns. Gore told the committee this would help end "an endless steeplechase to raise and spend campaign contributions" that pay for campaign ads on TV.

After meeting for more than a year, however, the committee in December 1998 came back to Gore with only a weak plea that each commercial station voluntarily give five minutes of campaign time per night. Other recommendations were similarly mild, but three could help the cause of public broadcasting:

■ **Create a trust fund.** "Congress should create a trust fund to ensure enhanced and permanent funding for public broadcasting to help it fulfill its potential in the digital television environment and remove it from the vicissitudes of the political process," the committee said.

■ **Possible trade-offs with commercial TV.** To cover the very live possibility that commercial broadcasters will get richer by using their DTV channels to simply broadcast four, five or more regular TV programs simultaneously (to "multicast" or "multiplex"), rather than devoting their whole channels to high-definition TV, the committee advised: "Digital television broadcasters who choose to multiplex, and in doing so reap enhanced economic benefits, should have the flexibility to choose between paying a fee, providing a multicasted channel for public-interest purposes, or making an in-kind contribution."

■ **A second educational channel in every city.** "When spectrum now used for analog broadcasting is returned to the government, Congress should reserve the equivalent of 6 megahertz of spectrum for each viewing community in order to establish channels devoted specifically to noncommercial educational programming. Congress should establish an orderly process for allocating the new channels as well as provide adequate funding from appropriate revenue sources."

Under other circumstances, this last recommendation might have caused celebration among public TV leaders, but the reaction was muted. Public TV didn't want more channels if they came without new funds to build and run the stations; it is already facing the costs of putting digital TV transmitters on the air and of upgrading to HDTV production. Moreover, with the digital transition, public TV already has the option of a historic expansion in its capacity: multiplexing four, five or six simultaneous programs.

"Selling is going on"

While Congress remained stymied in the status quo, public broadcasters themselves were cleaved philosophically and strategically regarding the commercial media marketplace.

One camp reconfirms the noncommercial ideals of the enterprise, despite uncertain funding prospects. "What makes noncommercial television different is its devotion to providing a service to viewers as opposed to attracting eyeballs," said Tom Howe, g.m. of North Carolina's state network. "Over time, the more commercial we become, the more that will change our programming practices." The other camp rejects the inevitability of this classic dynamic, pushes the envelope for new revenues and argues that stations will still pursue their missions and maintain quality, even if they begin airing ads.

Scholar Debra Merskin, a former advertising executive, contends that many public broadcasting institutions have already altered themselves to operate in the commercial world. She noted that many stations have developed sales forces, often comprised of people with commercial sales experience, who speak the language of ad-agency media planners in pitching a place for underwriting in a conventional media mix. The corporate underwriter also has changed, she said. Where previously many corporations would contribute to public broadcasters with no-strings attached, to burnish the company's image, today they assign marketing staffers to dole out underwriting money with an eye on the firm's overall advertising campaign.

"When one takes into account the Barney toys, video sales, logo marketing, public relations events and other integrated-marketing tools, it's apparent, at least to an advertiser, that selling is going on," Merskin argues. How apparent it is to viewers and listeners is another question. Studies have suggested that supporters of public broadcasting are willing to make concessions to commercialization, but they may lose faith in the industry if pushed too far.

In public radio, audience researcher David Giovannoni put out a warning in 1998 that listeners were already showing signs of "underwriter anxiety." According to a survey of listeners by Giovannoni's Audience 98 project, 77 percent said underwriting blurbs are becoming "more prevalent than in the past"; one-third said they're "getting more annoying"; and half were concerned that underwriters "may eventually force changes in the programming."

Listeners are particularly alert when funders become the subject of news. NPR felt the heat from listeners and critics after a major underwriter, the agribusiness giant Archer Daniels Midland, was embroiled in a price-fixing scandal in 1996. NPR News broadcast a lengthy investigation of ADM, but the network's reputation suffered from its longtime association with the company. *The Nation*, for instance, referred to ADM as "super-briber to the political world"—a take-off on the firm's on-air underwriting slogan, "supermarket to the world." And critics seized on the case as a symbol of the danger of corporate influence upon programming. Though corporate (and government) funders may hope for gentle treatment in the newsroom when their names get into the news, their primary impact on public broadcasters comes through their choice of which programs they will support.

Corporate self-interest in an underwriting choice has seldom been as clear-cut as in a TV documentary project developed in 1996 by KQED, San Francisco. The program's topic was arguably a worthy one that threatened no major damage to the commonweal, it should be said. KQED was eager to produce a profile of colorful vintner Robert Mondavi, a Napa Valley pioneer, and the station got initial funding from a nonprofit group backed largely by Mondavi's winery. Though KQED contended it maintained editorial control of the project, a treatment of the proposed special, leaked to the *San Francisco Chronicle*, outlined a favorable profile. "The whole process was polluted," Peter Sussman, president of the local chapter of the Society of Professional Journalists told the *Chronicle*. Abashed after weeks of public acrimony, the station cancelled the documentary, returned the money and adopted new guidelines for fundraising.

Commercial routes not taken

At least in part because many public broadcasting leaders remain wary of relations with the marketplace, the system did not pursue various major opportunities for commercial revenue.

One such opening was created by former PBS President Lawrence Grossman in the 1990s. After leaving NBC News in 1988, Grossman proposed several ambitious undertakings for public TV, both commercial and noncommercial. In 1993, major stations and PBS signed on to advance the idea of a modest-budget, noncommercial Horizons cable network that would have become the equivalent of C-SPAN for the arts and humanities. The sun never came up on Horizons. In 1997, Grossman returned to his 1980s idea of a "Grand Alliance" with other cultural organizations, and helped generate a wave of enthusiasm among foundation leaders for collaboration in use of public TV's digital channels among universities, museums, libraries and foundations.

PB
PB
See online:
Grossman's PTV
Weekend proposal.

Grossman's most controversial funding proposal also aimed to generate enlightening cultural fare, but would have broken the commercial barrier in a new way. In a study backed by the John and Mary R. Markle Foundation, he suggested that public TV stations turn over Friday and Saturday nights to a new network with the working name of "P-2" and later "PTV Weekend." This new network, parallel to PBS but separate, would sell ads to generate funds for production of high-quality cultural programming. It would coexist peaceably on the same stations that also air PBS public affairs and other genres of programming that cannot easily get corporate backing and need public-sector support, Grossman said.

Under the proposal, PTV Weekend would get its all-important

capital from commercial media firms that would co-own it with interested public TV stations. Grossman said the idea was inspired by Britain's acclaimed Channel 4, a commercial network with formal public-interest obligations. Of course, starting a commercial network on reserved noncommercial stations, even for two days a week, would require the approval of Congress. "It's an idea we have to take a look at," said Jack Willis, then president of KTCA in the Twin Cities. But Willis expressed concern that weekend commercials would start the system sliding down the "slippery slope": "Once you're relying on the income, you have to dance to the tune, broaden the audience, and downgrade programming more and more." As the single-channel analog era was ending, PTV Weekend had not won widespread support within the public TV system, but the idea could arise again with the coming of multicasting on digital TV.

In public radio, one well-publicized embrace of the marketplace was quite literal but equally fruitless. NPR President Delano Lewis gave one of his signature big hugs to Liberty Media executive Peter Barton at the 1996 Public Radio Conference after Barton gave a speech lauding the radio network and calling for collaborative ventures between Liberty and NPR. That night, Barton's company, an arm of cable giant TCI, paid for a lavish 25th anniversary party for NPR, where party-goers could see NPR's logo hanging on the walls with those of TCI's many cable networks. Lewis' ebullient embrace of Barton prompted independent producer Sandy Tolan to pen a *New York Times* op-ed piece headlined "Must NPR Sell Itself?" Wrote Tolan: "TCI and Liberty want to use NPR to gain public-interest credibility as meat for their own mission . . . 'creating shareholder value.'" A chagrined Lewis was compelled to downplay the embrace: "I hug everybody," he explained.

Footnote: A year later, the frustated Peter Barton had been doing a deal a week but none was with NPR, or with public TV, which he had also courted. He told a reporter: "My focus was with public television more than public radio." Going to see NPR was a way to reach managers who also run public TV stations. Besides, he said, he personally likes to listen to public radio.

New media: much to do, perhaps too much

Despite these funding frustrations, public broadcasting has developed a much sturdier machine for self-support than it admits during pledge drives. Like a healthy, diverse ecosystem, the system does not depend on a single stream of sustenance, and most of its revenue sources are growing. Total revenues (chart, page 47) passed the mark of $1 billion in 1985, by CPB's count, and neared $2 billion in 1997. Inflation absorbed more than half of that gain, but after a dozen years the system was still 40 percent ahead.

But this growth is not adequate to keep up with the growing cost of services as the system is currently structured, fulfill the system's longstanding promises and expectations—and, at the same time, equip it for digital transmission and let it develop new public services on the new pathways.

Looking ahead to new media, as Frieda Hennock and other leaders did in the infancy of FM and UHF broadcasting, 1990s public broadcasters looked to stake claims in new transmission technologies, but they initially had limited success. Taking the lead, APTS sought free or reduced-cost access to new "video dialtone" networks then expected from phone companies, but the FCC said no in 1992. Later, the Telecommunications Act of 1996 made elementary/secondary schools and libraries eligible for preferential rates on wired and wireless networks, but refused discounts for public broadcasters (and colleges, among others).

In radio, the FCC refused NPR's request for a noncommercial allocation on the coming digital satellite radio services, but the commission did hold the door open for public-interest requirements on satellite radio at a later time.

APTS's first win came in 1992, when it sought reserved channel space on TV direct broadcast satellites. Like the pioneers who won reserved FM and TV channels in past decades, it was asking early, before the DBS industry had licenses, money or political clout. Congress assented, requiring DBS operators to set aside 4 to 7 percent of their capacity for noncommercial educational channels. In August 1996, APTS beat back a court challenge of the set-aside, and the FCC followed through with rules in November 1998, setting the reservation at 4 percent and allowing the DBS companies to charge carriage costs.

These developments combine with others to give public TV a dizzying set of expansion options for the next millenium—none of them with guaranteed means of support:

■ **DTV multicast channels.** With compression technology, digital DTV can carry far more information in a standard TV channel than analog transmissions can. When a channel is not occupied with a high-definition program, it can carry four or more standard-definition (SDTV) programs simultaneously. Public TV's consistent plan has been to "multicast" during the day and air HDTV in primetime.

■ **HDTV.** Technologists first assumed that HDTV would occupy a whole DTV channel, but data rates are flexible in DTV. Some broadcasters say consumers will not have big enough screens to benefit from the highest 1,080-line HDTV standard for years; they and the computer industry are championing HDTV at lower data rates that would leave capacity for other services. If HDTV takes off, broadcasters may even find a way to air two reduced bit-rate HDTV programs at once.

■ **"Enhanced" interactive DTV and datacasting**. DTV planners expect that services with interactivity that mimics the Internet or CD-ROM discs will ride along with video programs on DTV broadcasts. Some will be entirely separate information products, while others will "enhance" the TV shows with additional pictures, text, sound and interactivity.

■ **New educational DTV channels**, proposed by the Gore Commission. These may

PBS's first experimental "enhanced" DTV broadcast came the night after the DTV debut of seven public TV stations in November 1998. In the tryout backed by Intel Corp., a multimedia team created a **supplementary "enhancement" to Ken Burns' Frank Lloyd Wright biography**, for viewing after the film was over (as Burns insisted). It was a very early demonstration; only a scattering of prototype receivers, built into ordinary personal computers, were available to pick it up. The few participants could explore an interactive treasure chest of images, text and video—digital data equal to one-third of a CD-ROM, downloaded to their computers through the air.

be a long shot, and there's no guarantee that existing public TV operators would get the licenses, but it could greatly increase distribution capacity. The FCC and Congress will have to consider the 1998 recommendation for an additional DTV channel to be reserved in every city for non-commercial, educational purposes. The reservations could be blocked by budget-cutters, who are already counting on proceeds from auctioning off the channels instead of assigning them to education. And public broadcasters have been cool to the idea. It is possible that nobody will lobby hard to make the recommendation come true.

When RCA introduced color television in the 1950s, it had the advantage of owning NBC, which built public interest with *Walt Disney's Wonderful World of Color* and other shows. For the national broadcast debut of HDTV, public TV took a leading role. Seattle's KCTS, which had been producing high-def documentaries and travelogues since 1989, made the premiere documentary, **"Chihuly over Venice,"** documenting the multi-nation glassblowing project of famed hometown artist Dale Chihuly. (Photo: KCTS.)

■ **Reserved channels on DBS.** Some of these channels on DirecTV, the largest DBS service, went to religious broadcasters and various nonprofits in late 1999, but two were expected to be operated by PBS—PBS Kids, which began operation in September, and PBS-You, a new adult-education channel.

■ **Possible new cable channels.** A $900 million foundation endowed by the Gannett newspapers fortune, the Freedom Forum, unveiled plans in January 1999 to partner with public TV station WETA to start a local public affairs channel in Washington, D.C. The project was called off before year's end for lack of local cable channels, but similar channels may arise later on.

■ **Upgrades of existing "overlap" channels in major cities.** In 1998, for the first time, PBS agreed to work with the Program Resources Group, an alliance of overlap stations, to consider developing a second stream of national programming to strengthen their schedules. A year later, however, the plan seemed to be stalled.

■ **The wide-open world of the Internet.** Beyond the predicted 500-channel world of cable is the possibility of future on-demand communications systems patterned on the Internet that offer, in effect, millions of video channels.

Challenges: accepting and affording the multichannel future

To seize these possibilities, however, most public broadcasters will have to change their mindsets. Public TV licensees mostly operate single channels and all but a few have shown little interest in developing complementary, counterprogrammed second or third channels in a community. They lacked an enthusiastic consensus to get into cable TV in the 1980s. Second stations that do exist have been underused. But audience researchers David and Judith LeRoy, among others, have preached a new multichannel gospel that may take hold. And DTV multicasting at last is giving all stations a direct stake in multiple channels. PBS is now developing multiple streams not unlike those proposed two decades ago by Hartford Gunn's System Planning Project.

Can public radio serve a public beyond the generally well-educated fans of classical music, jazz and NPR-style news? More than anyone else, **Hugo Morales** is testing that possibility as executive director of Radio Bilingüe, a five-station group that mainly serves Chicano farmworkers in California, largely in Spanish. Morales, born in the Mexican region of Oaxaca, worked in the fields of Sonoma County as a youth and returned to California after earning a law degree at Harvard. He started a public radio station in Fresno in 1980, adding four more stations and in 1993, with the help of foundations and CPB, a satellite network, Satélite Radio Bilingüe, which distributes to dozens of other stations across the country and in Mexico. CPB recognized the achievement in 1999, giving Morales the annual Edward R. Murrow Award (pictured). (Photo: *Current*.)

The prospect of all these new distribution channels led CPB President Bob Coonrod to make his most-quoted remark of 1998: With digital TV, "the technology has finally caught up with our mission." Public TV can fulfill more of its many educational and public-service objectives at once, while using "enhanced DTV" to supplement video with text and interactivity.

The expanded channel capacity is also expected to bring new revenue to public TV. Station leaders expect to be able to sell unused parts of their DTV bitstream to transmit digital material for business and education. Early in 1999, the FCC was considering what restrictions it should put on public TV's "ancillary and supplementary" uses of DTV channels. Some public TV stations already are sampling the benefits of a similar arrangement: PBS is leasing out space on stations' vertical blanking interval—unused space in the analog TV picture—for data transmission to home computer users and other customers.

Though revenue-producing use of the DTV bitstream could become a boon to the field, it could also lead to new clashes over commercialism with the field's traditional supporters. Worse, the revenue prospects could look so rich that Congress and other funders may assume that public TV can solve its own money problems by renting out a large part of its DTV capacity.

The high cost of switching to DTV amounts to a sky-high hurdle for public television, as it does for smaller commercial stations. Almost half of public TV licensees face transition costs that exceed their annual budgets, Louisiana Public Broadcasting executive Beth Courtney testified during a House hearing in 1998. Public broadcasting asked the government to put up $771 million of the estimated $1.7 billion cost, but the best offers were $450 million proposals from the Clinton Administration in 1998 and 1999.

Fortunately the FCC acknowledged the high costs in 1997, giving public TV stations until 2003—a year longer than even the smallest commercial stations were given—to begin broadcasting in digital. By November 1998, seven public TV stations had set up and turned on digital transmitters, but most others will have difficulty raising the funds to make the switch.

Public radio's networks are also starting to develop multiple program streams beyond the local stations. NPR announced in June 1999 that it was planning two channels for CD Radio, a forthcoming direct-to-listener satellite service, and PRI said it was planning one for the same satellite service. In an essay the previous year PRI President Stephen Salyer cited 11 formats that public radio producers and stations could develop collaboratively for new digital distribution media. NPR's board in July 1998 adopted a "strategic framework" that permits the network to develop new program streams as long as they don't "compromise the long-term viability" of member stations. (*Morning Edition* and *ATC* won't be on the satellite, at least initially.) To Wyoming Public Radio manager Jon Schwartz, an architect of the policy, it is NPR's chance to serve more of the public than just its present, well-educated, largely middle-aged, white listenership. "That's a great start," he says, but it is not all that the founders of the field, and Congress, had in mind for public radio.

Fortunately, public radio doesn't face an imminent, vastly expensive digital transition. Though the technology for digital audio broadcasting (DAB) has not been perfected or adopted, it appears that the cost and dislocation may be much less severe than in TV. But the public radio networks felt they had to join rather than strictly fight the challenge of digital broadcasting by satellite. CD Radio, the company with which they first announced deals, is one of two ventures that bought chunks of spectrum in a 1997 FCC auction—each stake large enough to accommodate 100 program streams. The two ventures, CD Radio and its competitor XM Satellite Radio, plan to launch service in 2000 or 2001. Establishing their services will be a long-haul proposition, if not a long shot, since the public will have to be sold on buying new radio receivers for stations they've never heard. But if it materializes, digital satellite radio may jolt radio broadcasters into going digital. "The incentive will be us becoming real," said David Margolese of CD Radio.

Public radio is worrying that satellite radio will eat into their audiences—with its narrowcasting of news, jazz and classical music—but it's also participating so that it won't be left behind by new media, as public TV was by cable.

One of the best ways public radio can protect itself, many broadcasters are saying now, is to provide strong *local* programming. "It is unlikely that a national (satellite) broadcaster will be able to provide the particular local service component that a good public radio station offers its audience," said Skip Pizzi, a technical consultant to public radio.

Toward public cybercasting

The emergence of the Internet as a widely used medium is challenging public broadcasters to keep pace with the Information Age. But well before the Internet boom, in 1985, WNET in New York established its Learning Link online service for teachers, eventually expanding it to dozens of cities. CPB moved tentatively toward online services in 1993 with its Community-Wide

In a variation on its policy of "parallel production" for multiple media, Boston's WGBH repeatedly offered live webcasts from *Nova* filmmakers climbing Mt. Everest. In 1996, Nova Online carried reports as the film crew joined efforts to rescue another expedition. In '97, the web site carried a live audio webcast from the summit, as the crew prepared a *Nova* documentary on oxygen deprivation. Then in '99, *Nova* filmmakers posted web dispatches as they searched for and found the body of a climber missing on the mountain since 1924. (Photo: WGBH.)

Education and Information Service (CWEIS) initiative. CWEIS offered grants to 12 public broadcasters to help develop "community networks"—providing online access to local educational and informational resources, and, in some cases, the Internet. CWEIS marked "the transformation of public radio and public television into public telecommunications," noted Bob Coonrod, then the top aide to Carlson at CPB. "We're helping to ensure that the core values of public broadcasting—access, service, and most important, local autonomy and community control—become an integral part of the National Information Infrastructure."

The outcome of the three-year CWEIS initiative was mixed, according to scholar Philip Thompsen, who studied the projects. He found that public broadcasters were more at home developing content, as in web sites, rather than facilitating dialogue. "It may be difficult for public broadcasters, conditioned to the roles of cultural gatekeeper and program producer," wrote Thompsen, "to exploit the unique strengths of community networks."

Thompsen also found that only two of the 12 CWEIS grants resulted in a community network that was still operating in 1997. Some others did, however, establish a presence on the Internet's World Wide Web, which by then had swept the online world, superceding local dial-up networks, replacing proprietary software with freely available browsers.

Initiated in 1993, the web took off so fast that many media companies were caught by surprise. One was PBS. In March 1995, the network's plan for online services was an echo of its TV distribution model: it bought a used two-way VSAT satellite system for $2.8 million, and was going to use it to periodically feed updated national material to the stations. To connect, local users would use proprietary online software to dial-up a modem at the nearest station. But by September, PBS had shifted its plans to the web, creating PBS Online. Stations also began creating their own web sites.

Three years later, by September 1998, PBS Online had built a site of 50,000 pages, visited by 2 million unduplicated visitors per month. Online usage peaked at times when PBS aired "web markers" in the corner of the screen of a documentary—reminders to viewers that they could find "webumentaries" with supplementary figures, outtakes from interviews and background documents on the web site.

Public radio was among the early settlers on the web. Computer audio innovator Carl Malamud included public radio programs among his early, pre-web, "cybercasts" on Internet Talk Radio. NPR was quick to provide its news reports in RealAudio format, and now streams audio files from its daily newsmagazines on the web. Dozens of local public radio stations offer their music schedules on the web as well.

Though some local radio managers fear the web will lure away their specialized audiences—and even their NPR News fans—the online audiences so far are not large. Of 45,000 Arbitron diaries filled out in the spring of 1996, only one respondent mentioned listening to radio programming online. And the audience listening to NPR Online on the web during its afternoon peak in 1998 was just 250 to 300 in 1998, compared to NPR's typical over-the-air audience of 1 million.

Transforming public broadcasting

The words ring out with immediacy: "We are persuaded that public broadcasting does have an integral role to play in bringing the benefits of an enriched information environment to the public and in helping to shape that environment in ways that are not dependent on the marketplace." But the year was 1979, and the sentiment was that of the second Carnegie Commission, commenting on the need for public broadcasting to evolve into public telecommunications. And, indeed, some public broadcasters have begun to morph.

Among them is KPBS, San Diego, a joint FM/TV licensee that has adopted "a publishing model." The station views content, not distribution systems, as central. "We consider how to best organize content creation and acquisition within the new technological world," says Michael Flaster, KPBS' associate g.m. for programming. For example, programming on the same topic may be distributed in different forms over KPBS' various distribution channels: FM radio, TV, the members' program guide and magazine, a closed-circuit video system, and the KPBS web site. KPBS also looks for outside partnerships, as in the case of the coffee-table book planned in conjunction with "California and the American Dream," a documentary being produced to mark the state's 150th anniversary.

The publishing model drives staffing decisions, too. The radio news department serves as, in effect, an "editorial department" for the entire operation, contributing to television and other media projects. "We hire and train people who can cross borders," Flaster says. "Our mindset recognizes that Renaissance producers could just as easily create radio, television or real-time 'movies' for the web."

Elsewhere, as the 1990s ended, dozens of public radio stations were retransmitting programming over the Internet, in effect becoming global broadcasters. PBS was airing interactive "enhanced DTV" material to supplement Ken Burns' latest biography, of Frank Lloyd Wright. Public radio networks were competing to syndicate text and interactive content to radio stations' web sites, following variations on the old model of audio networking.

Practitioners of the "old media," as TV and radio are now regarded, will have to deal with seismic shifts in their world. Futurist George Gilder envisions an information/entertainment appliance that he calls a "teleputer"—combining television and telephony with computers. When TV goes digital, the computer industry has crowed, there will be more computers capable of receiving the signal than TV sets. A wave of TV accessories for web surfing and computer accessories for TV tuning hit the market in the late '90s, and some fully integrated devices were on sale.

Even the long-lived medium of radio is evolving as technology permits—perhaps demands—that audio producers provide some visual accompaniment on the computer screen to the sounds coming out of the speakers.

Traditional thinking about audiences will have to change. Viewers wield their remotes with abandon, substituting cable and videos for broadcast TV, surfing the web instead of the tube, moving from video to audio to text and back with the click of a mouse.

Will public broadcasters "publish" in the newer digital forms? Will they maintain donor and tax support in a world of web-users who increasingly believe that information is free? Will they need revenue from partnerships with for-profit video and online publishers? And what if those companies come with fundamentally different values? How will public service communication—as scholar Greg Lowe suggests the new endeavor be named—maintain its distinctiveness?

The academic community has a role to play in revitalizing the form of broadcasting that was spawned on college campuses in the early days of radio. When the National Association of Educational Broadcasters closed in 1982, public broadcasters and academics lost their locus for intellectual interchange. A spate of recent books and scholarship marks an encouraging renewal of academic interest in the field. Here's hoping the academy will continue to invest intellectual capital in the study of noncommercial media.

Consolidating a third force

As we ponder the role of public broadcasting in the new-tech world, there are important lessons for public broadcasting professionals from an "old-tech" information provider: the public libraries.

Writing in the March 1997 issue of *Harper's* magazine, Sallie Tisdale describes the debate roiling in the library community, which curiously parallels public broadcasting's. "Today's library is trendy, up to date, plugged in," Tisdale writes. "You can get movies there and Nintendo games, drink cappuccino and surf cyberspace. . . . But the way things are going, in a few years it's going to be hard to tell the difference between the library and anything, everything else." Tisdale notes that high-profile new libraries like those in San Francisco and Portland, Ore., have traded off quiet reading rooms for public spaces to host puppet shows and Lamaze classes. Shelves that used to house old books have been torn down to make room for networked computer terminals, often funded by grants from Microsoft and the like.

The new libraries, less focused on their traditional mission, are more accessible, more popular. But Tisdale laments the loss of the silent refuge from the street and the marketplace: "No one seems to believe that there is a public need for refuge. . . . In a world of noise and disordered information, a place of measured thought is the province once again of the wealthy, because it is invaluable." She concludes her essay with a wistful description of being in such a place: a large, quiet, book-filled room, in which people of various colors and ages were in thrall of "the immense possibilities of stories." It was a branch of Barnes & Noble.

Shouldn't public broadcasting, by whatever name, be a "place of measured thought" amid the cacophony of the multichannel world? Lawrence Grossman floated a similar notion in his proposals of a "grand alliance": that public media, in concert with museums and libraries and other nonprofits, should comprise a "third force" of information providers, alongside the media conglomerates and the anarchic Internet volunteers who populate today's web. In this realm, the success of public telecommunicators' communicative efforts would be measured not only by "counting the house," but, to use a museum analogy, by the "quality of the collection"—the strength and value of the content.

This metaphor may be useful in guiding the field through its ongoing, inevitable transformation. To provide places of measured thought; calm, reasoned places to consider the broad spectrum of information and cultural expression that Americans need both to participate in the civic debate and to celebrate the human experience. This would be a worthy goal for public telecommunicators in the new millenium, one that respects the interests of the public whose name noncommercial broadcasters invoke, and in whose name they are licensed to serve.

1895
■ Guglielmo Marconi sends wireless signal on family estate in Italy.

1912
■ Iowa State College's station 9YI (named WOI since 1922) experiments with Morse code broadcasting.

1917
■ University of Wisconsin begins voice broadcasting with radio station 9XM, forerunner of WHA, under an experimental license.

1921
■ FCC issues first license to an educational institution, Latter Day Saints University in Salt Lake City.

1925
■ Nov. 12: Forerunner of PBS and NPR formed: Association of College and University Broadcasting Stations (ACUBS). (It later becomes National Association of Educational Broadcasters.)

1927
■ Feb. 23: Radio Act of 1927 signed into law, creating Federal Radio Commission (later FCC).

1928
■ November: FRC's General Order 40 shifts most radio stations' frequencies; 23 of the first 25 clear channels are affiliated with NBC. Favoritism toward commercial stations prompts Broadcast Reform Movement.

1930
■ Carnegie Corporation of New York, with NBC, creates National Advisory Council on Radio in Education (NACRE) to promote Cooperation Doctrine—alliances between commercial radio and educators. ■ July: ACUBS asks Congress to reserve channels for education. ■ September: Payne Fund begins funding Broadcast Reform Movement.

■ October: Joy Elmer Morgan appointed to organize movement's National Committee on Education by Radio (NCER).

1934
■ June 19: Communications Act of 1934 signed into law, replacing FRC with FCC. ■ September: ACUBS changes constitution; new name is National Association of Educational Broadcasters (NAEB).

1938
■ Jan. 26: FCC establishes new class of noncommercial educational radio stations in high-frequency band.
■ Cooperation doctrine subsides, NACRE closes, consensus develops for reserved channels.

1939
■ RCA demonstrates TV with first public broadcast at World's Fair.

1940
■ FCC reserves five of the 40 channels in new high-frequency band for noncommercial educational stations. (Though planned for AM, stations go to FM as technology develops.)

1945
■ June 27: FCC moves FM service to VHF band, expands noncommercial FM reservation to 20 channels (88-92 MHz) of the total 100 FM channels.

1948
■ FCC freezes licensing of TV stations, allows educational FM stations to operate with 10 watts or less power.

1949
■ FCC authorizes 50th noncommercial FM station. ■ WNYC begins "bicycle network," shipping taped radio programs from station to station. ■ April 15: Pacifica begins operation of KPFA in Berkeley, claimed to be first listener-supported station.

Early deejay, WILL, University of Illinois. (Photo: WILL.)

A History of Public Broadcasting

1950

■ February: Iowa State College launches WOI, first TV station owned by educational institution, though it operates commercially (in 1994, Iowa State sells WOI). ■ Oct. 16: NAEB and educators organize Joint Committee on Educational Television (JCET) organizes (it later changes its name twice, eventually becoming the Joint Council on Educational Telecommunications in 1966).

1952

■ April 14: FCC's Sixth Report and Order allocates local TV channels, reserves 242 for noncom educational TV. ■ October: Ford Foundation funds Educational Television and Radio Center in Ann Arbor to distribute programs. ■ In latter-day tryout of Cooperation Doctrine, Ford also begins Sunday arts magazine *Omnibus* on CBS, hosted by Alistair Cooke. (It airs five seasons, the last on ABC.)

1953

■ May 25: The University of Houston signs on the first noncommercial educational TV station, KUHT.

1955

■ KQED in San Francisco pioneers the public TV auction.

1958

■ Sept. 2: Congress passes National Defense Education Act, which aids numerous instructional TV projects.

1959

■ Jan. 24: Under new president John White, Educational Television and Radio Center adds "National" to its name (it later becomes National Educational Television, NET). ■ July: NETRC moves from Ann Arbor to New York City.

1960

■ December: Eastern Educational Television Network (EEN) incorporates after 1959 demonstration of hookup between Boston and Durham, N.H.

1961

■ Educational Radio Network established ("Eastern" is added to name in

Julia Child and WGBH producer Russ Morash (above) popularized good cooking and virtually invented how-to TV with *The French Chef* in 1963. As reported in a profile by David Stewart, when Child first appeared on a book show, she brought along the ingredients for an omelette, a copper bowl and a whisk. Hundreds of shows later, she's in a new series with Jacques Pepin. Morash went on to create *The Victory Garden, This Old House* and *New Yankee Workshop*.

1963). ■ Midwest Program for Airborne Television Instruction (MPATI) experimentally broadcasts ITV to six states from airliner circling above Indiana.

1962

■ May 1: President Kennedy signs Educational Television Facilities Act, bringing first major federal aid to pubcasting (predecessor of today's Public Telecommunications Facilities Program, PTFP). ■ July 10: All-Channel Receiver Act, aiding UHF channels, signed into law. ■ Sept. 9: New York City finally gets a public TV station, as WNDT (later WNET) goes on-air. ■ FCC approves Lorenzo Milam's KRAB-FM in Seattle, first of "Krab Nebula" community radio stations.

1963

■ Jan. 25: WGBH begins airing Julia Child's first *French Chef* series (later distributed nationally). ■ July 25: FCC allows Instructional Television Fixed Service microwave for education.

1964

■ FCC authorizes 100th noncommercial educational TV station. ■ June 10: FCC authorizes first statewide educational TV translator network, in Utah. ■ Dec. 7-8: NAEB First Conference on Long-Range Financing proposes presidential commission on future funding.

1965

■ Nov. 10: Carnegie Corporation of New York establishes Carnegie Commission on Educational Television (Carnegie I). ■ Fred Rogers' program, *Mister Rogers' Neighborhood,* debuts on EEN regional hookup (goes national on NET in 1968).

1966

■ Aug. 1: Ford Foundation proposes to the FCC (in vain) that profits from a nonprofit communications satellite system for all broadcasters would go to public broadcasting.

1967

■ Jan. 26: Carnegie I releases report proposing federal aid and an extension of educational TV called "public television." ■ Feb. 23: WETA premieres *Washington Week in Review* (it goes national on PBS in 1969). ■ March: NAEB Second Conference on Long-Range Financing reviews Carnegie report. ■ April: NAEB report, *The Hidden Medium,* promotes aid to educational radio as well. ■ Nov. 5: Ford Foundation launches *Public Broadcasting Laboratory (PBL),* live Sunday-night magazine program. (CBS starts *60 Minutes* a year later.) ■ Nov. 7: President Johnson signs Public Broadcasting Act of 1967, authorizing federal operating aid to stations through new agency, CPB.

1968

■ March: CPB incorporates. ■ KQED, San Francisco, innovates in news programming with *Newsroom,* begun during newspaper strike.

1969

■ NET begins regular interconnection for educational TV; *The Forsyte Saga* is a hit. ■ CPB begins general support grants to stations (later called Community Service Grants). ■ Precursor of Internet, ARPANET, hooked up by researchers. ■ Nov. 3: PBS is incorporated. (Its board chooses Hartford Gunn as first president, February 1970.) ■ Nov. 10: *Sesame Street* debuts.

1970

■ Feb. 26: NPR incorporates; Don Quayle is to become first president. (Lee Frischknecht becomes second president in 1973.) ■ November: NET and WNDT merge, creating WNET. ■ Nov. 9: PBS carries NET's "Banks and the Poor," generating major controversy. ■ Nov. 20: Maryland PTV launches *Wall $treet Week*.

1971

■ *The Great American Dream Machine* and *Masterpiece Theatre* debut. ■ April 20: NPR begins service with live broadcast of Senate hearings on ending Vietnam War. ■ May 3: NPR begins *All Things Considered.* ■ NAEB's National Educational Radio Network merges with NPR. ■ National Public Affairs Center for Television (NPACT) is created. ■ Oct. 21: Nixon aide Clay Whitehead challenges public TV in speech at NAEB meeting.

1972

■ June 30: President Nixon vetoes two-year CPB authorizing law; a reduced one-year bill is enacted later. ■ John Macy resigns as CPB president, succeeded by Henry Loomis. ■ Frank Pace, CPB's first chairman, also quits, succeeded by Tom Curtis. ■ PBS forms Adult Learning Service. ■ *The Electric Company* debuts. ■ Nov. 4: PBS airs WNET's first *Great Performances.* ■ WGBH Caption Center prepares first open-captioned national broadcast, *The French Chef*.

1973

■ Jan. 11: WNET begins *verite* documentary series *An American Family.* ■ Association of Public Radio Stations (APRS) is formed to lobby for field. ■ May 15: MacNeil and Lehrer team up on NPACT's coverage of Senate Watergate hearings. ■ May 31: CPB and PBS make peace with Partnership Agreement, letting PBS schedule the interconnection. ■ September: With Ralph Rogers as chair, PBS reorganization cuts parental ties with CPB, adds board of lay leaders.

Watergate hearings coverage drew tens of thousands of letters. Pictured: NPACT's James Karayn and Martin Clancy. (Photo: PBS.)

1974

■ March 3: WGBH inaugurates *Nova.* ■ PBS establishes Station Program Cooperative (SPC) to aggregate station funds for national programming and Station Independence Program (SIP) for pledge specials. ■ *Upstairs, Downstairs* debuts on *Masterpiece Theatre.*

1975

■ April: PBS launches first national pledge drive, Festival 75. ■ Sept. 15: National Federation of Community Broadcasters incorporates. ■ Oct. 20: WNET starts *The Robert MacNeil Report* (in 1976 renamed *The MacNeil/Lehrer Report).* ■ Lawrence Grossman named president of PBS; Hartford Gunn, vice chairman. ■ Dec. 31: President Ford signs five-year funding act anticipating a new feature: advance appropriations. In 1976, Congress follows up with appropriations through fiscal 1979.

Fans visited 165 Eaton Place weekly for 55 episodes in the 1974-78 run of *Upstairs, Downstairs.*

1977

■ May 4: NPR takes on public radio's

lobbying functions, merging with APRS. ■ Carnegie Corporation establishes Carnegie Commission on the Future of Public Broadcasting (Carnegie II). ■ NPR expands *All Things Considered* to the weekend and launches *Jazz Alive!* ■ Aug. 1: Frank Mankiewicz begins work as NPR president.

1978

■ March 1: Public TV's satellite interconnection begins operation. ■ July 3: Supreme Court upholds FCC indecency ruling against afternoon broadcast of George Carlin's "filthy words" routine on Pacifica's WBAI in 1973.

1979

■ January: Public TV splits lobbying function from PBS. (In 1980, new group will be named National Association of Public Television Stations. Later, it's called America's Public Television Stations, APTS). David Carley is first president. ■ Jan. 30: Carnegie II releases report. ■ Aug. 23: CPB creates Television Program Fund. ■ Nov. 5: NPR launches *Morning Edition.*

1980

■ March: Closed captioning, developed by PBS, premieres on three networks, including PBS (*Masterpiece Theatre*). ■ March: NAEB launches trade newspaper, *Current.* ■ May 3: Minnesota Public Radio begins national feeds of *A Prairie Home Companion.* ■ June 20: NPR completes first national satellite network for radio. ■ August: WNET launches *Dial* program guide for major stations (it loses millions, dies in May 1987). ■ "Death of a Princess" on WGBH's *World* outrages Saudi royalty. ■ KCET offers Carl Sagan's *Cosmos.*

1981

■ February: Walter Annenberg pledges $150 million over 15 years, launching Annenberg/CPB Project to make college-level video courses; he breaks off funding in 1990 and begins new math/science project to train grade-school teachers in 1991. ■ March: President Reagan seeks $88 million cut in CPB funding, achieves $35 million cut in fiscal 1983. ■ Oct. 2: FCC's Temporary

Commission on Alternative Financing (TCAF) begins work. ■ Nov. 3: NAEB membership votes to dissolve bankrupt association.

1982

■ June: Bruce Christensen succeeds David Carley as president of NAPTS. ■ Nov. 4: Station consortium raises curtain on *American Playhouse.* ■ WNET lets *Nature* loose on PBS.

1983

■ Feb. 23: Many public TV stations air live open-heart surgery covered by KAET, Phoenix. ■ April 8: FCC allows public radio to use FM subcarriers for profit-making. ■ April 15: American Public Radio incorporates (it changes its name to Public Radio International in 1994). ■ April 19: NPR President Frank Mankiewicz steps down from management role as financial crisis becomes known; he resigns May 10. ■ Aug. 2: CPB joins stations in bailing out NPR. ■ Sept. 5: First hourlong nightly news program debuts: *MacNeil/Lehrer NewsHour.* ■ WGBH and consortium launch *Frontline.* ■ WGBH produces *Vietnam: A Television History.* ■ Oct. 27: NPR elects Douglas Bennet as president, succeeding Mankiewicz. ■ December: NBC News announces hiring of PBS President Lawrence Grossman as its president.

1984

■ March: FCC loosens rules, allowing "enhanced underwriting." ■ April: Bruce Christensen of APTS named PBS president. Peter Fannon succeeds him at APTS in January 1985. ■ July 3: U.S. Supreme Court overturns law prohibiting editorials by CPB-assisted stations, acting in case brought by Pacifica and others. ■ Chicago's WTTW is first station to air TV stereo sound full-time. ■ *Christian Science Monitor* launches Monitor Radio (ceases June 1997).

1985

■ May 22: Public radio stations approve NPR business plan: they receive the funds that CPB previously sent directly to NPR. ■ June: CPB President Edward Pfister quits in dispute over planned Moscow trip. ■ June 30: Public broadcasting rev-

Though he sometimes does a duo act for events like Morning Edition's 10th anniversary party a decade ago, **Bob Edwards** ordinarily solos as anchor of NPR's most-listened-to program. (Photo: Andrea Mohin for *Current*.)

enues pass $1 billion by end of fiscal year 1985. ■ Nov. 2: NPR debuts Scott Simon's *Weekend Edition* on Saturdays. ■ CPB begins aid to Public Television Outreach Alliance.

1986

■ January: CPB hires Martin Rubenstein as president (and fires him Nov. 13). ■ CPB establishes Radio Program Fund. ■ September: Co-host Susan Stamberg leaves *ATC* after 14 years. ■ Sept. 30: NPR makes final payment on $7 million debt. ■ WGBH introduces Descriptive Video Service for vision-impaired viewers.

1987

■ January: Bill Moyers, gone since 1981, announces return to PBS. ■ Jan. 21: Henry Hampton's *Eyes on the Prize* debuts. ■ March: CPB drops proposal for political content analysis of programs. ■ June 13: Garrison Keillor's last *Prairie Home Companion* before (temporary) departure from public radio (he returns in September 1989 with *American Radio Company of the Air*). ■ July: CPB promotes Donald Ledwig to president. ■ Dec. 7: NAPTS names David Brugger president, succeeding Peter Fannon. ■ Dec. 10: Senate rejects Ernest Hollings' trust fund plan. ■ NPR begins producing *Performance Today* and *Weekend Edition Sunday,* and distributing *Fresh Air* and *Car Talk.*

1988

■ February: APR hires Stephen Salyer as president. ■ Oct. 11: WGBH launches *The American Experience*. ■ November: Congress directs CPB to create a program service to aid independent producers (the resulting Independent Television Service is created in June 1991).

1989

■ January: KUSC and APR launch *Marketplace.* ■ March: Whittle Communications stirs controversy by offering free satellite dishes and TV sets to schools that show daily Channel One newscast with commercials. ■ October: PBS names Jennifer Lawson as its first chief programming executive. CPB adds $23 million to her budget.

1990

■ Feb. 16: PBS launches PBS Home Video. ■ Alvin Perlmutter proposes Voter's Channel with aid from Markle Foundation to cover 1992 politics. (PBS doesn't take the offer, and the plan falls apart in June 1991.) ■ Sept. 23-27: Ken Burns' *The Civil War* breaks PBS audience records; he follows with *Baseball* in 1994.

1991

■ June 19: Walter Annenberg pledges $60 million over 12 years for new math/science project at CPB. ■ July: "Tongues Untied" wins condemnation and applause. ■ Heritage Foundation hires Laurence Jarvik to study public broadcasting. ■ NPR debuts *Talk of the Nation.*

1992

■ January: American Program Service is new name of EEN Interregional Program Service. ■ March: CPB hires Richard Carlson as president. ■ March: Robert and Linda Lichter release political content analysis of PBS documentaries. ■ Aug. 26: President Bush signs CPB reauthorization act with Senate amendment requiring CPB to monitor "objectivity and balance" in programming. ■ October: Congress requires DBS operators to set aside 4-7 percent of capacity for noncom educational use. (U.S. Court of Appeals upholds set-aside in August 1996; FCC goes with 4 percent in November 1998.)

1993

■ January: NPR Board ends annual dues struggles by "locking down" stations' dues increases to their rate of revenue growth. ■ Feb. 5: CPB report to Congress proposes expanded "ready to learn" preschool programming. ■ March: PBS suffers flap over pledging of *Barney & Friends.* ■ May: Bruce Christensen says he'll leave PBS presidency; in December, PBS names Ervin Duggan as successor. ■ July: Twentieth Century Fund publishes task force report on public TV. ■ August: NPR names Delano Lewis as president. ■ Sept. 16: Radio Bilingüe starts Satélite radio service for Latino public radio stations.

Under attack as elitists in 1995, public broadcasters pointed to rural stations like West Virginia's **WVMR-FM** (the fiddler was shown on ABC's *Nightline*) In 1998-99, public radio stations reached consensus to boost CPB aid to rural stations, which have less chance of private fundraising.

1994

■ January: NPR moves into new D.C. headquarters. ■ July 1: APR becomes Public Radio International. ■ July 11: PBS launches pilot of Ready to Learn Servic for preschoolers. ■ October: American Indian Radio on Satellite (AIROS) network starts up. ■ November: Republicans win majority in House; new Speaker Newt Gingrich soon announces plan to "zero out" CPB funding.

1995

■ January: PBS Board plans to penalize stations airing 30-second spots; furor erupts; and penalties are later tabled. ■ March: PBS and MCI announce programming and online deal; it never gets going. ■ July 17: CPB creates twin Future Funds for public radio and TV. ■ September: PBS Online debuts. ■ September: Markle Foundation backs Lawrence Grossman study of his proposal for two nights of ad-supported weekend programming on public TV. (The idea goes public in June 1997, but falters.) ■ November: PBS announces production deal with Reader's Digest Association; publisher backs out within two years. Duggan pledges to hold down stations' program dues under new Station Equity Model. ■ PBS and APTS launch governance reviews.

1996

■ Jan. 2: CPB Board adds radio station audience and fundraising criteria for grant eligibility, effective October 1998. ■ January: PRI launches limited distribution of *The World*. ■ February: Rep. Jack Fields introduces trust fund bill, but it doesn't advance. ■ July: PBS names Kathy Quattrone to succeed Jennifer Lawson as chief program executive.

1997

■ Jan. 24: Richard Carlson resigns as CPB president. ■ February: PBS Board revises bylaws, increasing managers on board. ■ April 3: FCC sets 2003 deadline for public TV stations to begin DTV simulcasting. ■ April: Group of public TV stations pledges not to air 30-second spots; others already have them on-air. ■ June 30: Public broadcasting's total

revenues pass $2 billion by end of fiscal year 1997. ■ Oct. 1: CPB announces promotion of Robert Coonrod to presidency. ■ October: NPR and PRI presidents propose merger, their boards say no. ■ Nov. 5: Public TV stations create National Forum of Public Television Executives at convention in Austin.

1998

■ March: Minnesota Public Radio sells mail-order subsidiary for $120 million. ■ April: Children's Television Workshop announces Noggin cable venture with Nickeoleon. ■ May 18: U.S. Supreme Court rules Arkansas state network has journalistic discretion to exclude minor candidate in on-air debate, overturning Eighth Circuit decision of August 1996. ■ July: PBS announces program development deal with Disney/ABC subsidiary Devillier Donegan Enterprises. ■ Nov. 9: Seven public TV stations are among first DTV broadcasters; PBS premieres "Chihuly Over Venice," first national broadcast of a program produced and edited in HDTV. ■ Nov. 10-11: The seven stations air first test broadcast of enhanced DTV, adapting Ken Burns' "Frank Lloyd Wright." ■ Nov. 11: Following Delano Lewis's retirement, NPR hires Kevin Klose as president. ■ December: Gore Commission recommends additional educational TV station in every market, backs trust fund; White House, Congress and FCC take no action.

1999

■ Jan. 1: American Program Service renamed American Public Television. ■ Feb. 1: Former PBS Home Video distributor Michael Nesmith wins $47 million civil judgment against the network. (In July, PBS settles with Nesmith for an undisclosed amount.) ■ June: NPR and PRI announce plans to provide channels to CD Radio satellite service. ■ July: House leaders erupt as Washington hears about WGBH mailing list deals with Democrats. ■ Sept. 6: PBS begins transmitting PBS Kids service for DBS and DTV. ■ Sept. 9: Ervin Duggan resigns as PBS president. ■ December: DirecTV commits to carry new PBS-You adult education channel.

Aufderheide, P. (1999). *Communications policy and the public interest*. New York: The Guilford Press.

Aufderheide, P. (1991). Public television and the public sphere. *Critical Studies in Mass Communication*, 8, 168-183.

Avery, R. K. (1996). Contemporary public telecommunications research: Navigating the sparsely settled terrain. *Journal of Broadcasting & Electronic Media*, 40, 132-139.

Avery, R. K. (Ed.). (1993). *Public service broadcasting in a multichannel environment: The history and survival of an ideal*. White Plains, NY: Longman.

Avery, R. K., Burrows, P. E., & Pincus, C. J. (1980). *Research index for NAEB journals, 1957-1979*. Washington, D.C.: National Association of Educational Broadcasters.

Avery, R. K. & Pepper, R. (1979). *The politics of interconnection: A history of public television at the national level*. Washington, D.C.: National Association of Educational Broadcasters.

Blakely, R. J. (1971). *The people's instrument: A philosophy of programming for public television*. Washington, D.C.: Public Affairs Press.

Blakely, R. J. (1979). *To serve the public interest: Educational broadcasting in the United States*. New York: Syracuse University Press.

Blumler, J. G. & Nossiter, T. J. (Eds.). (1991). *Broadcasting finance in transition: A comparative handbook*. New York: Oxford University Press.

Broadcasting and the public sphere [Special issue]. (1989). *Media, Culture & Society*, 11(2).

Bullert, B. J. (1997). *Public television: Politics & the battle over documentary film*. New Brunswick, NJ: Rutgers University Press.

Burke, J. E. (1979). *An historical-analytical study of the legislative and political origins of the Public Broadcasting Act of 1967*. New York: Arno Press.

Calabrese, A. & Borchert, M. (1996). Prospects for electronic democracy in the United States: Rethinking communication and social policy. *Media, Culture & Society*, 18(2), 249-268.

Calhoun, C. (Ed.). (1993). *Habermas and the public sphere*. Cambridge, MA: MIT Press.

Carnegie Commission on Educational Television. (1967). *Public television: A program for action*. New York: Bantam.

Carnegie Commission on the Future of Public Broadcasting. (1979). *A public trust*. New York: Bantam.

Cater, D. & Nyhan, M. J. (Eds.). (1976). *The future of public broadcasting*. New York: Praeger.

Croteau, K., Hoynes, W. & Carragee, K. (1996). The political diversity of public television: Polysemy, the public sphere and the conservative critique of PBS.

Journalism and Mass Communication Monographs, 157.

Day, J. (1995). *The vanishing vision: The inside story of public television.* Berkeley: University of California Press.

Dornfeld, B. (1998). *Producing public television, producing public culture.* Princeton, NJ: Princeton University Press.

Engelman, R. (1996). *Public radio and television in America: A political history.* Thousand Oaks, CA: Sage Publications, Inc.

Ford Foundation. (1976). Ford *Foundation activities in noncommercial broadcasting, 1951-1976.* New York: Ford Foundation.

Fowler, M. S. & Brenner, D. L. (1982). A marketplace approach to broadcast regulation. *Texas Law Review*, 60(2), 207-257.

Friedland, I. (1995). Public television as public sphere: The case of the Wisconsin Collaborative Project. *Journal of Broadcasting & Electronic Media*, 39, 147-176.

Gibson, G. H. (1977). *Public broadcasting: The role of the federal government, 1912-1976.* New York: Praeger.

Habermas, J. (1989). *The structural transformation of the public sphere.* (T. Burger, with the assistance of F. Lawrence, Trans.). Cambridge, MA: MIT Press.

Horowitz, D., & Jarvik, L. (Eds.). (1995). *Public television and the public trust.* Los Angeles: Center for the Study of Popular Culture.

Horowitz, R. B. (1989). *The irony of regulatory reform: The deregulation of American telecommunication.* New York: Oxford University Press.

Hoynes, W. (1994). *Public television for sale: Media, the market, and the public sphere.* Boulder, CO: Westview Press.

Jarvik, L. (1997). *PBS: Behind the screen.* Rocklin, CA: Prima Publishing.

Lasar, M. (1999). *Pacifica Radio: The Rise of an Alternative Network.* Philadelphia: Temple University Press.

Koenig, A. E. & Hill, R. B. (Eds.). (1967). *The farther vision: Educational television today.* Madison: University of Wisconsin Press.

Lashley, M. (1992). *Public television: Panacea, pork barrel, or public trust?* Westport, CT: Greenwood Press.

Leach, E. (1983). *Tuning out education: The Cooperation Doctrine in radio, 1922-38.* Washington, D.C: Current Newspaper. Republished 1999 by Current Online, www.current.org/coop.

Ledbetter, J. (1997). *Made possible by . . . : The death of public broadcasting in the United States.* New York: Verso.

Lowe, G. F. & Alm, A. (1997). *Public service broadcasting as culture industry: Value transformation in the Finnish marketplace.* European Journal of Communication, 12(2), 181-195.

Lowe, G. F. (1998). Competition and restructuring: Value transformation in Finnish public radio. *Journal of radio studies*, 5(2), 99-115.

Macy, J. W. (1974). *To irrigate a wasteland.* Berkeley: University of California Press.

McCain, T. A. & Lowe, G. F. (1990). Localism in western European radio broadcasting: Untangling the wireless. *Journal of Communication*, 40(1), 86-101.

McChesney, R. W. (1999). *Rich media, poor democracy: Communication politics in dubious times*. Champaign, IL: University of Illinois Press.

McChesney, R. W. (1993). *Telecommunications, mass media, & democracy: The battle for the control of U.S. broadcasting, 1928-1935*. New York: Oxford University Press.

Morrisett, L. N. (1973). Rx for public television. In The John & Mary R. Markle Foundation (Ed.) *Annual Report 1972/73*, 6-20. New York: The John & Mary R. Markle Foundation.

Newsom, C. V. (Ed.) (1952). *A television policy for education*. Washington, D.C.: American Council on Education.

Pepper, R. (1979). *The formation of the Public Broadcasting Service*. New York: Arno Press.

Powell, J. W. (1962). *Channels of Learning: The story of educational television*. Washington, D.C.: Public Affairs Press.

Raboy, M. (Ed.). (1995). *Public broadcasting for the 21st century*. Luton, England: University of Luton Press.

Robertson, J. (1993). *TeleVisionaries: In their own words, public television's founders tell how it all began*. Charlotte Harbor, FL: Tabby House Books.

Rowland, W. D. (1986). Continuing crisis in public television: A history of disenfrancisement. *Journal of Broadcasting & Electronic Media*, 30, 251-274.

Rowland, W. D. (1980). The federal regulatory and policymaking process. *Journal of Communication*, 30(3), 139-149.

Rowland, W. D. & Tracey, M. (1990). Worldwide challenges to public service broadcasting. *Journal of Communication*, 40, 8-27.

Scannell, P. (1989). Public service broadcasting and modern public life. *Media, Culture & Society*, 11, 135-166.

Starr, J. M. (forthcoming 2000). *Air wars: The fight to reclaim public broadcasting*. Boston: Beacon Press.

Stavitsky, A. G. (1994). The changing conception of localism in U.S. public radio. *Journal of Broadcasting & Electronic Media*, 38, 19-33.

Stavitsky, A. G. (1995). Guys with suits and charts: Audience research in U.S. public radio. *Journal of Broadcasting & Electronic Media*, 39, 177-189.

Stavitsky, A. G. (1995). *Independence and integrity: A guidebook for public radio journalism*. Washington, D.C.: National Public Radio.

Stavitsky, A. G. & Gleason, T. W. (1994). Alternative things considered: A comparison of National Public Radio and Pacifica Radio news coverage. *Journalism Quarterly*, 71, 171-186.

Stewart, D. (1999). *The PBS companion, A history of public television*. New York: TV Books.

Stone, D. M. (1985). *Nixon and the politics of public television*. New York: Garland Publishing.

Streeter, T. (1996). *Selling the air: A critique of the policy of commercial broadcasting in the United States*. Chicago: University of Chicago Press.

Tracey, M. (1998). *The decline and fall of public service broadcasting*. New York: Oxford University Press.

Twentieth Century Fund Task Force on Public Television. (1993). *Quality time?* New York: The Twentieth Century Fund Press.

Index